Police Powers and Politics

# Police Powers and Politics

## Robert Baldwin and Richard Kinsey

Quartet Books
London  Melbourne  New York

First published by Quartet Books Limited 1982
A member of the Namara Group
27/29 Goodge Street, London W1P 1FD

British Library Cataloguing in Publication Data

Baldwin, Robert
   Police powers and politics
   1. Police—Great Britain
   I. Title      II. Kinsey Richard
   363.2'0941      HV8195.A2

   ISBN 0-7043-2333-8

Typeset by MC Typeset, Rochester, Kent
Printed and bound in Great Britain by
Mackays of Chatham Limited, Kent

# Contents

# Acknowledgements

It is not possible for us to mention all those who have helped and encouraged us to write this book. The Chief Constable and officers of the 'Research' Force assisted enormously and without their co-operation much of this book could never have been written. They may well disagree with some of our conclusions, but we can only hope that they may find something of value in these pages in return for allowing us to share their experiences. To those who read the manuscript or were otherwise subjected to our obsessions, apologies are perhaps more in order than thanks; but we thank them none the less and in particular: John Alderson, Bob Alston, Stuart Anderson, Andrew Ashworth, Francis Bell, Derek Blyth, Duncan Campbell, Chris Cooper, Ian Cowden, David Cowell, Hazel Genn, Tom Harris, Stuart Hay, Felicity Jones, Maureen Kinsey, Neil MacCormick, Gus Macdonald, Peter MacIntosh, Ken Mackinnon, Euan MacLean, David McLuckie, Sandy Neilson, Ian Nisbet, Colin Rintoul, Alistair Robertson, Andrew Ross, Joanna Shapland, Willie Stephen, Robin Turton, Peter Wilson and, as ever at the end, Jock Young. For their patient help with the manuscript we specially thank Noel Harris, Janet Law, Sheila Macmillan, Conan Nicholas, Chris Parker, Isabel Roberts, Beverly Roger and Rosemary Stallan.

# Introduction

Law and order is a central concern in British politics. Each time crime statistics are published, media coverage focuses on some aspect of 'the rising tide of lawlessness' in our country. It is always a good angle for a news story and one that most sets of statistics cater for in some way. Thus, when, in March 1982, Scotland Yard published figures on London crime, there were few headlines rejoicing 'Homicides down from 204 to 103' but, instead, attention was drawn to the tiny sector of crime (three per cent) categorized as robbery and violent theft which had increased by a third.

Not only the media keep anxiety alive. The Metropolitan force in 1982 fuelled public concern by concentrating also on the 'mugging' category of offence. Assistant Commissioner Gilbert Kelland said that 'the most worrying factor' in the figures was that nearly a quarter of victims of violent crime were over fifty years old. For the first time the Metropolitan Police disclosed figures giving the colour of offenders and purporting to show that twice as many black people as whites were involved in mugging offences. The Police Federation responded to the general climate of worry (rather than the decreased homicide figures) by taking out adverts in the national press on 16 March calling for the restoration of capital punishment. On the same day, the Chief Constable of Greater Manchester, James Anderton, warned of a conspiracy to hamstring the police and to take them over by democratically elected police authorities. Such politically motivated control of the force was, he said, 'something without which the dream of a Marxist totalitarian state in this country cannot ultimately be realized' (*The Guardian*, 17 March 82).

Whatever the media distortions, or the difficulties of using crime statistics, and, however much James Anderton is criticized for his wild language, there *is* genuine anxiety in this country both with levels of crime and concerning the role that the police may play in reducing this. Here our approach is to cut through the quick and easy responses on crime and its control (harsh punishments, unrestricted policing) and examine how best the law and the police may combine to serve the needs of the community.

In this book we ask what sort of powers the police should have. Should they, for instance, be allowed to detain people for questioning without having to give reasons, or conduct random stop-and-search operations, or fingerprint sectors of the population in order to isolate a suspect? Would that aid detection and bring popular respect for the police or would it alienate the public and so render detection even more difficult?

To answer these questions, we argue, is not a simple matter of having lawyers review past policies and draw up neat rules. We first have to look at what the law (and other systems of control) can do to influence how police forces go about their jobs. This demands, therefore, that we understand something about how police officers do their work, how they are organized and rewarded, controlled and socialized. Only by doing this, will we be in a position to judge whether, for example, passing a new law governing police action, will stand any chance of actually changing police behaviour.

Even assuming that we do comprehend everything about police work and the role to be played by legal or other rules in regulating police activity, we would still have to answer another more fundamental question: 'What sort of police force do we want?' It may be that we could devise a number of workable but very different systems of policing for Britain – for example, hard-line regimes based on confrontation with the public or ones that emphasize the value of policing with public consent. We have to have an idea of the kind of policing we aim for since the kind of powers we give our police will affect the way that they go about their job and vice versa. Draconian powers, we believe, will inevitably lead to policing by confrontation.

Sig Essay
vol

A recurring theme in the following chapters will be that those who have considered the reform of police powers in the past have done so in a vacuum. They have tended to see lawyers, prosecutors and policemen as the experts on criminal procedure but, in doing so, have forgotten to look to the interests of the wider public. It is a more general indictment of our law reform system that in changing the law on, say, prisons, hospitals and criminal procedure, governments tend only to consult the 'professionals' and not prisoners, patients and suspects. As a result, the 'consumers' interests' are left out of calculations in favour of those of the official organizations directly concerned.

It is a special concern of this book to deal with the organizational aspects of police work. We accordingly concentrate on the day-to-day relationships between officers and public together with the routine processes of street work and detection rather than public order and security issues or the more dramatic aspects of police operations portrayed in the media or seen in inquiries such as that involving the Yorkshire Ripper. We do not offer an exhaustive analysis of police work or its history but instead deal with what we see as those aspects of the job that have and will have, a major influence on the form that policing takes and the manner in which control is exercised over policing. If, for example, we are reviewing the power to arrest we should not merely have lawyers 'clarify' the law after consulting the police and prosecution services but should look at such issues as the policing policies involved, the role of arrest within police organizations, the effectiveness of using arrest in crime control and detection, the results of arrest on the individual arrested and the public's reaction to arrest powers. Only by viewing police powers in their broadest sense will we come to a realistic view of the roles they play in police behaviour, in the prevention of crime and in its detection. If we take this approach then we may disabuse ourselves of a variety of unhelpful fictions such as, 'more police power means less crime' or even 'clearer law means fewer police breaches of the law'.

We start to explore these issues by looking, in Chapter 1, at the job we expect of the police and how common-sense ideas of policing have become divorced from reality. In Chapters 2 and 3, we take a closer look at key aspects of police organization, both on the street and in detective work. These chapters will give an indication of the kinds of pressure that police officers are expected to work under, pressures that cannot be ignored by those who set out either to devise police powers or to protect the civil rights of those who come into contact with the police. Chapter 4 examines accountability and discipline at the local level and describes how alongside formal systems of control there are informal rules and understandings of at least equal importance.

When the law itself is considered in Chapter 5, it is seen that rules on police powers which were once relatively clear have become eroded as policing methods have changed and how, in parallel with developments in policing, we are drifting towards a system of criminal justice in which the real work of establishing innocence or guilt is conducted not in the court but in the police station.

What happens when the real issues are neglected is seen clearly when we consider the way in which governments have attempted to reform the rules of criminal procedure. In Chapter 6 we tell how extended police powers were introduced in Scotland against massive public protest and how during the legislative process many of the problems that should have been faced were abandoned at the hands of lawyers. Chapter 7 recounts how a similarly narrow approach was set in motion in England and Wales by the Royal Commission on Criminal Procedure. We review the philosophy of the Commission and find that, in spite of its detailed researches, and expenditure of £1,189,800, it has still failed to explore the fundamental principles upon which its recommendations rest.

Having criticized the lack of vision of past law reformers, we examine in Chapter 8 what many people see as the progressive influences on modern policing and the sources of future hope: the community policing philosophy of John Alderson and the Scarman proposals following the Brixton disturbances. These approaches we find attractive on their face, as many others have done, but, on further analysis, we are driven to conclude that community policing methods, in themselves, supply no simple answer for those who question what kind of force or what kind of police powers we want.

Chapter 9 reviews the choices now facing us and offers our own conclusions. Because we argue against the strictly legalistic approach to police powers only part of the chapter deals with specifically legal proposals; the rest looks at the forms of police organization and the policing styles that are needed in this country.

# 1

# Slogans or Policies?

'What I felt distressed about was that on television my own party were trying to act with slogans in an area which does not permit slogans. They were taking easy solutions in an area which requires a great deal of hard work from a great many very sensitive and sensible people, right through the law and order services . . . Slogans . . . won't solve the complex problems in themselves and can't.'

(Home Secretary William Whitelaw,
Tyne Tees Television, 10 January 82)

It is a great temptation, when dealing with police issues, to substitute slogans for analysis. Few lay people are interested in the details of police work until they become personally involved in the criminal justice system. As a result, the police are misunderstood; extraordinary demands are made of them; and superhuman capabilities are attributed. Sir Robert Mark has claimed that of all the public services the police are the most taken for granted and he has doubted whether 'one in a thousand Englishmen could give even a vague outline of our organization, accountability or method of control'.[1]

Before starting any analysis of police work, a number of confusions, simplifications and misleading assumptions that have persistently dogged debates in this field must be cleared up. First, any notion that 'more police and greater powers' is the way to deal with a 'crisis in law and order' needs to be dispelled.

This idea draws heavily on the recurrent folk memory of a 'golden age', sometime before, after or during the last war, when it seems petty crime was virtually unknown. In different variations on the same theme we are told that there was no television violence – indeed no television; there was no extra- or pre-marital sex – apparently there was no sex at all, for there was no 'younger generation' and no 'permissiveness'; unlike today, discipline was effective and authority respected. According to this picture, there is now a crisis in the moral order, represented by an explosion in crime, especially amongst younger people. In the 'perplexed society' the crisis demands new methods and exceptional measures to be taken by the police before it is too late.

Statistics of recorded crime can lead to exaggeration of the nature and extent of crime and the generation of 'moral panics'.[2] The numbers must, however, be treated with extreme caution: there are many variables at play which may have little to do with the actual amount of crime occurring in the streets. Thus, for example, the incidence of arrests and reported offences may be strongly affected by the way manpower is deployed, changes in the law or new policing policies. The paradox is that more effective policing may produce alarming figures. More officers on the beat, more efficient communications (e.g. wider availability of telephones) and greater public sensitivity to certain types of offence may well result in more crimes being reported to the police and so being recorded. This may suggest an outbreak of crime where none exists. By circular argument, the more police are used the more crime appears to grow and the stronger are calls for more police officers.

Whatever we make of the statistical numbers game, however, we can draw two conclusions. First, the steadiness of the overall increase in recorded crime does not substantiate the idea that there has been a sudden and dramatic intensification of criminal activity. Second, the social history of crime reveals that the steadiness of the rise in recorded crime is matched by the equally steady recurrence of a belief in impending social and moral collapse, which almost without exception focuses upon street crime and violence.

In 1795 Patrick Colquhoun introduced his classic *Treatise on the*

*Police of the Metropolis* with these words:   ~ class  bias .

> In vain do we boast those liberties, which are our birth-right, if
> the vilest and most depraved part of the community are suffered
> to deprive us of the privilege of travelling upon the highways, or
> of approaching the capital, in any direction, after dark, without
> danger of being assaulted and robbed; and perhaps wounded or
> murdered.[3]

In 1863 the *Cornhill Magazine* took an identical line, announcing
that: 'Once again the streets of London are unsafe by day or night.
The public dread has become almost a panic.'[4]

The following extract is taken from the parliamentary debate on
the Criminal Justice (Scotland) Bill 1980:

> As never before, our urban and, indeed, some of our rural,
> areas, are dangerous. One can no longer travel alone safely on
> the last bus or on some trains and it is certainly dangerous to go
> to football matches and some discos.
>
> The danger is greater today than it was in the days of our
> parents or our grandparents. Should we be surprised? Since 1945
> the well-intentioned, articulate academics and reformers have
> had their way, often aided and assisted by woolly political
> thinking and woolly, inept political action. Old values and old
> standards have been debunked and rejected. The situation in
> Scotland today is evil, violent and frightening in many areas.[5]

(It is perhaps instructive to note that in 1980 when this comment
was made the number of assaults and robberies recorded by the
police in the Strathclyde area [which contains over half of the
Scottish population] fell by 4 per cent and 6 per cent respectively.)

The notion that more police means better policing has been a
recurring theme not only of political rhetoric but in post-war police
planning. It is often assumed to be self-evident, as can be seen from
a Home Office review of manpower carried out in the early 1970s,
where it was stated: 'In trying to answer the question of how one
knows when the country has enough policemen, the only firm
conclusion to be reached is that, since the war, there certainly have
not been enough.'[6]

It is, of course, easy to say that there are not enough police or
that policing is 'inefficient'. It is, however, much more difficult to
determine what is the best level of policing or what is an efficient
use of manpower with any certainty. When can it be said there are
finally enough police? How is the quality of the police work to be
assessed? How is crime prevention to be measured? How are
community relations and satisfaction on the part of police and
public to be evaluated?

Confusion on these questions has led government departments,
policy-makers and analysts to express the frustrations engendered
by the consequently exaggerated demands placed upon them:

> It is one thing to describe the functions of the police, but quite
> another to measure their success in carrying them out. The
> Royal Commission in their interim report of 1960 recommended
> that 'in fixing the authorised establishment of the force the
> criterion should be the number of police officers required to give
> adequate police protection'. It hardly needs to be said that an
> adequate standard of police protection is not something that can
> be defined in absolute terms.[7]

As a result, and perhaps understandably, key questions on the
quality and efficiency of policing have been ducked, in favour of
solutions amenable to statistical formulation and analysis. We can,
after all, count the number and cost of motor cars, personal radios
and policemen, whilst 'social costs' remain a highly contentious
matter of political opinion and subjective evaluation. So, instead,
the emphasis was placed upon the simple increase of manpower
and provision of more sophisticated labour- and time-saving
devices:

> No scientific way of resolving the problem has been found or
> seems likely to be found. Once this conclusion has been reached,
> if only for the time being and on the basis of present experience,
> it becomes manifest that the role of scientific operational research
> and modern management methods is to improve the effective-
> ness of police methods, using the best equipment, *rather than to
> seek to establish just how many police are ideally required.*[8]

The easy option, then, was to rely on increasing the numbers and output of the police and to postpone – 'at least for the time being' – the difficult questions about the quality of policing. Indeed it was the responsibility of neither the police nor the planners to do more, for it was for 'the community' to 'reach a decision somehow on what level of unsolved crime and inadequacy of patrolling it regards as tolerable'.[9]

It is hardly surprising, but unfortunate, that these conclusions were not made public. Few governments would relish the idea of going to the electorate with a programme of 'inadequate' policing, however realistic. None the less, it is interesting that in 1972, in private, the Home Office recognized that the 'community' should make a decision 'somehow' – even if there was no indication of how that might in future be done. In practice, of course, the answer to all these problems was to become a purely financial one and the policy-makers were never required to debate their assumptions in public or to face the unresolved questions which lurked beneath the policies they implemented. The result has been that, over the past thirty years, arguments, which should have been about the quality of policing, degenerated into haggling over the cost of more police.

From the data presented in Tables 1 and 2 it can be seen that since 1950, both in England and Wales, and in Scotland, there has been a steady rise in police strength so that by 1980 total numbers had almost doubled. This is important to keep in mind, as the publicity given to difficulties in recruitment and to the problem of wastage (premature retirement) has created an impression that the number of police has actually fallen. As can be seen, this is not true. Until recently there was some difficulty – especially in some of the bigger city forces – in offsetting wastage, but since the vastly improved rates of police pay following the implementation of the Edmund-Davies Report[10] this is no longer the case.

While there has been a continued rise in the actual strength of the police, there has been a truly remarkable increase in the number of civilians employed. Civilians now add as much as an extra 25 per cent to total manpower, thus releasing many more police officers for operational duties. Never before have there been so many well-qualified and well-equipped personnel, yet, in 1978, David Gray, the Chief Inspector of HM Constabulary in Scotland, was

# Table 1: The Rise in Actual Police Manpower in England and Wales

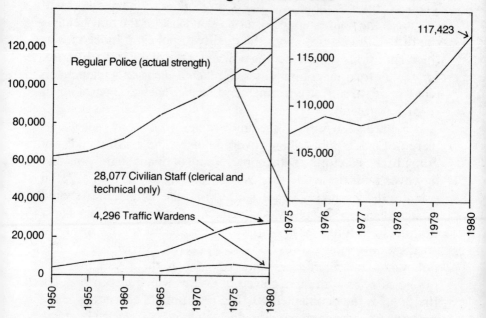

# Table 2: The Rise in Actual Police Manpower in Scotland

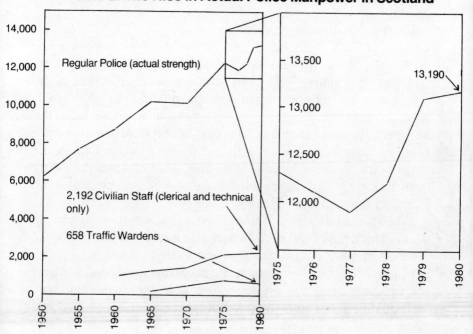

none the less prompted to comment in the Introduction to his Report for that year:

> Records show that in 1938 there were 6,923 police and 88 civilians in Scottish forces. There are now nearly twice that number of police and the civilian establishment has increased from 88 in 1938 to 4,482 at the end of 1978. In effect our police force has more than doubled in the last 40 years. Population in Scotland has increased by only about ten per cent since 1938 and one could well ask where all the policemen have gone.

The answer to Sir David Gray's question lies in the internal reorganization and bureaucratization of the police since 1945. Once again, however, considered analysis has given way to belief in the golden age of law and order. In this variant, the streets were protected by bands of jovial bobbies, taking cups of tea and slices of Hovis with worried parents, and a clip round the ear was the only weapon in the arsenal of deterrence.

The image of the 'friendly local bobby' is another simplification in the policing debate and is well worn. The following example comes from an editorial in *The Times* of 1908:

> The policeman in London, is not merely a guardian of the peace, he is an integral part of its social life. In many a bad street and slum he not merely stands for law and order, he is the true handyman of our streets, the best friend of a mass of people who have no other friend and protector.[11]

This idea, both in terms of the theory of policing and in terms of its particular history, is complex and important. There is a strong sense in which the idea of the friendly policeman is a contradiction in terms. Privacy can never be invaded by friendship, which demands that confidences are kept. For the police, however, privacy is a barrier to their work. A criminal investigation demands that private lives are made public; further, personal obligations and ties cannot be allowed to influence judgment, duty and justice, yet friendship demands precisely that. There is thus an inherent tension in police work – the protection of freedom and privacy demands the invasion of freedom and privacy.

Even historically, the 'friendly bobby' image contains little truth. One of the leading social historians of the English police, T. A. Critchley, has described the office of the seventeenth-century parish constable as being held in such low regard as to be deemed 'appropriate only to the old, idiotic or infirm'.[12] As has been thoroughly documented, eighteenth-century opposition to any idea of a regular police force was intense, widespread and successful. Peel's Metropolitan Police Act 1829 thus became law, in Critchley's words, 'only after three-quarters of a century of wrangling, suspicion and hostility towards the whole idea of a professional police'.[13] Indeed, in relation to the village policeman, even as late as 1842 *The Times* kept up the barrage of criticism: 'We perceive with great satisfaction that a strong feeling is gaining ground in different parts of the country, and in most respectable quarters, against the continuance of the rural police system.' The editorial concluded that Peel's system of policing had furnished a machine capable of being employed 'for the purposes of arbitrary aggression on the liberties of the people'.

Such language seems to sit strangely alongside the editorial of 1908 cited above, with its references to the 'people's friend', the 'handyman of the streets' and so on. Yet what it marks is one of the most successful public relations exercises ever mounted by the police in Britain.

The original image of the friendly bobby was deliberately constructed and successfully employed by Peel himself to counter the fears, not only of the working classes but of the middle classes, which had been provoked by the idea of the 'New Police'. Opponents had characterized Peel's and earlier proposals as ushering in a centralized system of police 'spies', *'agents provocateurs'* and arbitrary power. The model of the Parisian police was constantly held up as anathema to the idea of English constitutional liberty, and reference to 'Continental methods' was sufficient to send shivers of alarm through the soul of true-born Englishmen. Even the word 'police' was alien to the English. In 1763 the rather inappropriately named *British Magazine* had carried the following comment:

The Word *Police* has made many bold Attempts to get a Footing
. . but as neither the Word nor the Thing itself are much

understood in London, I fancy it will require a considerable
Time to bring it into Fashion; perhaps from an Aversion to the
French, from whom this word is borrowed; and something under
the Name of Police being already established in Scotland,
English prejudices will not soon be reconciled to it. Not so long
ago, at a Bagnio in Covent Garden, on my complaining of some
Imposition, I was told by a fair North Briton, that it was the
regular established *Police* of the House. This, I own, is the only
Time . . . I have heard it used in any *polite Company*; nor do I
believe it has made any considerable Progress (except in the
News Papers), beyond the Purlieus of *Covent Garden.*[14]

As we have seen, it was not to be until the end of the nineteenth
century that the police were 'brought into fashion' by *The Times*. In
1829, however, Peel had most certainly been conscious of the
suspicion and distrust surrounding his 'New Police' and of the
belief that such innovations represented a fundamental threat to
and interference with the privacy of the individual. To this end, the
first *General Instructions* issued in 1829 to the Metropolitan Police
emphasized that the role of the police above all was to prevent
rather than to investigate crime. Whilst investigation meant 'interference' and the invasion of privacy, prevention, on the other
hand, demanded no more than a public presence on the streets.
Thus the newly appointed officers were told:

It should be understood at the outset, that the object to be
attained is the prevention of crime.
To this great end every effort of the police is to be directed.
The security of person and property *and the preservation of a
police establishment* will thus be better effected than by the
detection and punishment of the offender after he has succeeded
in committing crime.[15]

While it would be misleading to suggest that Peel was not aware of
the deterrent value of the 'certain detection' of crime, his emphasis
was clearly placed upon the presence of the *uniformed* officer,
visibly performing his duty in the streets and *in public*. The distinc-
tive, but deliberately non-military, blue tail-coat, blue trousers
(white in summer) and black glazed top hat thus, for both func-

tional and political reasons, ensured visibility as the officer patrolled his fixed beat within the new police divisions. There was to be no doubt where and who the policeman was, precisely in order to allay fears for freedom and privacy. Plain-clothes investigation, epecially, was avoided.

Over and above this, however, the policeman was given precise instruction on what would now be called public relations. The force orders required him to be 'civil and obliging to all people of every rank and class' and to be 'particularly careful not to interfere idly or unnecessarily in order to make a display of his authority'. He was required to have 'a perfect command of temper', never to be moved 'in the slightest degree by any language or threats that may be used', but above all he was told that: 'In the novelty of the present establishment, particular care is to be taken that the constables of the police do not form false notions of their duties and their powers.'

They were thus warned to be extremely careful in the use of their powers of 'interference and arrest' and, wherever possible, to rely upon public consent and co-operation rather than upon formal legal powers.

Thus the public face of the police was that of the trustworthy, upright and politically independent officer, the helper and friend in need. In Critchley's words, from the very start, the police were presented as being 'in tune with the people, understanding the people, belonging to the people and drawing its strength from the people'.

At the same time, however, the police were expected to keep a watch on the people they policed. The tension between the protection and invasion of privacy was present right from the start. Thus, Sir Leon Radzinowicz points out that, complementary to the public presence of the officers on their new beats, the force orders also set up a new 'information service' for the purposes of which every constable 'was expected to get to know his beat and section thoroughly and learn to recognize those living in them'.[16] The constable was thus not only expected to know, he was expected to know about the people.

Despite the care taken by Peel, reaction and distrust was powerfully voiced throughout the next fifty years. The extension of the model of the New Police throughout the provinces ensured continued topicality, whilst incidents such as the 'Popay Affair' in 1833, in which a police *agent provocateur* was employed to infiltrate the National Political Union, lent even greater credibility to principled objections to the threat to liberty. Following the Popay Affair, a Parliamentary Select Committee had specifically criticized police methods. In particular, it was urged that the use of plain-clothes officers should be strictly confined to those cases where detection was otherwise unobtainable. Anything approaching the use of police spies was deprecated as a practice most abhorrent to the feelings of the people and 'most alien to the spirit of the Constitution'.[17]

Such events and opinion were of singular importance to the later development and organization of the police. Within the Metropolitan force they were effectively to delay the formation of a plain-clothes Criminal Investigation Department, very much against the wishes of the Commissioners of Police, for some fifty years. Thus, in 1842, the detective force of the Metropolitan Police amounted to a mere six officers, and discussion of enlargement provoked the following comment from *The Times*: 'If it be dangerous and perhaps unconstitutional, to maintain a few government spies, what will be the effect of impressing that character on the whole police force of this vast metropolis?'[18]

Twenty-five years later, there were still only sixteen full-time officers, and it was not until 1878 that the idea of the police was sufficiently well received among the middle classes to tolerate the setting-up of a specialist criminal investigation department. Over the next ten years, however, the situation changed dramatically, and the new CID expanded from 250 to some 800 officers. By the turn of the century, the new provincial forces were rapidly following suit.

By this time, the friendly uniformed bobby, created by Peel, had become associated with the idea of 'helping the public'. It is, of course, contestable whether the bobby was ever so widely welcomed by the working classes as *The Times* was suggesting by 1908, although there is no doubt that middle-class opinion had shifted quite radically in favour of the police as the politics of the nineteenth century were realigned in the face of growing trade unionism and the labour movement.[19]

For present purposes, however, it is only necessary to recognize that the CID was presented in a very different light from the uniformed branch of the force. While the uniform branch dealt directly with the 'public', the investigative work of the CID was directed only at the 'criminal'. The present position is described by Sir Ronald Howe as follows: 'The Uniform Branch works alongside the *public*, dealing with traffic control, patrol activities and crime in the streets. The CID on the other hand works alongside the *criminal* . . . its sole job being to track down the criminal.'[20]

Thus, the original distinction between prevention and investigation is maintained in the organizational separation of two arms of the law: the uniform branch and the plain-clothes CID. Previous anxieties are allayed by matching this separation to two supposedly distinct social categories, namely the *public* as opposed to the *criminal*. The public (as they are defined by the police) need not fear for their freedom and privacy.

We have spent some time looking at the genesis of this image of the friendly policeman. It is important for a number of reasons. First, the idea of the friendly bobby symbolizes the idea of policing by consent. This conception of policing stresses the mutual interdependence and respect of public and police, and emphasizes the provision of a service to the public rather than a conception of the police as separate from and controlling society. It stresses that the privacy of the citizen must be respected above all else. Thus the police constable must obtain consent before that privacy is interfered with, and the powers of the police must be 'strictly confined'. It stresses that protections and rights be afforded to limit undue interference and to guarantee the consensual base.

In theory at least the use of covert or coercive police methods was subordinated to a public and open model of police work. In no sense, therefore, does policing by consent imply that the police officer is to be given full and extensive powers based upon an unquestioning trust. Trust in the friendly bobby was secured by the publicity of his office, and by the limitation rather than by the extent of his powers. There is a danger, however, that in recent years the idea of policing by consent and the image of the friendly bobby have been reworked to imply precisely the reverse of their original meanings. Today, it would seem that the image suggests that the police should and can be entrusted with whatever powers are necessary to enable them to do anything they think appropriate.

Ӿ Closely associated with the idea of the friendly bobby is one of the
official myths of British policing, namely that the police constable
is the moral lynch-pin of the entire force. Upon the wisdom,
personal qualities and experience of the ordinary bobby are supposed to ride the efficiency, uniqueness and respect accorded to
the force. This is institutionalized in the law, where the constable is
held personally responsible for the manner in which he exercises
his powers and fulfils the duties of his office. In giving evidence to
the Royal Commission in 1960, the Association of Chief Police
Officers (ACPO) described the position of the PC as follows:

> He is not an agent of any other authority, central or local, or
> indeed of any superior officer. He is *personally* responsible for
> all his actions and although he is a citizen, mainly exercising the
> powers and duties of a citizen, he also exercises other powers
> conferred on him by law by virtue of his office; in exercising
> these powers he does so on his own initiative and is liable in law
> for any impropriety. His authority is original, not delegated, and
> exercised at his own discretion by virtue of his office.[21]

We shall see in later chapters that the law to which the constable
is subject is barely comprehensible, even to the academic lawyer.
As may be imagined, this can place the 'ordinary' constable in an
extremely precarious position. One Chief Superintendent we
spoke to summed up the PC's dilemma as follows:

> A police officer gets half a second to decide what action to take.
> Later that action might be diagnosed right through the courts
> where eminent legal brains have days and months to mull over
> their books and decide what he should have done. In practice it
> has to be intuitive. It's one of the unfair things. Young PCs are
> expected to decide in a flash what to do and then get criticized
> later. And they'll be expected to stand by what they've done. I
> mean, we'll be as hard on them as anybody else.

The young PC might be excused for thinking that there are double
standards employed here, yet in the public utterances to the Royal
Commission ACPO were in no two minds on the issue:

This Association wishes to stress that this doctrine of the personal responsibility of the Constable is the most important principle underlying the British Police System. It is more – it is the root and branch of our democratic way of life. [22]

Such a fundamental principle demands that we should be clear about its many implications but two in particular need emphasis. First, the nature and standards of police action are seen to rely on the individual integrity and moral qualities of the constable, who alone is responsible for his actions to the courts. The most important controls upon the police are external to the force, matters of personal morality and public legality; internal discipline is of secondary importance:

> in the discharge of his responsibilities, moral qualities of a high order are called for. There must be high standards of personal discipline, to which the Discipline Code of the service is purely supplementary. [23]

These are high-sounding phrases and on the face of it admirable – as ideals. But if we look at the converse of the principle, we see a second implication of no little significance, namely, there can be no collective responsibility attributed to the force for failure to meet up to expectations. By definition, all instances of wrongdoing are instances of personal failure and inadequacy. Explanations are sought not in terms of policy or organization of the force, except, perhaps, in the failure to recruit the right sort of person who displays the superhuman qualities demanded by the public, official agencies and senior police officers alike. The Interim Report of the Royal Commission of 1962 typifies this approach:

> In a country jealous for the liberty of the subject, powers of arrest are not to be lightly conferred or wantonly exercised; and the constable must be vigilant both to use his authority adequately and instantly as the occasion demands, and at the same time never to exceed it. We are satisfied that this individual responsibility is more onerous than any delegated to, or assumed by a member of any comparable profession or occupation. Responsibility of this kind to be properly and reasonably exer-

cised, demands high moral standards and a nice exercise of judgment.[24]

This displays an exaggerated assumption of individual responsibility and the imagery upon which it draws. If we look at the actual practice and conditions of police work we find that the discretion and the options open to the individual policeman are in reality far fewer than theory would lead us to believe. The nature of police work itself, the excessive workloads and shortage of manpower, the organization of the police on the ground – these are some of the more obvious factors which combine to limit very severely how the individual police officer will react in different circumstances. Police officers of all ranks are called upon to defend their actions and decisions as if they were solely a matter of individual choice. This necessarily presents the problems of policing in a false light and disguises much of what is of real cause for concern – such as the public's response to the working methods of the force as a whole. Problems of policing would be relatively easy to resolve if it were simply a matter of individual officers changing their ideas and making different decisions.

Limited knowledge of what the police actually do is tacitly supplemented by a conception of what they ought to do. This is instanced in the following passage from the Interim Report of the Royal Commission on the Police 1960, where various images are brought together, initially to define ideal police practice, but in the end to stand as a description of actual practice:

> the constable is expected to act with authority, commonsense, courage and leadership. He rises to the demands made on him. Physical toughness, mental alertness, a long-established reputation for honesty and fair dealing, tact, kindness, courtesy and a sense of humour; such qualities are taken for granted; and it is a remarkable tribute to the police that they are very rarely lacking.[25]

An alternative but more realistic description is given by a young Liverpool police constable interviewed by James McClure:

It's basically you can be nosy. A lot of people won't admit this, but you can be nosy without being called nosy. It's yer job to be. Apart from the rubbish pay and rubbish conditions, I enjoy it. It offers – it's very hard to explain – the unusual? You were the man at the scene, you were there, everybody's lookin' at you.

That's one thing about the uniform, it gives you confidence. You tend to notice a bird and think: Oh, that's beautiful! I'd never have done this in plain clothes, I don't think, but once I followed her for about two hundred yards, three hundred, and eventually stopped her. Hi? – y'know.[26]

Sir Robert Mark provides what is perhaps a more telling example, this time an 'alternative version' of the Judges' Rules on the treatment of suspects (for discussion of which see Chapter 5).

I can remember a very successful, fairly senior detective in Manchester, who, when dealing with hardened criminals, had his own version of the Judges' Rules. It consisted of greeting the prisoner with the blunt enquiry, 'Will you talk or be tanned?' If the reply was in the negative, sometimes colourfully so, the prisoner was removed smartly to the lavatory where he was upended and his head jammed down the bowl. It usually took two to hold him, whilst a third repeatedly pulled the chain until a waggling of the feet indicated a more compliant attitude. He then signed a form headed by the usual caution against self-incrimination.[27]

Sir Robert concludes that in his view 'the Rules afford . . . the classic example of the enormous gulf between those who enforce the law and those who administer it'. The problem runs much deeper than this, however. The imagery, and especially the tendency to assume that the police are perfect, actually impedes responses to policing problems and renders debate ineffective, if not impossible. A number of identifiable obstacles flow directly from this confusion.

First, from the point of view of the police, the demands made of them by the public are unreasonable. Failure to live up to expectations results only in an intensification of what is seen to be ill-founded criticism. As a result there is a tendency to close ranks and react defensively. A Scottish Chief Constable displayed the resentment typically occasioned by what is seen as an impossible contradiction when he stated that: 'At the end of the day, we do what the law says. If they say stand on your head and tie your hands behind your back, then that's what we'll do. But don't expect the clear-up rate or detection rate to be singularly good, because it won't be.'[28] The police, in this way, are placed under considerable pressure to bend the rules and to engage in irregular practices to meet the demands placed on them.

Second, on the part of the public, it is assumed that whatever the police actually do is both necessary and legitimate. There is a sense in which, by definition, the police can do no wrong even if this means breaking the law. The police are placed above criticism. Thus, for example, powers under the Criminal Justice (Scotland) Act 1980 to detain suspects for interrogation without arrest and charge were introduced explicitly to 'legalize' widespread practices of interrogation.

A third problem, is that the images employed provoke an emotional rejection of criticism. This is compounded by the assumption of perfection. Criticism of perfection is always negative. However much the critic may protest his or her good intentions, he or she will always appear destructive and debate will inevitably polarize.

Finally, the assumption that the police can be made perfect is fundamentally flawed. It assumes not only that ideals can be realized, but that there is one, identifiable set of standards about which there is or can be complete agreement. In such a utopia there would be no need for a police force. In the reality of a democratic society the assumption of perfection simply disguises the need for a politics of policing by denying its existence.

Confusions and exaggerated ideals, such as those we have discussed, do not merely impede discussion but can be positively damaging to policing. To demand too much of the police is to create a spiral: to fulfil expectations the police 'bend the rules' and exceed their legal powers. Defensiveness is thus reinforced by a need to disguise actual shortcomings. The police are forced to withdraw into themselves and insulate themselves from criticism. Less information flows between police and public, policing itself suffers. Demands are increased and the spiral tightens.

Such isolation of the force manifests itself in a number of ways; its source is to be found, however, in the obligation assumed by the police to 'eliminate' crime or, in some cases, even to rescue society from itself.

Realistically, the object of policing can only be to contain crime, but Sir David McNee for example, as is expected of the Commissioner of the Metropolitan Police, must publicly adopt the very high moral position which requires of the police that they prevent all crime. There can be no police tolerance of even the most minor offence. Although some 75 per cent of recorded crimes are property offences valued at less than £25, it would be wrong, Sir David McNee argues, to regard such offences as trivial:

> I suppose it really depends on what is meant by trivial. But I suspect that few crimes are seen as trivial by their victims, many of whom are the more vulnerable members of our communities. The trauma which many people suffer as a result of criminal behaviour – despite its triviality to the dispassionate academic eye – is not easily assessed.[29]

Few people would want to disagree with the broad sentiments expressed here: the very fact that people report the offence shows their level of concern. By the same token, however, the fact that the vast majority of offences are not reported to the police suggests fairly forcibly that a level of crime is tolerated in society and dealt with by alternative means.[30] Although research on this point is limited, it is reasonable to conclude that the reluctance to involve the police speaks to the fact that police involvement in, and prosecution of, crime is not seen as 'trivial' either. We can be quite certain that in many circumstances individuals and communities seek and prefer to have the freedom to police themselves rather than to invoke the very serious consequences of a criminal prosecution in every instance. Were it the case that 'all the necessary powers to deal effectively with criminal behaviour' were given to the police, as the Commissioner requires, the result might be a crime-free society – although all historical evidence suggests that this is unlikely – but, whatever else, it certainly would not be a free society. Again it seems that the image of the perfect police force, which, in this case, functions to prevent and eradicate all crime, is at odds with the reality of social life.

In sum, where, in response to idealized demands, the police perceive their function as the elimination rather than containment of crime, then legal limitation of their powers, which is an essential element of policy geared to policy by consent, will be perceived negatively. The law will be perceived as an obstacle to the performance of their duty, to be avoided or to be got round by devious means. In turn lawyers and law-makers are perceived as the opponents of the police in a perverted battle of wits. Thus, for example, in 1965, Sir Robert Mark referred to the criminal trial as 'less a test of guilt or innocence than a competition . . . a kind of show jumping contest in which the rider for the prosecution must clear every obstacle to succeed.'[31] Lawyers are employed to exploit every loophole, to utilize every trick in the book to ensure that 'the guilty go free'. Where they can find no legal technicality, they resort to corrupt practices. In his 1973 Dimbleby Lecture, Sir Robert returned to the theme with extraordinary vehemence:

> The criminal and his lawyer take every advantage of these technical rules. Every effort is made to find some procedural mistake which will allow the wrongdoer to slip through the net. If the prosecution evidence is strong the defence frequently resorts to attacks on prosecution witnesses, particularly if they are policemen. They will be accused as a matter of routine of perjury, planting evidence, intimidation or violence. What other defence is there, when found in possession of drugs, explosives or firearms, than to say that they were planted? Lies of this kind are a normal form of defence.[32]

The lawyer is rapidly identified as public enemy number one: 'Experienced and respected metropolitan detectives can identify lawyers in criminal practice who are more harmful to society than the clients they represent.'[33]

It is not, however, just the lawyers who take advantage of the rules. The police do also: Sir David McNee himself has described both the expectations and the practice of the police. He said:

> One of these legitimate demands is that policemen have high

moral standards and work within the law they are expected to uphold. Deliberate misuse of his office is the worst sin a police officer can commit; it is a complete betrayal of trust.[34]

Only a few lines away, however, Sir David says:

> many police officers, early in their careers, learn the art of manipulating the law to their advantage, and, in the investigation of crime, begin to use methods which border on trickery and stealth.[35]

The problem, as McNee sees it, is that the police are expected to prevent crime, to detect offenders and to bring them to justice, but that 'current law and legal procedures do not facilitate that aim'. It cannot be right, he argues, that police officers:

> should have to rely on bluff and stealth – and on occasions force – in order to carry out their duties effectively. All the necessary powers to deal effectively with criminal behaviour must be clearly within the law.[36]

Such complaints are as old as the police themselves. Almost two hundred years ago, Patrick Colquhoun wrote as follows:

> it is a melancholy truth not to be contradicted, that the major part of the hordes of criminal people who infest the metropolis, although committed by Magistrates for trial on very satisfactory proof, are again vomited back on society in vast numbers year after year, and are encouraged to renew their former practices by the facilities they experience in escaping justice.

He then continued with words of uncanny likeness to those of Sir Robert Mark:

> But this is not all – the adroit thief often escapes, from his knowledge of the tricks and devices which are practised through the medium of disreputable practitioners of the Law, while the novice in crimes generally suffers the punishment attached to conviction.[37]

What is new to today's version of the complaint is the assumption that the police and the police alone have access to the 'real' workings of the system and that, as such, the police have a monopoly of practical knowledge and expertise: they are 'the professionals'. The failure of lawyers and law-makers – who have 'vested interests' and 'doubtful motives' – must be rectified and their responsibilities assumed by the police. Thus Sir Robert Mark campaigns for changes and self-consciously enters the political arena:

> It is important to understand that no one but the police sees collectively the failure of the criminal process. We alone know the numbers of crimes not followed by prosecution of the offender, of crimes committed on bail, of acquittals of those who are only too obviously not innocent. We alone experience the collective effect of the difference between the theory of criminal justice and its defects in practice, which undermines its efficiency and lessens public confidence in it. In Britain the police are coming to realise that the public interest requires us to gather and make known information of this kind to the public itself rather than those who have vested interests in the making or practice of law.[38]

Exclusive possession of expert knowledge by implication gives the police the right to speak and be heard above the parliamentary voice. The issues are too detailed for the ordinary legislative process and for ordinary law-makers to deal with adequately. Thus, when Parliament approved the introduction of an independent police complaints procedure, Sir Robert Mark was to comment:

> When the Prime Minister told the House that the Police Bill was the will of Parliament, he tactfully omitted to mention that, if every member of the House was compelled to sit an examination paper consisting of ten simple questions about the working of the police disciplinary system and the pass mark was set as low as 20 per cent, not 5 per cent of them would be likely to pass. So much for the will of Parliament.[39]

If parliamentarians did not enjoy Sir Robert's full confidence, the jury fared even worse. This was his opinion:

> if the one person in the criminal justice process most fitted by
> education, training and experience to decide the issue, namely
> the judge, is to be denied that right (to decide the verdict), how
> much more illogical is it to confer it upon any one of 12 random
> jurymen, least fitted by deafness, stupidity, prejudice or one of a
> hundred other reasons so to do?[40]

Such attitudes are clearly coloured by notions of technical efficiency and professionalism. At the same time, however, they
reveal a more deep resentment and a tendency on the part of the
police to adopt a position of confrontation. Increasingly they
perceive themselves as under attack from all quarters. In their
evidence to the Royal Commission on the Police the Superintendents' Association voiced these feelings directly:

> The fears of the Police Service are that only the police and, on
> track record, a minority of the legal profession will speak for law
> and order in the enforcement sense. On the other side will be
> ranged the big guns of every minority group and sociological
> agency – many with doubtful motives – propounding the theory
> of a violent and unfeeling Police Service whose only aim is to
> inconvenience or convict as many innocent persons as possible.[41]

Here the police are typified as desperately striving to save society
from itself. Reference is often made to the police force as
the last bastion in the war against crime; to a 'perplexed society'
which looks to the police for the answer to declining standards of
private morality and public life alike. This is the rhetoric of Sir
Robert Mark, who claims that 'We are no longer just the shock
absorber, or the oil which lessens the frictions of society. We are
now the bastion to which people at every level look for reassurance
and comfort.'[42]

This image of the beleaguered force has a particular resonance
for today's police. Policing is portrayed as an increasingly specialist
function of a *separate* and *expert* body. This is very much in line
with the process of centralization, rationalization and specialization
which has marked the development of police organization through-

out the post-war period. It confirms beliefs in police professionalism. The process itself enhances the social and political status,
especially of senior officers, which, in turn, reinforces a belief on
their part that they speak for the silent majority of ordinary folk.

For such reasons, the police demand reforms of the law. To the
policy of more police and a better equipped professional force is
added the demand for more and wider powers. Thus, it appears
that police chiefs are increasingly prepared to confront society – as
can be seen from the 'shopping list' presented by Commissioner
McNee to the Royal Commission on Criminal Procedure in 1978.
The Commission was asked, *inter alia*, for powers to hold suspects
for questioning for up to seventy-two hours, to detain witnesses, to
set up road blocks, to search persons and vehicles and to fingerprint
whole communities. The shopping list, if nothing else gave a disturbing view of the level of public co-operation that Commissioner
McNee was either presupposing or building into his system of
policing.

In Chapters 2 and 3, we shall have cause to question the nature of
the relationship between police and public still further when we
look at different strategies of policing and the forms of police
organization that these require. Crucial to the style of policing is, of
course, the manner in which the police perceive their relation to the
public and how they define the public that is to be policed. The
sense of isolation and sensitivity to criticism we have mentioned,
the claim to an exclusive monopoly of expertise and the extent to
which the police assume a responsibility to stop rather than contain
crime are key factors in determining the kinds of strategies and
tactics to be employed, and consequently the powers required to
put those strategies into effect.

To achieve a rational system of policing it will be necessary to make
concrete changes in the law and the organization of the police. In
particular we shall argue that there is a need to redefine the extent
of police powers and the purposes they are intended to serve. It will
be necessary to introduce procedures to review and scrutinize their
use and to punish their misuse. Adequate guarantees of individual
rights and means of redress must be secured in order to guarantee a
policy of policing by consent. In terms of the social organization of

the police, thought must be given to training methods and to career structure, as well as to the implications of new technology if the introduction of alternative strategies is to be facilitated. In terms of police organization, there has been no clear understanding of what the so-called police function actually is, let alone of what it ought to be. These issues are given priority in this book because too frequently critics tend to dismiss them. On the one hand, it is said that the law is unimportant because in practice the police can do what they want (rules can always be bent and laws 'interpreted'); on the other hand, especially among some civil libertarians and lawyers, there is a tendency to emphasize the law and ignore mundane considerations such as the conditions of employment and the nature of the job done by the police. What is really necessary, is to spell out what can and cannot be done through law and to provide a legal framework of control. The practical conditions of work however: the pressures and strains of promotion, the obligations of mutual support, and so on – are just as important as the formal rules.

## Further Reading

Alderson, J. C. and Stead, P. J., *The Police We Deserve*, Wolfe, London, 1973.

Bailey, V. (ed.), *Policing and Punishment in Nineteenth Century Britain*, Croom Helm, London, 1981.

Bottomley, A. and Coleman, C., 'Criminal Statistics: The Police Role in the Discovery and Detection of Crime', *International Journal of Criminology and Penology*, 4, 1976.

Clarke, J. *et al.*, *Policing the Crisis*, Macmillan, London, 1978.

Clarke, R. V. G. and Hough, J. M. (eds.), *The Effectiveness of Policing*, Gower, Aldershot, Hants, 1980.

Critchley, T. A., *A History of Police in England and Wales, 1900–1960*, Constable, London, 1967.

Holdaway, S. (ed.), *The British Police*, Edward Arnold, London, 1979.

Lewis, R., *A Force for the Future*, Temple Smith, London, 1976.

Mark, Sir R., *Policing a Perplexed Society*, Allen & Unwin, London, 1977.

*In the Office of Constable*, Collins, London, 1978.
Martin, J. P. and Wilson, G., *The Police: A Study in Manpower*, Heinemann, London, 1969.
Thompson, E. P., *Writing by Candlelight*, Merlin, London, 1980.
Whitaker, B., *The Police in Society*, Eyre Methuen, London, 1979.

# 2

# The Organization of Police Work I: 'Fire-brigade' Policing

'He will be civil and obliging to all people of every rank and class
. . . He must remember that there is no qualification so indis-
pensable to a police officer as a perfect command of temper,
never suffering himself to be moved in the slightest degree by
any language or threats that may be used.'
             (General Instructions to the Metropolitan Police, 1829)

The last chapter looked at what the public, legislators and Chief
Constables like to believe of the police. This chapter and the next
investigate the contemporary practice of the 'two arms of the law' –
the uniform branch and the plain-clothes branch of the service.
Evidently every aspect of their work cannot be covered so the two
most important movements in police work and strategy are emphasized. First, we look at the development of what has been termed
'fire-brigade' policing and the redefinition of the work and
organization of the uniform branch since the last war. The following chapter examines the development of plain-clothes police work
and the use of local intelligence-gathering for what has been termed
'pre-emptive' police work.

The purpose of this account is neither to apologize nor to lay
blame for any wrongdoing or failure, but rather to understand what
it is about the way in which the job is defined and organized which

itself creates difficulties and contradictions for police officers from the Chief Constable to the PC on the streets.

It cannot be disputed that individual officers can and do deliberately break the rules for reasons of their own self-interest, that there are instances of corruption and brutality which are to be deplored, and for which fault lies with the individual. Such occurrences are not the central concern here, however. Our interest is with those conditions of work which systematically and routinely recur in such a way as almost to guarantee that policing will not be done according to the rules.

In his Report on the Brixton Disorders, Lord Scarman regretted the inadequacy of recent research on conditions of police work. In particular he pointed out that:

> The conflict which can arise between the duty of the police to maintain order and their duty to enforce the law, and the priority which must be given to the former, have long been recognised by the police themselves, though they are factors to which commentators on the police have in the past paid too little attention.[1]

While abuse of power and individual excesses are not to be condoned, it is essential to analyse policing from a position which respects and expects human fallibility. Police constables are not perfect. As we shall see, they take short cuts round the law, bend the rules and cover up for each other. Some skive on the job, many lose their tempers and become frustrated with the public. As in most occupations, theory gives way to what 'works' and what is easiest.

In Chapter 4 we shall look critically at the system of internal control and external accountability. To an extent, however, it is inevitable that individual failures and transgressions will occur. What can and must be avoided, however, is the creation of conditions which make *collective* failure inevitable. Unfortunately, as police work is presently organized, that stage has already been reached.

Although many people most readily associate police work with catching criminals and 'thief-taking', it would be incorrect to see this as the primary function of the uniformed PC. Put crudely, 'thief-taking' has become more and more the prerogative of the

CID (we shall examine the associated problems in the next chapter), while the work of the uniform branch of the service has been directed more to the rather loosely defined 'provision of ground cover' and the prevention of crime.

By tradition, the job of the uniform PC is to 'guard, watch and patrol'. The model was provided by Sir Robert Peel and was securely institutionalized during the nineteenth century. Increasingly, however, that preventive role has been reduced, and the constable's job in 'providing ground cover' has been defined in terms of the 'rapid response' to calls from the public. At the same time, local contact has given way to an overtly deterrent function. This is clearly visible from Home Office analyses of the use of police manpower.[2]

Although it is recognized that operational duties will 'blur and overlap', for Home Office planning and policy purposes the functions of the police are divided into four categories: *Ground Cover*, to which between 50 and 60 per cent of manpower is devoted; *Crime Investigation and Control*, 20 per cent; *Traffic Control*, 10 per cent; and *Additional Services*. It is this last category which is of particular interest, as it shows the relatively low priority given to methods of crime prevention other than deterrence. Thus, while in excess of 50 per cent of manpower is devoted to 'ground cover', the Home Office Review 1972 stated that the category of 'Additional Services' covers a 'miscellaneous range of *mainly minor duties*' such as licensing work and lost and found property:

Also included under this heading would be the traditionally accepted police function of being there to befriend and help those in need and to help in all manner of minor and major emergencies; and to their role in community relations and other functions designed to help in cementing the bonds of society.[3]

It should also be noted, however, that the uniform branch has not been exempt from rationalization and specialization, even in the area of general ground cover. Thus one of the most prominent features of post-war police policy has been the concern to reduce the amount of time taken to respond to calls for assistance from the public. As a result, less emphasis is placed upon the general duties of 'guard, watch and patrol', and relatively little time is given over to investigation. For the uniform PC a 'capture' is now very much a bonus and, as we shall see, in the station we studied a uniformed officer could expect to make *no more than two arrests in any month* – by far the larger proportion of these being for street offences, such as breach of the peace, drunk and incapable, or drunk driving with only the very occasional 'good capture' for a housebreaking or car theft.

To Sir David Gray's question 'where have all the police gone?' might be added 'and what are they doing?' We suspect that many people would be as surprised as we were by the answers to these questions and by the pace and pressure of work inside (and outside) a police station. For that reason this chapter describes the kind and conditions of work in a typical 'unit' station operating a 'fire-brigade' service, based upon observations made over a period of two and a half months during which time permission was obtained to accompany police officers in their daily work. One month of that time was spent working through the cycle of a complete shift in a busy unit station. We have drawn extensively upon the men's own comments as they were given to us on tape. We do this to illustrate the limits to the individual PC's 'discretion and responsibility' and to provide a basis for later analysis of the legal and political control of police behaviour. (No WPCs worked on the research shift: with apologies the male pronoun will be used.)

Policing of city centres or more sparsely populated rural areas bears little resemblance to the kind of work and conditions which prevail in the policing of a large residential area of mixed housing such as we describe. It is, however, in the latter locations that the problems of contemporary policing come most clearly into focus: where the panda system operates, where difficulties in police/community relations surface most harshly, and where workloads are at their highest. It is also in such areas that, for the majority of people, policing is most important, where relationships between the police and the public are either built up or come unstuck.

Before looking at the conditions of police work in the eighties, we must provide a context. To do so we review briefly the major development of police strategy in the sixties and seventies which can be seen to underlie many of the problems faced by the police today, namely the policy of 'Unit Beat Policing'. This system was the policy-makers' answer to a perceived shortage of manpower and inadequate 'ground cover' and, by the early seventies, it was generally accepted in the police service to have been a highly effective innovation.

We then look at 'fire-brigade' policing in practice and the conditions of work which typify and sharpen the problems of contemporary policing 'at the sharp end'. In our description and analysis of this kind of work we are not only looking at the failure of unit beat policing, we are also looking at a fundamentally changed context of policing to which in future all policy and innovation must pay heed.

## Unit Beat Policing

The theory was good . . . It was an expedient in a way – to counteract rising crime and the shortage of officers. The idea was of a conspicuously marked vehicle – the panda car – put into an area to show the flag. That was the purpose of the panda.

If the truth were known the idea was copied from the American system . . . in Chicago, Detroit and New York where they had the black and white cars . . . easily seen. That's why they're called pandas.

The idea was they'd move round the areas at less than twenty miles an hour and be seen by the public . . . so you could flag one down when you needed one. It was a good idea – but it didn't work out. (Chief Superintendent)

Unit beat policing was first introduced in the mid-sixties.[4] It caught on rapidly, and, by the early seventies, it had become the standard method of policing residential areas in the towns and cities of Britain. In conception the idea was simple and attractive. As it turned out it generated more work than it could handle.

For the general purposes of policing, a force area is broken down into a number of 'divisions' and then, again, into further 'subdivisions'. The strategy of policing adopted at subdivisional level will differ according to the characteristics of the area. In a town centre, for example, greater emphasis would be placed on foot patrols than in the larger and more densely populated outlying residential districts.

In a typical unit beat policing system a subdivision or 'unit area' would be divided into eight 'areas'. Each two of these areas would make up one panda car beat which would be patrolled throughout the twenty-four-hour working day. It was intended that the car was to be manned by a single constable, and controlled from subdivisional headquarters (the 'unit station') by means of radio. Each of the eight areas was to have an 'area constable', who would wherever possible, live within his own area. The area constable was to have overall responsibility for the day-to-day policing of his area. When he was off duty, however, he would not be replaced, ground cover being provided by the panda. The area PC was to be allowed a wide measure of discretion, both as to the hours he was to work and in deciding how the area was to be policed. For both area men and car men there was to be no fixed beat or route to be followed, the necessity for 'checking in' at fixed points having been superseded by the introduction of the personal radio.

In addition to the car man and the two area men, each car beat was to be covered over the twenty-four-hour period by a detective constable, so that a team of four men would be attached to any one car beat. Between them they would carry out the basic functions of prevention and detection of crime and rendering assistance to the public. Supervision of these duties throughout the unit area was to be carried out by the shift sergeant who was provided with an additional car.

Once in operation, the heart of the system is the subdivisional control room. From here the station clerk (a PC) maintains continuous radio contact with the men outside, channelling information and instructions to and from divisional and force headquarters. The men are thus controlled from the centre and directed to incidents as and when they occur.

The primary purpose behind the introduction of the panda cars was thus to ensure a rapid response to emergencies, while leaving officers free for as much time as possible to fulfil the traditional police function of 'guard, watch and patrol'. The presence of the constable on foot in the areas was intended to compensate for any lack of contact between the car men and the public and to ensure continuing ground cover at times when the car men were busy, while the more time-consuming job of investigation was handled by the detective constable.

Backing up the station clerk, co-ordination of information was to be achieved by the introduction of the 'collator'. The collator is a constable whose function is to 'sort, file and disseminate items of information received from patrolling officers'.[5] The fund of local knowledge and general information which was previously available only to the local police constable, now – because the job had been broken down into different parts – had to be brought together and fed out through the system. Thus a centralized system of 'divisional criminal intelligence' was made available to all officers. This intelligence-gathering procedure was to prove singularly efficient, and, with the advent of computerization, is now the subject of some controversy.

Uppermost throughout the general approach was the desire to rationalize the use of police time by specialization and thus to increase the number of police on the streets. The priorities were clear:

> The system aims to increase the work capacity of operational officers by keeping them on active patrol for longer periods; and to increase their efficiency through the regular supply of information from the collator. The system has been made possible by the development of personal radios which all members of the team can use and by the provision of many more police cars.[6]

The obsession with numbers and equipment at the expense of any consideration of the quality of policing is evidenced in the ease with which *personal* knowledge and experience of an officer is sacrificed in favour of the specialized intelligence-gathering function of the collator.

As we shall see, the unit beat system has not met with anything like the success hoped for it. In one important respect however, the system has been successful, even if that success has been double-edged. Response times to emergency calls have been significantly improved – in most cases down to a matter of two or three minutes.

This has been important for a number of reasons. First, it has fundamentally changed public demands. However much the system may now be criticized, it is unlikely that today's public would be satisfied with the kind of service offered twenty-five years ago as it is described here:

You can't skive off so easily nowadays . . . 'cos of the radios. All right, you used to have the old flasher system on top of the boxes. But say my time for ringing in was 11.30 – at five past twelve I might be back and see the flasher going, but nobody was to know if I left it. You can't do that now.

I remember you'd come back to your box and find half a dozen people waiting for you . . . and maybe some notes pushed under the door. *You'd* decide which jobs to do first and who had to wait, and if they'd been waiting an hour already it was hard luck. (PC, 26 years' service)

*CRITICISM*

Second, because it is now so much more easy to report incidents to the police, demand and workloads have risen out of all proportion, although it is impossible to put a precise figure on the increase.

Third, the rapid response has itself come to be regarded as the hallmark of police efficiency – it is one of those few aspects of police work which can be measured accurately and improved upon by internal changes. (Unlike, for example, detection rates, improvement upon which rests very much on factors outside the immediate control of the police – such as the availability of evidence or the co-operation of witnesses.) This is one of the reasons why the system has come under unbearable pressure. There is a kind of self-destructive logic to the process: the more quickly more calls are dealt with, the more calls are made and consequently the more work there is.

At the time of its inception there could have been no idea of the extraordinary pressure to which unit beat policing was to be subjected nor of the consequences. The sheer pressure of work – whatever the cause – has thwarted the intentions of the planners in almost every respect.

The system rests upon the effective co-ordination of the area men, the car men and the detective constables, and upon their ability to function as a team. The practical effects of increased workloads have been to limit severely if not wholly prevent this from happening. Constant pressure on manpower has tended to devalue the role of the area man: he is the first one to be pulled off his normal duties if there is need elsewhere in the division or if there is a man short in the station. It is the area man who performs

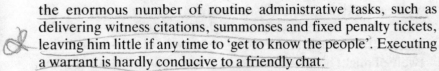

the enormous number of routine administrative tasks, such as delivering witness citations, summonses and fixed penalty tickets, leaving him little if any time to 'get to know the people'. Executing a warrant is hardly conducive to a friendly chat.

A further problem faced by the area men stems from the job description itself. Many policemen do not want the job, as they feel that 'drinking cups of tea with old ladies' is not 'real police work'. Lord Scarman noted this with concern in his Brixton Report (paras 5.48–50) and instanced the failure of 'operational' policemen to communicate with the so-called 'hobby-bobbies' as one of the underlying causes of the deterioration in police public relations. It is possible to exaggerate this point. There are some extremely committed and hard-working area men who gain a great deal of personal satisfaction from what they do. It has to be said, however, that this is more in spite of than because of the system and often works solely because the individual officer is prepared to spend off-duty time working within his area. A car man represented the opinion of many of his colleagues when he told us:

> Area men? A lazy man's job. Instead of going out and getting to meet the public, as they should, they go out and find six or seven howffs and use them continually, going back to the same place, time in, time out. Instead of serving citations and speaking to the people and getting to hear their points of view, they go up to the door and 'there you are' – exit stage left, running!
>
> Some of them – the good ones – they'll go out and make a point of getting to know who so and so is. They'll read the summations and they'll say 'Oh, that's Joe Bloggs who's been fixed. I didn't know about that.' So they go out and get their own ideas of what's been happening in their area. And they know exactly, they've got their fingers on the pulse. They can tell you who's got a car and's disqualified, who's been spending money recently and's not working. They can tell you . . . but there's very, very few good ones. (PC, 14 years' experience)

As things have developed, the area constables tend now to regard themselves as 'forgotten men'. The fact that they do not work the same shifts as the car men and sergeants, that they are less directly and less frequently engaged in the more visible and publicly recognized aspects of police work – captures, chases etc. – and, paradoxically perhaps, because they have greater freedom from supervision, they can very easily come to see themselves as marginal if not expendable.

Such difficulties are not helped by the common policy which requires that young officers should be given as wide an experience of as many sorts of police work as possible, with the result that a young policeman, with perhaps two or three years' experience, can find himself at the age of twenty or twenty-one doing six months as an area man. Some enjoy it, but most regard it as a waste of their time: 'you can't possibly get to know an area in six months, and anyway, what am I supposed to know about kids?' Subsequently the job is avoided like the plague.

The area man's job has further become devalued in his own and others' eyes by the increasing amount of petty beat complaints which are gladly handed on to him by other officers to be 'written off' and 'resolved the best way possible'. All too frequently his task becomes a thankless one of increasingly problematic public relations.

The specialization of the unit beat system has further disadvantages from the point of view of the men themselves. By entrusting criminal enquiries to a detective constable, both car men and area men are rarely able to see a 'good' case through from beginning to end. Here again the difficulty of ensuring co-ordination between the different elements of the team is in part to blame, as is the inordinate workload. In consequence, however, a very high premium is placed by the men on 'making a capture' for themselves and this brings the attendant danger of over-zealousness.

It is, by definition, the car men rather than the area men who are the more likely to make arrests at the scene of the crime, so that a further feature of the practice of unit beat policing has been the identification of the area men as the 'goodies' and the car men as the 'baddies', especially among younger people. Such labels tend to emphasize the over-eagerness of the car men to get 'involved' and to reinforce the idea that the introduction of the panda cars (rather than the total system) has alienated the public from the police.

By the end of the seventies many of these features, which it can be argued were inherent in the system, had become increasingly obvious and the unit beat system had all but collapsed under the weight of work. As one Chief Superintendent put it, 'It's not so much that our men aren't involved in the community – it's just that they're involved in the wrong way.'

## A 'Fire-brigade' Service in Action

[Unit beat policing] was a good idea. But it didn't work out . . . because of the rising number of incidents they have to attend. The treble nine calls are stacked up now . . . three or four at a time . . . and you have to take the priority calls first. It's unfortunate. The pandas stopped being there to show the flag and went onto 'fire-brigade' policing . . . just answering calls, one after another. (Chief Superintendent)

A 'fire-brigade' service means just what it says: providing a rapid response to emergency calls. Almost without exception the policemen we spoke to were of the same mind, that 'fire-brigade' policing is not 'good policing'. Nor is this approach confined to policing in cars. There are still large parts of our towns and cities which are patrolled predominantly on foot, for example in the city centres where it would be impractical to do otherwise. To an extent some of our comments also apply to the working of such beats, where the introduction of personal radios and the general increase in the amount of reported crime have significantly affected the nature of the job, both in terms of discipline and supervision and in terms of the kind of work done:

Supervision is very tight now with the radios and it has to be with so many young officers working the town beats. But the fixed beat is not so rigidly enforced now as it used to be . . . because of the amount of incidents that happen. With the police officer being taken away to calls it's not so easy to work the old system. Very seldom now is he able to complete an hourly turn round the beat without being interrupted. In the old days you could walk round an hour's turn without getting a job to do. That very rarely happens now. (Chief Superintendent)

However, we have chosen to concentrate on the panda system for two reasons. First, for the purposes of studying the police it is a lot easier to accompany officers in a patrol car and to attend incidents in 'plain clothes' than it is to walk the beat with an officer where the 'observer' sticks out like a sore thumb and becomes an object of curiosity to passers-by. From a car, on the other hand, there is a natural assumption on the part of the public that the 'third party' is either a prisoner or a CID officer. Occasionally this proved embarrassing, but generally a semblance of normality was maintained. The second, and really the more important, reason is, of course, that the panda system as it presently operates and as it is being developed is the focal point of the problems of modern policing.

The unit station described here was not chosen by any careful process of selection, but on two general criteria. First, it was the station which the local police themselves thought would best illustrate the difficulties as well as the variety of their work. In so far as the police perceptions of the difficulties and contradictions of their work was seen to be an important aspect of the study, it seemed justifiable to follow their advice. It should perhaps be said that there was no question of being required to observe this particular station nor, so far as ever became apparent, of anything being 'laid on' for the purposes of research observation.

Second, the area policed was fairly diverse, and suggested itself as one which might be found in any large town or city. While it is always dangerous to make such claims, it is unlikely that the problems encountered in policing this particular area differed significantly from those of many other unit stations throughout the country.

The centre of the unit area contains most, and some of the worst, housing in a large and visibly run-down local authority scheme. Down either side of it run two of the major roads out of the city. The scheme is a place which many people pass by, but few have cause to visit. Those who do are very often surprised by the level of obvious poverty and decay in what is generally thought of as a wealthy city. This is by far the most heavily policed section of the unit area and the most hard hit by crime. It provides at least 50 per cent of the work of the station, which is situated in the centre of it.

As one moves south and west, the standard of living improves noticeably. At some distance from each other, and surrounded by a clutter of bungalows and smaller private dwellings, there are two further, compact and neat local authority schemes. Here, there are no metal shutters over the shop windows, and there are well-established playing fields and good amenities.

Further out again, one comes to the old village, now comparatively built up, with a substantial population of owner-occupiers. By the time the outer boundary of the unit area is reached in the prosperous south-west, the surroundings are more countrified and the private houses 'over the hill' more substantial.

The unit area makes up one subdivision of 'R' (Research) Division. A second unit station and two further 'town sections' (worked on twelve foot beats and controlled from the divisional station to the north) carry the full divisional responsibility to a total of 160,000 residents. The total population living within the unit area is approximately 60,000, of whom 35,000 are local authority tenants.

The first obvious question to ask is how many men work from the unit station? Unfortunately, it is not possible to give a direct answer to this, as the manpower of the force is allocated at divisional rather than subdivisional level. This necessitates a brief look at manpower in the force as a whole.

The operational 'establishment' of each division is assigned at force level. Each division is then responsible for allocating ground cover in its own subdivision. The total 'authorized establishment' of the force (i.e. the level up to which the force is allowed to recruit) provides for a ratio of one policeman to every 362 members of the resident population. As at the present time the actual strength of the force is up to its authorized establishment so that there is on paper no shortage of men. However, the ratio of 1 : 362 is very misleading. To begin with, once allowance has been made for internal secondments and for personnel employed in the traffic division, in CID and at HQ the ratio of uniform officers to the population in 'R' Division becomes 1 : 625.

For a number of reasons, short-term manpower shortages create an almost constant and unpredictable drain on resources, with the result that a daily juggling act has to be performed to ensure that basic cover is provided in the different subdivisions. In a sense there is constant need to 'rob Peter to pay Paul', with the result that it is difficult to maintain a stable contingent of men in each station although this is given high priority and whenever possible, especially in busy stations such as the unit station under consideration, every effort is made to keep the same team of men working together.

For such reasons it is only ever possible to give a target figure for manpower at subdivisional level. For this particular unit the 'best possible' figure is something like fifty-four officers, which would include one Chief Inspector, one Inspector, four sergeants, and forty-eight PCs. Also working out of the station is a CID establishment of one detective sergeant, six detective constables and one acting detective constable. However, in so far as the CID take over from the uniform branch as specialists, they are relatively uninvolved in the initial response and first contact, and rarely featured in the day-to-day work of the station. Two civilians – a clerk and a typist – are also employed.

From this, it can be seen that the ratio of police to population in the residential area has now fallen from a starting point of 1 : 362 to a ratio at street level of 1 : 1111.

At first sight, a target of fifty-four men to police 60,000 might not look at all unreasonable. However, the operation of the shift system necessitates a further division of the strength by four if we are to see the target strength at any one time during the day. This gives a maximum of twelve police constables on duty and a ratio of approximately 1 : 5000.[8]

More or less in line with the theory of unit beat policing, the unit area is itself divided into four car beats and nine 'areas'. However, due to pressure of work, nine areas are worked not by nine but by a total of thirteen area constables. The area men work a different shift pattern from other officers. Their hours are more flexible – they can usually choose to work between 8 a.m. and 4 p.m. or 2 p.m. and 10 p.m. They are rarely called upon to work a night shift, unless it is to replace one of the car men. More often than not, between the hours of 10 p.m. and 9 a.m. the majority of the area men will be off duty, although at the weekends two or three area men will be required to work a cover shift from 6 p.m. until 2 a.m.

We can now see that, through the later part of the evening and the night, it would be *hoped* to have at most nine constables, one sergeant and either the Inspector or Chief Inspector on duty. One constable is necessarily desk-bound at the station (the station clerk, who takes all the calls and passes on the radio messages to the men). This leaves as the target four double-manned panda cars, plus a sergeant in his own car, making a total of nine men on the street to police a population of 60,000 at what is regularly the busiest time during the twenty-four-hour period.

It needs to be emphasized that this is the most optimistic view of the situation. During any month on average well over one hundred working days are lost for reasons of sickness, for court appearances and for other duties, so that even when the morning juggling act is completed the actual figure may be substantially lower. Over the monthly cycle of the shift, it was found that on average, at any one time (day or night) there were between six and seven uniform constables (including the area men) actually on duty. Thus we have moved from a ratio of 1 : 362 to one of 1 : 10,000. Therefore at a station which has been numbered among the ten busiest stations in Britain, an average night shift will see six police constables, in four cars, policing in excess of 60,000 people.

It is also worth noting that according to the most recent statistics for 1980, over one-third of police constables in Britain are twenty-five years of age or younger. On shift 4 (the 'research' shift at the unit station), of the eight PCs who were most often on duty in the cars – rarely if ever were they all on duty together – two had between four and five years' service and were aged twenty-two and twenty-three respectively, one had served two and a half years and was aged thirty, and three were probationers, with less than two years' service who were 'there for the experience'. There were two constables with more substantial service of seven and fourteen years each.

The four most senior men had primary responsibility for each of the four car beats, but (although it was avoided by the shift sergeant whenever possible) the probationers would quite regularly have to go out either alone or in twos. The target was to have each of the four cars double-manned, especially during the evenings and during the night shift, with the sergeant in a fifth car to 'float' round the areas ready to attend more serious or complicated incidents and generally to help out the less experienced men. Throughout this period of research the ideal target was met only once – during a day shift.

On paper, the basic work of the unit is, in accordance with theory, shared between the car men and the area men, with the CID taking over the more serious investigations after initial contact and report from the uniform branch. To that extent the system in operation accords with the model of unit beat policing but there is little if any further resemblance. For the car men especially, boundaries between areas have become meaningless as the pressure of work has risen; for both car men and area men the traditional function of guard, watch and patrol has given way to attending calls and filing reports. The idea of a team of men working a particular area has been entirely forgotten and, in practice, the car men, the area men and the CID form three identifiable and separate groups, both socially and in terms of the kind of work they do.

As we shall see, statistics can only give the vaguest indication of the nature and conditions of police work and for that reason they have to be handled with care. None the less they are of some interest, although it should be noted that for various reasons – the most obvious being that there simply is not enough time – a vast quantity of trivial incidents and work is simply unrecorded and unrecordable.

In an average month, a total in excess of 600 'treble nine' calls will be attended by the cars, as will approximately the same number of less urgent calls made directly to the station. In responding to these calls each car will travel approximately 50,000 miles per annum within the three and a half square miles of the unit area, aiming for a response time of between three and four minutes. It is hardly surprising that the blue light is seen so often and that the label of 'fire-brigade service' has been earned. In addition, the car men will execute, or attempt to execute, some eighty warrants per month. As persons wanted on warrant are not likely to make the job easy, this can prove repetitive and frustrating. It is impossible to estimate the amount of time spent on traffic-related matters. This kind of work, such as watching for speeders or drunk-drivers, tends to be done at odd moments when time permits the officers to 'go out and find work'.

In any month, some 400 crimes will be reported to the CID. Over half of these (the less serious) will be handed back to the area men for routine investigation. Each criminal investigation will entail visits to interview witnesses and complainants, possibly several times over. About one quarter of reported crime is cleared up, and some ninety arrests made per month. As we noted earlier, this is an average of less than two arrests per man per month.

In addition to dealing with the less serious criminal investigations, the area men will also deliver, in person, approximately 300 witness citations and summonses for appearance in court during the month. These also frequently require return visits, and, in an area dominated by high rise flats, can prove both tiring and time-consuming. The area men also have to deal with the mass of minor beat complaints – stray dogs, noisy neighbours, malicious damage etc. – many of which are passed on to them by the car men (who are only too glad to be rid of them).

Even so, the figures have little real meaning. Statistics cannot convey what it is like to attend at a serious road traffic accident, or the sense of intrusion when searching someone's house – perhaps that of a parent of a child in trouble; how it feels to be stone cold sober in the middle of a pub brawl, or of how a young policeman feels attempting to sort out a domestic dispute between people old enough to be his parents.

An Inspector with over twenty years' service explained how the work can affect the young officer. His hardened exterior was belied by his words:

A lot of young lads around about the twelve- or eighteen-month stage go through a bad spell. They become affected by what they see and what they have to do. Most of them get over it, but others don't. They develop real problems. Some of them leave, some of them take to drink, some get very fat, their marriages break up . . . You can see it happening. They become bad policemen if they get to that stage. Officious *and* vicious. They tend to over-react very badly on occasions. Others, of course, just seem to retreat into their shells. Nothing happens to them . . . no feelings.

Of course, you've got to suppress your feelings and I suppose it shows. Certainly, I know that for many, many years of my service I made a thing of suppressing my feelings. The stiff upper lip is permanent . . . never cry, never show any emotion; you know, you're not really a person. Not until you've learned to live with it . . . I suppose.

Of course, reactions differ and it is not possible for a senior officer to require that certain emotions be displayed in particular situations. Such reactions can, however, be intensified, repressed or displaced as a result of the general conditions within which the men work.

For the individual officer the conditions of his work are beyond his control. For young officers especially, who may have had no experience of anything else, they appear as necessary preconditions of police work in general and they become resigned to the system. As such, the conditions of work inevitably colour the officers' perceptions of what is possible 'under pressure', and this in itself can in consequence limit and determine the quality of service provided. We shall now look at the various factors which in combination have created the pressure of work which undermined the theory of unit beat policing. In looking at the experience of the daily work of the unit station, therefore, we are seeking to identify which problems are the consequence of policy and organization, and to that extent possible to change, and which are necessary features of police work in general.

One of the most important inadequacies of statistical accounts of police work is the inability to show the distribution of work over the twenty-four-hour period and consequently the pressure which can occur at different times. It is important to emphasize that for all practical purposes this cannot be done statistically for the simple reason that there is no such thing as an average day. This is not to say that the work cannot be boring. At times it can be tedious in the extreme, the same old complaints and the same old complainers reappearing with what becomes a monotonous frequency, but there is little pattern to it. Some jobs can be organized, such as the delivery of witness citations and the execution of warrants. These are initiated by the police and can be carried out at times which are convenient and most likely to be successful. It is possible to say that some incidents are more likely to be reported at certain times than others – people returning from work report daytime housebreakings in the early evening, road traffic is bad on winter mornings and so on – but there are no ways of knowing how many and how often such incidents will occur. It is not unusual for the car men to have 'treble nine' calls stacked up, for the station clerk to complain that 'it hasn't stopped all day', and yet for the next shift to complain that nothing has happened.

It is not easy, therefore, to convey the constant pitch of police work and activity, and the amount of nervous energy consumed even during the not infrequent moments of peace and quiet, for, even at such times, there can be no real relaxation, precisely because no one knows what might happen. Indeed, when something does 'break' more often than not it is a relief, as energy otherwise expressed in an endless stream of humour and practical jokes is suddenly converted into action. Nothing is regular about police work. Interrupted meals, cold cups of coffee, complaints of indigestion, are a constant feature of station life, which policemen would willingly forgo. No one can say whether a particular shift will be busy or quiet and allocate men accordingly. Everything is geared to what *might* happen and the time when resources are stretched to the limit.

It is self-evident that problems will result in relations between police and public simply as a result of the pressure on time. It is in the nature of the work that, where they are in a position to do so, police officers will give priority to certain calls. Of course, what may seem to the police officer a trivial or routine matter to be dealt with in a spare moment, will usually appear to the complainant in a very different light, and he or she will resent delay. Very often the police will have only limited information as to the nature of the incident, and a succession of calls to 'emergencies' can prove to be tiresome 'rubbish' to be got out of the way as quickly as possible in order to get on to the next call. All too easily, the result can be a string of complaints of officiousness or lack of interest on the part of the police.

While by far the largest part of the working day is spent dealing with minor complaints, none the less the work can swing between extremes, with no opportunity for readjustment. The abrupt variation of work can again give rise to situations where frustration and irritation surface naturally. Two consecutive incidents observed late one Saturday night illustrate this. The first involved a family feud which had resulted in a particularly brutal beating with an iron bar and multiple stabbing. Following an anonymous 999 call shortly after 11 p.m., the victim was found semi-conscious. The blood, vomit and excrement was cleaned up, and rudimentary first aid given. The victim refused to make a statement or to lodge a complaint. Two police constables in attendance were instructed to search adjacent, unlit and unoccupied premises, where it was thought the culprit might be hiding. They met with no success. As they left the building a second 999 call came through, requiring them to attend an incident at a restaurant round the corner. No details were given. This, it transpired, concerned a dispute about the price of a meal. There was no criminal offence involved, but a very disgruntled customer none the less insisted that a complaint should be made, a charge brought because the food was too expensive and that surely the police were going to 'do' something. For the outside observer the contrast between the two situations was extreme. It was difficult to contain the reaction to the brutality and danger of five minutes earlier and even more difficult not to express anger at what appeared to be the perverse stupidity of the second complaint.

The pressure on the officers' time is further increased by the amount of administration they must get through; a major source of irritation and frustration – again not revealed in the statistics – is the amount of time taken up and apparently wasted in paper work. For example, once an offence is reported, no matter how trivial and before any further enquiries are made, police officers will attend and note full details of the incident: the nature of the offence, the locus, descriptions of stolen or damaged property or personal injuries; an officer will take the names and addresses and possibly quite lengthy statements from potential witnesses; a suspect may be arrested and charged who must then be taken to the Central Charge Office (at the city centre) where a decision must be taken whether to allow bail or to lock him up for the night. Alternatively, the detaining officer may decide to take the suspect down to the unit station for questioning, thus setting in motion a different set of procedures. More likely, where no arrest is made, the PC will return to the station from where he or she will contact CID main office, having already transcribed full details from notebook to crime report form. The CID will give the report a number and detail to whom the report should be handed on. Even then the PC's work is not completed. It will probably be seen fit to enter a general description of the incident on the daily summations for the benefit of the next shift and for easy reference for senior officers. A further report should also be entered in the car log-book. In other incidents a PC may be tied up all night at the scene. For example, at a house fire the police cannot leave until the property has been made secure and a PC may spend several hours of a night shift just waiting for the corporation joiner to arrive. Self-evidently the impact of even a minor incident on manpower can be quite drastic: two or three serious incidents can virtually denude the streets.

The burden of feeding paper into the system has a number of related consequences. First, to save time much police work is simply not recorded, with the result that there is no reliable indication of the full extent of work available to policy-makers and those higher up the tree whose job it is to evaluate the use of time. As a result this strengthens the suspicions of the beat policemen that headquarters is out of touch with the reality of working the street and 'how it is done in practice'. This in turn legitimates the use of routine methods which are at variance with force orders and 'the book'. Thus in the station studied some incidents – for example minor traffic offences or assaults – were frequently ignored for the purposes of the record. More often, however, they were 'written off'. It should be noted that this is not an example of the 'nice exercise of judgment' applauded by the Royal Commission on the Police (see above, p. 15) so much as a necessity imposed upon the policemen by time and circumstance:

> *First PC:* I don't know if the other PCs do it as much – like I've never worked up the hill – but I find I write an awful lot of stuff off where maybe you could go into it a bit deeper. But . . . you know . . . you say 'Ah, well, just another typical breach, they've had their punch at each other – forget it.'
> *Second PC:* You get the hang of situations. You know whether to get yourself involved or just to write it off and give the impression you've done all you can.
> *Sergeant:* We have to do it like that. If he dealt with everything that comes along he'd be out for a day and in the office for three. The younger lads – they're not experienced in a way – they find out very quickly that they get snowed under if they try to do everything by the book.

For many officers the objection to 'driving a desk' goes much deeper than a simple dislike of form filling and bureaucracy. It conflicts with their private definitions of 'real police work' and its fundamental purposes which is to be out there on the street 'making captures'.

*Sergeant:* This is the thing about police work, ninety per cent is just boredom, repetitive. But it's the other ten per cent which you can't predict.
*Second PC:* For me there's nothing better than to come across something you can really get your teeth into . . . like a chase in the car or chasing someone on foot. Last Monday we got someone for breaking in – that's great. All that's down on paper is a statistic at headquarters saying that someone got caught for that, but we're happy.

As mentioned earlier, the 'good capture' is rare. Arrests are usually for street offences and even the duty to guard, watch and patrol and maintain a deterrent presence on the streets is transformed by the sheer pressure of work. It is evident that in general relations between police and public can and do come under strain, as the service provided appears inadequate. However, the nature of contact itself as well as the outcome is largely dictated by the job itself:

This place here [on the large estate] I would say that the biggest majority of people are civilized people. We don't really get to see them . . . we just deal with the garbage at the bottom of the bucket. But when you do get to speak to them you're quite content to go into their houses and have a chat and a cup of tea with them . . . speak to them pleasantly without saying any 'fucking this' or 'fucking that', 'see that cunt', you know? Whereas if you're speaking to the priggies out on the main road, and you say to them 'excuse me, move along' they stand there and look at each other . . . 'Hey! Would you listen to him.' But if you drive along and you roll down the window, stick your thumb out and say, 'Right, fuck off!' they go. We've proved this time and time again. They understand 'fuck off', they don't understand 'please move'. So therefore you've got to speak to them in that language and then you've got to drive across the hill there and speak to them with a 'Yes, sir' and a 'No, sir'. (PC, 14 years' service)

Maintaining a presence in the streets rapidly becomes one of simply 'dealing with priggies'. Methods are employed which would not be officially sanctioned:

> I wouldn't let so much go if I was a sergeant in a better area. There's an awful lot I could tighten up on. There's a lot goes on down here I don't like, but I know it has to be if we're to do anything with it . . . if we're going to win and be seen to be winning. We have to cut corners, take short cuts and do things which wouldn't be acceptable elsewhere. (Sergeant, 7 years' service)

We can also see here that, closely allied to the frustration occasioned by paperwork, is frustration with legal procedure. The law often requires the recording of information and procedures which appear to the officers on the ground as conspiring to make their job more difficult, if not impossible. Supervisory officers will, for this reason, tolerate quite flagrant flouting of the rules of evidence, for example, for the overriding purpose of keeping 'order'.[9] The danger of intensified distrust and suspicion as a result of routine rule infraction by the police – however justified it may appear – is all the greater.

All these pressures clearly affect relations between police and public. Equally important, however, is the manner in which different pressures combine to weld a group of men together as a team, with its own internal loyalties and definitions of what is possible and practicable. This further consolidates the sense of separation, exclusion and exclusiveness which readily fosters a potential rejection of outsiders.

Given the intensity of the work, the psychological stresses and physical dangers encountered, it would be remarkable were a feeling of camaraderie not to prevail. The unpredictable nature and uneven distribution of the work make further demands on teamwork. Just as the workload can vary between shifts so it can between different beats. In the unit area studied here one car in particular regularly had a much heavier workload than the others.

For this reason it was kept double-manned at all times, but even so the system would have broken down completely if the other cars had not been prepared to back each other up and give immediate assistance whenever necessary, especially if an officer was in trouble. From this point of view the reliability of an individual officer, his ability to 'fit in' and his willingness to help out is, in the eyes of his colleagues, the most important 'quality' an officer must possess if the team is to survive. In the busy unit stations everybody must work for each other otherwise the 'whole thing falls apart'. A 'good shift' is at a premium and the role of supervisory officers – of the sergeant in particular – is often crucial. The shift sergeant was as aware of this as anyone:

> One shift used to be terrible down here. The sergeant was a lad with twenty-nine years' service and he didn't give a damn any more. He was getting out and that was it. He never hit the streets, he just sat in the office and did the typing. Consequently the boys went out and they had to fend for themselves. The whole shift fell apart. Now they've got a new sergeant – a young sergeant – and the shift's beginning to blend back together again and become effective.

Increasingly in such stations the sergeant is a working policeman and must be 'one of the boys'. His supervisory role is less important than it was. But, from the point of view of all supervisory officers, the maintenance of morale – which, given all the external difficulties, is difficult – is good reason to tolerate irregularities and to allow a certain 'flexibility' in relation to the discipline code. This can prove to be quite a tight-rope to walk. On the one hand, too strict an enforcement of formal discipline can cause resentment, while serious discipline offences or illegality can cause trouble and inconvenience for everybody. A careful balance has to be kept and can all too easily be lost. In the station we studied an unspoken code operates. Thus, for example, indiscriminate violence is not tolerated and an officer who gains a reputation for looking for trouble will soon find his calls for assistance going unanswered. There are, however, circumstances in which the use of violence is regarded as legitimate, and it is seen necessary to apply 'welfare'. Again, this is regarded as a function of the conditions of work and often, straightforwardly, as a matter of self-protection:

> We've got our own ideas, our own rules. But there's no govern-
> ing point saying we'll hit this one or we'll not hit that one. You
> can never say. Sometimes it doesn't happen for months . . . but
> it happens.
>
> We had that caper last week – the kids breaking into the shop.
> OK, we did the usual . . . if you don't tell us the truth you're
> going to get bounced all over the station. But there was never
> any intention of lifting a finger to any of them. A few quiet words
> of threat to give them the idea we knew who we had. But there
> was no intention to beat the shite out of them if they didn't tell
> us. If you do that they'll swear blind to anything – just 'cos
> they're getting their head kicked in. There's no point . . . we'll
> get them another time anyway.
>
> But then you've got the other situation where they start to cut
> up rough. And whenever they start cutting up in this station – in
> any station – they've lost. If they take a swing at a cop it's fatal.
> That's the only time when it's a dead cert; and the idea is don't
> treat them gentle.
>
> The only reason is that if he does it and gets away with hitting a
> policeman, he goes up to court and gets fined £25 at £3 a week.
> That's no deterrent to stop him hitting a copper. The only
> deterrent is to hit him back fucking harder than he hit you and to
> let him know that it's not just one – there's two and a half
> thousand of us that'll keep on hitting him.

There is a clear recognition of the mutual needs and responsibilities between the men and supervisory officers, so that in the
daily running of a unit station a well-respected senior officer can
and will rely on his men to protect his position by keeping out of
trouble and not overstepping the mark. On the other hand, quite
serious 'bending' of the law – albeit with some reluctance – is often
seen as necessary 'if the job is to be done'. In such circumstances
loyalty is critical and, in so far as the police regard such illegal
practices as forced upon them, it is also necessary and legitimate to
cover up for each other and protect themselves from the prying
eyes of the outsider.

Clearly this can pose problems for the purposes of research and the validity of our observations may be contestable for that reason. However, while the consequences may be unpalatable, so long as present conditions hold, adaptation and the bending of the rules appears inevitable. When the men were asked about their reaction to outsiders it became increasingly clear that they considered themselves to be caught in a contradiction forced upon them by the conditions of their work and the demands made of them:

> We have accepted you this past month because you were here for a purpose: to find out and connect it with your job, and to go back and teach students what it's like. We've accepted that. But the more outsiders you get in, the more wary you become. I could just imagine if the media got hold of the things that a practical policeman does when he's catching criminals and trying to get something legal – or something that looks legal – on paper. If they were ever to get hold of that there'd be a bloody outcry. But people don't realize that's the only way . . . the *only* way. There is no other way you can do policing. (PC, 5 years' service)

At this point, we want to raise, but leave open, two questions. First, what real choices are there for officers to do otherwise? Second, to what extent are they individually responsible for the system of policing within which they work?

## After the 'Fire-brigade': The Command and Control Computer

> The main object of computer-based command and control can be summed up by saying that it is designed to assist in the best use of available manpower. In order to do this two major objectives are tackled.
>     Firstly, the system is designed to ensure the fastest attendance at urgent and important incidents of the correct resource for that type of incident. This should preferably be without the worry of artificial police division or precinct boundaries increasing response times. Secondly, is the provision of the correct type of management information to appropriate levels of management.[10]

It is apparent that the rise of 'fire-brigade' policing was not a deliberate outcome of policy so much as the cumulative product of piecemeal responses to problems as they arose in the wake of the collapse of unit beat policing. Further, it would seem that unless there is a radical rethinking of received ideas about the purpose and organization of police work, the scope for policy initiatives and change will remain so limited and constrained by the demands of the work-system that there can be little prospect of improvement. Policing will continue to stagger from one crisis to the next.

The holy trinity of policy – more men, more powers, better equipment – has lost credibility. Even in a station such as the one we have described, where an increase in manpower seems the obvious way out, the problem is known to be more complex:

> We tried an experiment down here and put four men – four area men – onto one of the areas to see how that would work. We did that for three months – and we generated statistics we never would have had. Simply because they saw a policeman, people reported things they would never think of coming to the station for. So we thought that, instead of four men to an area, the ideal situation would be to have two to cover the one area. But then one of the areas where I recommended that only one man should stay on, suddenly had a spate of trouble and hit the headlines – all because half a dozen yobboes were doing all these jobs. (Chief Inspector)

The problems are well known to the police, yet the response, which in many forces is seen to promise an answer – computer-aided 'command and control' systems – rests upon the same old ideas: greater output per man hour and better, even more expensive, equipment. Despite the inherent conservatism of large-scale organizations, it is difficult to avoid the conclusion that, given the awareness of the problems together with the sophistication and expense of the new technology, there has been a conscious decision to implement the style of policing described in the above section. In effect 'fire-brigade' policing is becoming policy.

The command and control computer is in principle a direct extension of 'fire-brigade' policing, the difference being that the territorial area covered is much greater and that, instead of relying on the station clerk to select and dispatch resources within the subdivisional area, deployment of resources is centralized at divisional or new 'Area' headquarters. The inefficiency of the station clerk is not the only difficulty to be surmounted, however:

> If this problem were not enough in itself the increasing use of telephones by the public, the increasing expectations of the public as to police response conditioned to an important degree by the impact of television programmes about the police, were to further complicate matters. Queueing problems were beginning to arise in message handling in control rooms and in the use of radio channels.[11]

At its simplest, the computer will be used to keep track of all resources and to plot their availability to respond to calls. When an incident is reported, a VDU operator in the control room will type into the computer all details as they are received – the name and address of the complainant, the locus, the nature of the incident etc. The computer will then automatically display all details of traffic patrols, pandas and even foot patrols in the vicinity. The VDU operator then selects and dispatches the appropriate resource forthwith. The computer is informed of the action taken and the system is ready for the next call.

The introduction of computerized command and control systems dates from as early as 1968. The Director of the Police Scientific Development Board, Mr Arthur Burrows, described the initial decision to implement the system in Birmingham as follows:

> The initiative came in the first place from the Home Office . . . In 1968, the then UK and now EEC Roy Jenkins noted on his overseas visits that computers were beginning to appear in police control rooms. He had noted no such tendency in the UK and asked why. The Home Office decided to run an experiment to find out if the police service should be encouraged to make more use of the then novel computer. The City of Birmingham agreed to be the guinea-pig for the initial experiment.[12]

The Birmingham system became operational in 1972. This was followed in 1973 by a more sophisticated scheme in Glasgow and, following this, the system was further developed for the purposes of mixed rural/urban policing in Staffordshire. By 1977 systems were fully operational in each of these areas, and since then they have mushroomed. In the fifty-one British police forces, there are now thirteen such computers in use and eleven proposed or under development.

A typical command and control system will have various standard features for the purposes of 'rapid response'. These include:

*Incident Handling* – all 999 calls are routed through the central operations room and details logged. Details are stored on this facility and can be utilized subsequently as a 'management information' resource.

*Street Index* – as each incident is reported, the locus is matched to the appropriate divisional area and ascribed a location code. Again this information is retained for subsequent analysis if needed.

*Resource Availability* – this file holds details of the positions of the officers on the streets and what they are presently engaged in. This is made possible by a device known as a 'coded tone generator' which is fitted to the cars and which transmits its location on VHF directly to the computer. At present these systems are still relatively crude and rely upon officers operating what is called a 'button box' to send the information. Improvements are to be expected, as is the availabiity of a commercially viable system for operation with the UHF personal radios carried by the foot patrols.

*Automatic reminders* – if for some reason a call is not dealt with within a certain length of time a reminder will be flashed up on the VDU requiring a particular man or car to update their position, their status, the result of the call etc.

The perceived advantages of the system are fourfold. First, it is said to offer better control over incidents. They cannot be forgotten or 'written off'. Second, there is a more efficient use made of resources. Under the old system the station clerk would have less idea of what was actually going on out on the streets and precisely where the men were at any particular time. Third, it provides a record of demand and resource use for management and planning purposes, and fourth, it reduces the amount of paper work required, especially in incident logging. The major objective however is to improve on response times. Superintendent Fraser describes the capacity of the proposed Merseyside system: 'Merseyside's system will be implemented in 1982. It will have some fifty VDUs linked to the computer and will be designed to handle more than six thousand incidents at any one time. The maximum response time acceptable will be five seconds.'[13] One can only assume that the five-second response time refers to the computer rather than the unfortunate PC; however, the emphasis upon time is seen to be at the heart of the system.

It is also at the heart of a contradiction. However laudable the project, and however important a rapid response may be, a few seconds here or there can be of little significance if it takes twenty-five minutes for the public to place the call.[14] It could very well be argued that all the equipment and the finance is being directed to the wrong objects. Much greater emphasis should be placed upon prevention, rather than waiting for the incident or offence to occur, and a greater awareness of the need to ensure community relations is necessary if such systems are to fulfil the important, but limited, potential they actually possess. A dissatisfied public is not going to make best use of the service offered.

There are two principal reasons for seeing concentration upon command and control as a further step away from prevention in general and community involvement in particular. In the first place, the size of the areas policed is increased and there is less demand made upon local knowledge. Second, the work expected of the police officer is such as only to compound the problems already encountered between police and public in fire-brigade policing.

Although the precise arrangements will vary according to the needs of the local force, the basic idea which pervades command and control systems is that bigger is better, or at least more 'efficient'. Rationalization requires 'economies of scale'. The result is that in many forces subdivisional control of resources will be abandoned in favour of divisional or 'area' control. This will require substantial force reorganization, particularly in rural and mixed rural/urban forces, as has been the experience in South Wales and Northumbria. In such areas, the model to be employed divides the force into a number of large operational communications areas, each with its own, self-contained operations room (AOR). The AORs and subdivisional stations will be linked to the force computer by VDU and teleprinter. *State Research* reports that while the old divisional and subdivisional structure will remain in such areas, it will be far less important and effective when operational control is centralized at Area level: 'In Northumbria, for instance, the eight divisions and twenty-two subdivisions will give way for basic operational purposes to three areas.'[15] The simple point is, of course, that the basic administrative unit must be big enough to merit the application of the technology used. Thus, by their very logic, command and control systems stand opposed to local knowledge and close involvement with small populations. Unless these systems are subordinated in programmes designed to counteract such tendencies, the difficulties of contemporary policing will only be exacerbated.

The second area of risk opened up relates to the conditions of work and the service provided. Enough has been said already of the dissatisfactions engendered by the rapid response, but the likely response of the officers themselves in such conditions is worth considering.

One of the constant problems for police administrators and senior officers alike is their lack of contact with and immediate control over the PCs on the street. To a great extent, knowledge and control over beat officers is even beyond the shift sergeant, who must be able to rely upon his 'relationship' with his constables. As a result, there is the traditional emphasis upon the responsibility and trustworthiness of the individual as the guarantee of order and discipline within the force. The advantage of such a situation is that it allows for the 'give and take', which as we have seen, is so necessary within the present conditions. Robert Reiner in his study of the police neatly summarized the findings of many investigators before him when he wrote:

Throughout the development of police forces, administrators have devised a variety of systems of organisation to maintain some degree of control. But the formal rules of supervision are filtered through the policeman's culture, and the actual operative procedures are the result of this set of informal understandings, which the wise supervisor shares.[16]

The implementation of command and control clearly reduces any space for the development of such understandings. What kind of relationship does one establish with a 'button box'? A senior officer, with specialist knowledge in the field, explained what happens:

> I know that in some of the smaller areas that used to be autonomous there is some resentment in having to be controlled by big stations elsewhere controlling big areas . . . In the past if I knew that one of my men was sitting in the station, I'd just nip out and tell him to go to a job. Now I've got to report the incident first of all to the central controller – who might be twenty miles away, but who has all the command and control information. *He* will then decide who's going to do the job. So from that point of view, control at the local basis has disappeared and this has caused resentment. There's a 'big brother' type of feeling creeping into a lot of local stations.

Such disadvantages spill right down to ground level. The computer does not discriminate between men and the different skills they possess. A sergeant can determine which particular man to put on a particular job, who knows the complainant best, or where trouble is likely to blow up on the night. Such knowledge is not available to the VDU operator and the computer. The other side of the coin is, of course, that any room for individual initiative and choice is finally excised. As a result, the system effectively dehumanizes the police. They are perceived as cyphers, as each step in the decision-making process is removed from their competence. Such developments cannot but affect the manner in which the job is done.

It could be argued that the dissatisfaction, frustration and resentment engendered will be transitional; that as a new generation of policemen is reared, the new methods will be accepted and the bad ways of their older colleagues will be forgotten. When that day comes, however, as one rather tired and cynical Chief Superintendent said to us: 'We'll be able to wind 'em up, let them go and stop work.'

## Further Reading

Bunyard, R. S., *Police: Organisation and Command*, Macdonald & Evans, Plymouth, 1978.

Cain, M., *Society and the Policeman's Role*, Routledge & Kegan Paul, London, 1973.

Chatterton, M., 'Police in Social Control', in J. F. S. King (ed.), *Control Without Custody*, Institute of Criminology, Cambridge, 1976.

Holdaway S. (ed.), *The British Police*, Edward Arnold, London, 1979.

Martin, J. P. and Wilson, G., *The Police: A Study in Manpower*, Heinemann, London, 1969.

Mervyn Jones, J., *Organisational Aspects of Police Behaviour*, Gower, Aldershot, Hants, 1980.

Pope, D. W. and Weiner, N. L., *Modern Policing*, Croom Helm, London, 1981.

Punch, M., *Policing the Inner City*, Macmillan, London, 1979.

Reiner, R., *The Blue Coated Worker*, Cambridge University Press, Cambridge, 1978.

Reiss, A., *Police and Public*, Yale University Press, New Haven, Conn., 1971.

Reiss, A. and Bordua, D. J., 'Environment and Organisation: A Perspective on the Police', in D. J. Bordua (ed.), *The Police: Six Sociological Essays*, Wiley, New York, 1966.

# The Organization of Police Work II: Local Intelligence

## Introduction

> It is the opinion of this committee that with respect to the occasional employment of policemen in plain clothes, the system as laid down by the heads of the Police Department affords no just matter of complaint while strictly confined to detect breaches of the law and to prevent breaches of the peace should those ends appear otherwise unobtainable. At the same time, the committee strongly urges the most cautious maintenance of those limits and solemnly deprecate any approach to the employment of spies in the ordinary acceptance of the term, as a practice most abhorrent to the feelings of the people and most alien to the spirit of the constitution. (Report of the Parliamentary Select Committee on the petition of Frederick Young and others, 1833)

By tradition and logic, the use of police spies is incompatible with the concept of policing by consent. From details made available to us in the course of our researches, it became apparent however that more than one person in ten, and probably as many as one in six males, residing within the force area was the subject of covert criminal intelligence reports.

On the basis of interviews and participant observation, it also became apparent that the collection of criminal intelligence was a major and increasingly important aspect of everyday police work: yet it is an aspect of policing which has received little, if any, serious consideration with respect to the debate on police powers. It is a major and fundamental omission from the Report of the Royal Commission on Criminal Procedure, which made no reference, even in passing, to the practices and developments which will be described in the course of this chapter, yet they are of central importance both to the question of the legal definition and limitation of police work, and, indeed, to the future of policing in general.

There is no formal definition of criminal intelligence nor any official guidelines for its use. Even a working definition is difficult to provide since the practice itself is vague. From one point of view, it is an attempt to record and make generally available to all officers that fund of local knowledge and information that previously was built up and retained for the personal use of the officer who walked the local beat. From another, it is the covert collection, analysis and distribution of personal data which amounts to little else than the systematic invasion of privacy.

At first sight its use seems relatively easy to establish. First, it is seen as an aid to the detection and investigation of crime. Information on the present whereabouts, associates and haunts of locally known 'villains', knowledge of their current financial state, the cars they are using, who they are living with and so on can be of direct help, it is argued, in the investigation of offences. Second, such information is said to be valuable in the prevention of crime and for ensuring that the police know what the people most likely to commit crime are up to, even before they do anything illegal.

While nobody can dispute the relevance of certain sorts of information to police work, difficulties are met when the attempt is made to say *who* should be a legitimate target of intelligence, to define *what* information is valuable or useful and what is merely malicious gossip, to place limits on the amount of intelligence which is justifiable and on the time span and life of the information collected.

Such is the nature of the subject, that there is very little publicly available material for guidance on these questions. For this reason, we shall again draw on observation of the practice of intelligence collection and its use in the 'research force' we studied. It would, therefore, be unwise to generalize unthinkingly from some of the particular details we describe. But there is no doubt that similar practices and systems of intelligence are widely used by the British police forces in general. That this is beyond question is witnessed by the immense amount of public money presently being invested in 'police-dedicated' computerized information systems throughout the country.[1]

Although it may be difficult to give a precise definition of criminal intelligence, it is possible to say what it is not. The material held is not a criminal record, nor is criminal intelligence to be confused with Special Branch records on political activists. The methods routinely employed are not those of special surveillance – the world of the criminal intelligence officer is not one of telephone taps, listening devices, and political intrigues.

Thus, to say that one person in ten is a subject of or 'of interest' to local intelligence is not to say that that person has a criminal record. Criminal records are kept both nationally and locally but are completely separate from criminal intelligence files. Somebody with a criminal record is not automatically made a subject of criminal intelligence reports, and it is by no means a requirement that a subject of criminal intelligence should have a current or previous conviction for crime. In the force we studied, we were told that considerably more than fifty per cent of subjects, possibly as many as two-thirds, had no criminal record. It is not possible to be more precise on this point as it appears that the police themselves do not keep, and are not required to keep, an accurate statistical account of their records.

It is worth emphasizing that, in our experience, criminal intelligence appears to have no explicit political function. Intelligence on political dissidents is held separately by the Special Branch. There may be some overlap, but, just as persons of interest need not have been involved in any specifically criminal activity, so it appears that political activity or allegiances is not a relevant criterion either.

The information gathered and held on local intelligence is, in itself, neither confidential nor of any great import. It is certainly of no national significance. In the main it is made up of pub talk, gossip and hearsay. As such it would have no standing in a court of law, which of course is one reason why its existence is rarely made public. Most people who are the subject of criminal intelligence would probably be surprised that the facility exists and that the police should be bothered to take such an interest in them.

The distinction needs to be emphasized, therefore, between national and local criminal intelligence. When criminal intelligence is discussed publicly, it is almost always in connection with national data banks and the justification is made in terms of the 'master mind' or 'professional criminal' whose sophistication demands the use of specialized and perhaps unorthodox methods. The subjects of local intelligence, however, are neither sophisticated criminals nor is the intelligence collected by particularly subtle methods.

Intelligence relating to serious crime is held both nationally and regionally. National intelligence is made available to local forces through the Police Gazettes. It is the product of a tightly organized and systematic surveillance of persons of particular interest. By contrast, local intelligence is gathered and collated by individual forces at divisional and often subdivisional level. It is far less organized and far more diffuse. As such, it hardly merits the name of 'surveillance', which entails the methodical, deliberate and continuing observation of particular persons for particular reasons. Local intelligence-gathering proceeds along entirely different lines. It is largely piecemeal, arbitrary and unco-ordinated. It relates to any information, from any source, about any person who might in the future prove to be 'of interest'. Local criminal intelligence is thus systematic in the collection and recording of information, but not in the selection of its material and its subjects. It is the lowest grade of intelligence, and until recently problems of storage and retrieval have reduced the extent of its use.

Even so, local criminal intelligence has always had its place in police work. During the first days of Peel's New Police an 'information system' was established and the local officer was expected to maintain a double-edged 'working knowledge' of the inhabitants of his area. It is only recently, however, that local intelligence can properly be said to be 'systematic' and that the observations and suspicions of the local officer have become a specialized resource.

There are various dimensions to the extraordinary growth of criminal intelligence in recent years: specialization within the force has devalued the skills and role of the constable and promoted in his place the specialist information and intelligence officer, and changes in the relation between public and police and the drift away from policing by consent have affected the nature of criminal investigation and served to place a new emphasis upon the use of information and intelligence. The availability and development of new computerized resources can be seen to encourage the police to redefine their role from one of mutual dependence to one of 'professional' independence of the public.

While such changes have come about separately, rather than as part of an overall or any Machiavellian plan, there is no doubt that the product now presents enormous potential for abuse. It was not denied by the officers we interviewed that the new computers presently being installed are capable of integration to form a national system for purposes of mass surveillance. Even at the present local level, however, covert intelligence-gathering represents a substantial challenge to orthodox ideas of 'policing by consent' and a challenge to the liberal conceptions of privacy and freedom. Whether that potential will be realized, will depend, in part at least, upon the extent to which present tendencies and developments go unchecked. This, in turn, will depend upon whether legislators, politicians and others maintain their persistent refusal to recognize the issues raised as immediate problems rather than futuristic fantasies.

Much of the present debate on policing has been impoverished, if not rendered irrelevant, by its failure to take cognizance of the practical implications of recent organizational and technological changes within the police. Serious, and indeed perennial, problems of policing have been glossed over. How would a new generation of 'community policemen' be put to work alongside the new generation of computers – to befriend, or to record intimate details of private lives? How will work and work practices be affected by the new resources? Will they lead to a wider use of powers of detention and interrogation? To what extent does greater police control over, and reliance upon, their own resources mark a significant shift in the relationship between police and the public, one that opens up new problems of accountability? How do these developments fit into the present context of the law and its proposed reform?

We shall postpone consideration of these questions to the last section of this and to later chapters. Before that, we look in detail at how local intelligence is collected, and how it is presently collated and disseminated. In addition, we examine the nature and capacity of the new computerized systems of criminal intelligence which are being introduced. Once this is done we shall return to the more difficult problems of evaluation.


## Collecting Local Intelligence: The Crime Patrol

> The people who give us most information are the shopkeepers. There's one down the street . . . they sell all kinds of things so lots of different people go in there. She gets tremendous information and passes it all on to us. People go in there and chat . . . Mind you, the shop gets broken into regularly so that's a bit of an advantage. (Chief Inspector)

There are some policemen who gain the reputation of being 'good thief-takers'. Such officers are described as having a 'nose' for crime. They can talk to anybody, hear things and pick up information where others will meet only silence. They become mines of information about the areas they work, and seem to possess an uncanny capacity to recall names, faces and places, sometimes literally years later. It is an extraordinary ability, sharpened to a fine skill.

It is disconcerting to be out on the street with such a person. A conversation or joke, for no apparent reason, is left in mid-air: a face is singled out for comment where the untrained eye sees only a mass of Saturday afternoon shoppers. A brief look into a pub prompts a catalogue of names, addresses and personal histories; a note that so and so is back in town and out with somebody else's wife; a reminder to go back later and have a chat with the landlord about someone. And always a string of questions: 'What brings him to this pub? – he usually drinks on the other side of town.' 'Where are they getting money for drink on a Wednesday? – they haven't worked for two months.' 'Who was that tall bloke in the corner? – he's not one of ours, but I know his face.'

Such men become the folk heroes of the local force. Their captures become the topic of 'piece-time' reminiscences – everyone has his own story about working with such a man. They are 'policemen's policemen'.

They have a special place in the informal rank order of the force. Their skill is held to be the essence of 'good police work'; their abilities and methods are emulated by younger officers; not only are they a fund of anecdotes and a repository of all the tricks of the trade, they are a resource upon which a favoured young officer can rely. To be apprenticed to such a man can help a career and get a young officer noticed, even if to begin with he simply shares in a reflected glory. One young constable who had just completed his first four years described his feelings on being teamed up with such a man:

> It's fantastic coming out of uniform to work with someone like Ginger. He knows everything about everybody. It's uncanny at times, he just seems to know when something's going to happen or who's done what . . . so you get a lot of captures with Ginger!
> . . . You watch him. He talks the same language as these people and they all know him – who he is – but they still tell him things, things they wouldn't even tell their mothers . . . You're learning all the time with Ginger, that's why they send us out with him. (PC, 4 years' service)

This peculiar skill and general ability is still recognized within the force we studied as the mark of a 'good policeman', but increasingly of 'the old style'. It is no longer enough on its own. The modern policeman needs other skills and qualifications. He must now pass examinations in 'human awareness', master the theory of man-management, gain experience of administration and of the specialist departments of the CID, community involvement, traffic enquiries and so on. The intuitive craft of the 'thief-taker' which was learnt on the streets is now becoming an anachronism among 'professionals'. In the name of efficiency his fund of local knowledge and capacity for intuitive judgment are being displaced, appropriated by technology, and the specialists. As a result the nature of local policing is being transformed.

In the 'research force', as seems so often the case in the development of police work, specialist intelligence-gathering came about as a spin-off from an altogether different project. During the late seventies, a particularly high level of shoplifting prompted the reallocation of beat officers in the town section to plain-clothes duties in and around the busy central shopping areas. They became known as the 'crime patrol'.

Great care was taken to ensure that the officer dressed for the part. The uniform of the CID – short mackintoshes or blue car coats – was studiously avoided and gave way to long hair, old Levis and working clothes. A generation of scruffy officers invaded a world still dominated by the traditional respect of the ex-serviceman for smartness and its equation with discipline. For the younger PC brought up in the sixties the opportunity to 'look normal' was taken up without regret. A CND badge became a favoured item of police apparel.

Initially the new crime patrol met with considerable success and large numbers of shoplifters were arrested and prosecuted until eventually word got around and the miscreants moved on to safer areas. Inevitably work of this kind is short-lived. Plain-clothes officers rapidly become known to the 'regulars' and consequently there has to be a fairly rapid turn-over if the element of surprise is to be maintained. It appears that teams of shoplifters have intelligence systems of their own.

However, two largely unanticipated advantages of the crime patrol soon emerged. First, it was found that the practice of stopping and searching suspects for stolen goods was made more easy and more productive when undertaken by plain-clothes officers. People were both less prepared for and less embarrassed by the experience, so that in addition to the increased likelihood of making a 'capture', it was found that 'suspects' were more likely to 'come across' (with information) to members of the crime patrol in preference to uniformed officers. This in part was because there was less visibility and in part because the police officers themselves could employ greater subtlety in negotiation either on the streets, or, more happily, over a quiet pint in the pub with no eyebrows raised. Second, a vast quantity of information was obtained from sources which had previously been allowed to lie fallow. Store detectives, who had built up their own information base and experience, were only too pleased to demonstrate to their employers that they were working closely with the 'plain-clothes officers' and the shopkeepers themselves rapidly started to pass a wide range of information to the crime patrol, which increasingly they saw as their own private police force.

In a sense, of course, there was nothing new in these procedures. It was more a matter of re-discovery of tried and tested methods. What was important was the development of a specialist squad for the purpose. To understand how this reorganization of basic police work came about, it only has to be remembered how, throughout the seventies, the workloads of the CID had increased alongside that of the uniform branch. Increasingly, the work of the CID had come to be centred almost exclusively upon the investigation of offences reported to them by the uniformed branch, while, as we have seen, the uniformed officers played less and less of an active role on the streets as their job became one of responding to calls. A gap in police work had opened up, which the crime patrol naturally filled. Their job was not to respond to calls, nor to investigate crime, but to be on the spot and keep in touch with the streets. Gradually the work of the crime patrol was redefined – they became specialists with their own place in the hierarchy:

> We don't work under the station sergeant like the uniform men . . . we're not given jobs to go to. Really we find our own work. We're a link between the CID and the uniform branch. We're not affiliated to the CID but we work with them a lot . . . passing on information mainly. (Crime patrol officer)

The initial object of dealing with shoplifters soon became only a secondary and increasingly unremarkable aspect of the work. Two years after the introduction of the first crime patrol in the shopping precincts their numbers had multiplied and their presence on the streets had become a regular feature throughout the city divisions. When asked to define their role there is now rarely any reference to their original purpose:

> What we generally do is just patrol the street, spot the criminals and follow them . . . collate information, collect as much information as possible and generally be there if someone's needed who's not going to be noticed as a policeman. We work very closely with the Divisional Intelligence Officer; we give him a lot of his information and he tells us about patterns of crime and things that we could give attention to. But it's very much off our own bat to decide what we do . . . We spend a fair amount of

time in pubs actually . . . 'cos obviously that's the criminal's
habitat – if they're not on the streets they're in the pub. It gets
kind of expensive.

While the emphasis of their work was to shift away from shoplifting towards the gathering of intelligence, the crime patrol are none
the less still geared to what might be termed the mundane or
routine side of crime. Their concern is with all aspects of street
crime, with the buying and selling of stolen goods, with slip-in
thefts, thefts from cars and so on, and indeed their arrest rate is
considerably higher than officers in the uniform branch (in 'R'
Division the crime patrol make approximately forty arrests per
month – five per officer as opposed to two in the uniform branch).
However their principal concern is with those people whom they
consider may, however indirectly, be involved in petty crime in the
future or who may be sources of information.

Each of the four city divisions now has its own regular crime
patrol squads, with as many as eight officers working in teams of
two, seconded for up to a year. The importance given to their work
can readily be appreciated if their numbers are compared to manning levels elsewhere. It will be remembered that in the unit station
described in the last chapter a complement of eight men would
have been regarded as the best possible and that was in one of the
busiest stations in Britain.

There is no doubt that the men working the crime patrols prize
the freedom of the job and the relaxation of discipline that goes
with it. On a cold winter's evening they are justified in choosing to
work in a pub. For most of the men it is also regarded as a step up
the promotion ladder, especially towards a more prestigious job
within the CID. But most important of all, is the identification of
the work of the crime patrols with the somewhat nebulous notion
of 'real police work'. The chances of 'making a capture' are significantly higher, and there is greater 'contact with the criminals' as the
men are actively encouraged to become involved and 'cultivate'
sources of information.

It would be wrong, however, to think of the work as in any sense
glamorous. Viewed dispassionately it is sordid and invidious, calling for a talent to 'con' people, to mislead and to betray confidences

and generally to use and manipulate others.

Even so, the job exercises an unholy fascination. To be out on crime patrol is to become a professional voyeur with a licence to poke and pry into private lives, and permission to live with respectability on the other side of all that is moral and permissible. However impoverished it may be in comparison, for many police officers this is as near as they will ever come to the image of detective work as popularized on the television.

Most of the working day is spent 'gleaning' and 'conning' information out of unwitting or reluctant sources. There is a regular trail round the shops, pubs and betting shops, on the look out for people who are known to 'come across'. At the end of the working day, however, this 'intelligence' is carefully transcribed into a 'pott book' and from there passed on to the Divisional Intelligence Officer.

Different methods are employed to elicit intelligence. 'Conning' information out of people requires some subtlety. Thus, one method routinely employed is the hidden question. For example, a shopkeeper might be asked whether old Mrs Smith is managing for herself now that she is on her own, in the expectation that information about her son will be volunteered. Disingenuous concern frequently conceals other motives. Another routine involves the mistaken identity or confusion of facts. For example, to establish the identity of an unknown third party seen to be associating with a local 'ned' the following conversation was observed:

*Patrol Officer:* And who's your friend?
*Ned:* Ask him yourself. You know me better than that.
*Patrol Officer:* Alright! Have it your own way . . . (returning to the subject some time later) Wait a minute, I know him. That's the man wanted for the job at the Coop. You're the other one, aren't you?
*Ned:* You must be joking. You don't get me that way.
*Patrol Officer:* You'd better tell us or you're both coming for a walk.

No matter how sure of his ground, the reluctant informant will 'come across' at this point, convinced by the 'con' and the ability of the officer, which frequently rivals that of a professional actor.

The implied threat of an 'overnight lie-down' (arrest with bail refused) is a favourite back-up to the 'con'. This often relies on ignorance of the law. Thus, for example, individuals may be misled into believing that the police will do them a favour and not lock them up for the night in exchange for information, when in fact there was no power to do so in the first place.

At this low level of intelligence-gathering, however, it is unusual for a potential informant to possess information worthy of a genuine trade-off. (This technique is more commonplace in relation to serious crime, where, for example so-called 'supergrasses' have been offered immunity from prosecution in exchange for information.) It is not unusual, however, for officers to give the impression that they are in possession of more evidence than in fact is the case, and that they will drop the charge or trade a less serious charge in return for a similar favour from a prisoner. The essence of a good 'con' is, then, for the officer to appear to be giving a concession, or, even better, to be compromising himself, when in fact he is not.

Outside on the streets, regular use of stop-and-search powers is made for no other purpose than to identify likely looking strangers or third parties seen associating with persons already known to the officers concerned. More often than not, the formal legal power remains unstated, merely a back-up to be invoked if necessary. In such circumstances, the stop and search becomes a stop and check for the purposes of identification only. Again the 'con' is used in preference, but if necessary the width of the legal power is usually enough to provide a legitimate cover story if it should prove necessary – which is unlikely. The usual legal resource, however, is not the formal power of arrest or stop and search under, for example, drugs legislation, but the much wider local legislation as, for example, under section 66 of the Metropolitan Police Act 1839, which provides that a constable may 'stop, search and detain . . . any person who may be reasonably suspected of having or conveying in any manner anything stolen or unlawfully obtained'.

The wide use of this power by the Metropolitan Police was singled out for criticism by Lord Scarman in his report on the Brixton disorders. However, noting that similar provisions had been adopted in local Acts applying to many inner city areas, Lord Scarman commented that: 'The power is, I am convinced, necessary to combat street crime. The formulation . . . is sound in that the power may be exercised only if there be reasonable grounds for suspicion.'

We shall look at the problems surrounding the definition of 'reasonable suspicion' in Chapter 5. Here, however, it is worth considering how, for the purposes of intelligence-gathering on the streets – a function which went unremarked in Lord Scarman's analysis – the notion of a 'suspected person' under the local legislation enforced in the research force is defined in the street.

The following is an extract from the formal training lecture given to probationary constables. The lecture begins with a working definition of reasonable suspicion but proceeds immediately to instruct the PC on the use of 'sightings':

A major extension of your normal police powers is the right under certain circumstances to detain and search people *without* making an arrest. If you have reasonable cause to suspect that any person is in possession of any money or other article, which have been unlawfully obtained . . . You may then stop, search and detain that person. Your suspicion must be based on reasonable grounds. Is he coming from a place where there have been a recent number of thefts? From cars, for example, or from the back of shops, or does he answer the description of a man who was seen leaving the locus of a crime? Is he wearing unusual clothes, such as gloves or training shoes?

The lecture then continues to instruct the young officer on the questioning of suspects. The officer is told that a 'check' with criminal records is 'vital' and to use the personal radio for the purpose: 'The suspect may have previous convictions for dishonesty, or have no convictions but is known to associate with known thieves.'

More wide powers, again given in local legislation, are available to arrest 'associates' of known thieves, for example, on the charge of loitering with *intent* to steal. For such purposes, reasonable suspicion is combined with evidence of 'association' which in turn, is 'proved' by evidence of previous 'sightings' of the suspect in the company of a known thief. The trainee officer is therefore told that:

It is essential to report all sightings to your Divisional Intelligence Officer. He records the information for divisional purposes and passes it on to the Criminal Intelligence Department at Police Headquarters. Once reported to this department, it becomes available to all members of the force. Do not keep knowledge of a criminal association to yourself. Failure to pass the knowledge on could result in an associate being allowed away.

Our point here, however, is not to criticize the particular content of the legislation nor to question its desirability, but to point to the uses of widely framed laws of this kind for the purpose of intelligence collection. Certainly, in the research force area, one of the products of 'saturation' policing (as of the kind that occurred in Brixton in the 'Swamp '81' operation) would have been a massive input into criminal intelligence.

A further aspect of such methods is, of course, that intelligence is disproportionately skewed towards certain 'suspect' populations, namely, 'criminals and their associates'. In practice this means young working-class males. On the basis of the statistics given earlier, it is not unreasonable to suggest that perhaps one in three of these are subject to intelligence observation.

While evidently enjoying the freedom and licence of working the crime patrols, the men were frequently ambivalent about the work itself. Occasionally they would stand back and object to their own employment as 'snoopers' and 'spies' and the use of what they termed 'legalized harassment'. They clearly doubted the value of much of the intelligence they collected, readily volunteering that 'most of it is garbage' and 'tittle tattle'.

Furthermore, despite the instruction given in the lecture quoted above, it is evident that the officers themselves keep much of the better information to themselves or see to it that it is only handed on to known and trusted colleagues. The reasons for this are comparatively straightforward: rivalry and competition within the job, and protection of sources and informants. We have seen the premium placed upon 'captures' by the working officer, therefore it is hardly surprising that few constables are prepared to spend their time 'cultivating a good squeak' only to see the kudos of making the ultimate capture pass to someone else. Bitterness and intense jealousies, especially between the CID and uniformed officers, whether in plain clothes or not, are thus still commonplace within most police forces, even though, as in the force described here, substantial efforts have been made to counteract the tendency. As a result, much of the information passed on to the DIO is the residue of trivia, gossip and hearsay, which just might be of interest but which on the face of it is of no immediate value to the officer concerned. In short it tends to be the least reliable and useful information that is recorded.

None the less, despite occasional ambivalence, officers of the crime patrol clearly relish the contact with 'criminals, potential criminals and suspects' and the 'neds'. It is seen as real police work within the 'capture-culture'. The concentration of this particular aspect of police work in the one job, however, has the effect of de-skilling and, in the eyes of other officers, devaluing the work of the foot patrols and reducing still further the general duties and status of the uniformed PC. It is no longer a necessary feature of the beat to seek out and maintain local knowledge and contacts. Some, of course, still do, but in those areas where the crime patrols work most frequently, many officers regard the work of the uniformed officer on foot patrol almost as a punishment. Anything 'interesting' is taken on by the crime patrol, leaving the uniformed officer little else but to answer his radio and general inquiries from passersby. There is little freedom and little responsibility, and for this reason few crime patrol officers welcome a return to uniform.


One of the major problems, therefore, that has resulted from the process of centralization, rationalization and specialization during the post-war period, is the manner in which the work of the police constable has been de-skilled, and (as a result) in which the intimacy of the policeman with the people has been broken. This is nowhere more apparent than in the use of specialist squads to gather intelligence. Thus, where previously the police might have been expected to use discretion and judgment based upon the intuitive knowledge gained through a wide experience of a particular area over a number of years, now 'intelligence' replaces experience and assumes the form of an unqualified, bald statement of 'fact', derived at best by dubious methods, and by young officers, seconded to the job for a relatively short period of time, while on their way up the career ladder.

Indeed, the job description itself demands that these officers meet and mix with only those sectors of the population that are considered, in advance, to be suspect or potentially criminal. The result is that suspicion is institutionalized as contact between the police and public is diminished. The obvious danger is that where this spills over into suspicion of the public in general, the experience and nature of police work is redefined. Many police officers are not unaware of this risk – it is inherent in the job itself:

> Suspicious? Well I suppose we are . . . it's the job. We're trained to be. When I go out with my wife she's forever telling me to stop working . . . you're always looking for something wrong. If you go out for a drink, you always get a seat where you can see everyone. That's why they say it's a twenty-four-hour job . . . You could say we're brainwashed – brainwashed by the job! . . . but don't quote me on that. It's just experience – that's all! (Chief Inspector)

## The Organization of Local Intelligence: The Intelligence Officer

> It doesn't have to be hard facts we deal with . . . This is the emotive grey area the civil liberties people are on about. It's anything of interest, or useful just for keeping tabs on people. There's paragraphs of stuff here. Sometimes useful, sometimes just garbage . . . what vehicles they're using, he was seen in a pub talking to so and so, and so on. (Divisional Intelligence Officer)

In the 'research force' each divisional station now employs a specialized 'Divisional Intelligence Officer' (DIO). Such is his[2] importance and the scale of his operations that he is often afforded his own office, which is a certain privilege for an officer of the rank of constable.

The DIO's office, probably more so than any other office within a police station, accords with popular imagery. The walls are hung with a collection of 'mug-shots', pinned randomly, one on top of another. 'Wanted' posters adorn the doors. One senses that for many officers this is the hub of 'real police work'.

Yet the intelligence officer's experience of the daily world of crime is entirely vicarious. His knowledge is always second-hand. It is culled from paperwork, from officers' reports, notebooks and forms filled in elsewhere. Snippets of information are brought together and an approximation of the world outside is compiled 'for police use'.

The DIO can 'know more about a person than he knows about himself', some of his 'regulars' are treated almost like old friends, and yet he is unlikely ever to meet them. He will know who drinks regularly in any pub, but could not describe the wallpaper or the beer. He lives in a world of card indexes, photographs and paperwork. More like a squirrel than a policeman, he is constantly looking for and storing up what might be useful in the future.

The intelligence officer's job was first introduced at the subdivisional level as part of the system of unit beat policing. As distinct from the Divisional Intelligence Officer, however, the task of the subdivisional 'collator' was to 'sort, file and disseminate items of information received from patrolling officers' in order to counterbalance the potential breakdown in local contact and information about the beat or 'area' resulting from the division of work between the CID officers, the area constables and the car men. Thus, to begin with, the emphasis was upon quite particular information received directly from the patrolling officers rather than upon the general low-grade 'intelligence' of the crime patrols and information culled from reports and paperwork.

As the system of unit beat policing came under increasing pressure it became evident that the uniformed officers were no longer in a position to provide the information demanded of them. Further, neither the area men, nor the car men, had the time or inclination to add to their paperwork. The problem was often resolved in a convenient compromise. An officer 'of the old style' would be brought off the street, who was able to treat his own local knowledge and experience as the source of information which he duly transferred to the card index. At the same time alternative available sources of information were located – the daily summations, the crime report forms and the mass of routine paperwork completed by the uniformed officers which are now regularly searched – and sifted by the office-bound intelligence officer.

As the weight of work increased on the uniformed branch and the unit beat system gave way to 'fire-brigade' policing, so the role of the collator changed. He was no longer there to supply information back out to the areas and to co-ordinate the activities of the men policing those areas, but more and more to channel 'useful' information to the specialist squads of the CID. In consequence, for the uniform men there was less and less reason either to use or contribute to the system, so that, by the late seventies, the collator in the subdivisional station became more and more the first stage on a supply-line to the newly appointed intelligence officers at divisional level. The present situation is described here by a Divisional Intelligence Officer:

> The first thing to be said about criminal intelligence is that it's not made use of by the PCs. It's so busy in most places that the beat man can't specialize at all. An immense amount of enquiry work has been taken off him so that any crime worthy of its salt will go to the CID. All the beat man gets is the petty stuff – broken windows, things like that – but for that he doesn't need to use the index. I very seldom get phone calls from them and most of the information that comes from the uniform branch comes from ex-crime patrol.

Thus, it can be seen that the local origins of the system have been transformed in the interests of a more 'rational' system of detection and investigation. We shall postpone consideration of the value of criminal intelligence for this purpose until later; the point to notice here, is how the system became increasingly geared to the centre and away from the needs of the local policeman. Thus, although the original role of the collator rapidly became impossible to fulfil, his importance grew as 'Divisional Intelligence' – for better or worse – became increasingly more important to criminal investigation. The original idea of unit beat policing, that information should be circulated among a small group of officers working a particular area, gradually gave way to the collator's supplying 'intelligence' to a centralized resource at divisional and latterly at force level. In place of information designed to act as a back-up and supplementary resource to four men working an 'area', divisional intelligence is intended as an investigative tool in relation to populations very often in excess of 200,000 persons. As we saw in the last section, the nature of the redefined task has entailed the introduction of specialist intelligence-gatherers.

There are thus two main sources of information available to the intelligence officer. On the one hand he has the intelligence gleaned off the street by the crime patrols, and on the other hand there is information derived from analysis of reports and paperwork provided in, and as a spin-off from, the routine work of the PC. Much of this latter work is still done at subdivisional level by the collators.

In practical terms, the DIO's work is arduous and, where uncomputerized, relatively mechanical. Most of his day is taken up weeding and selecting information from a mass of paperwork and reports which is then meticulously transcribed onto a manual card index system. The system can vary in sophistication from station to station. In most, basic indexes are kept which will include a 'nominal index' containing all known personal details of someone deemed 'to be of interest' including any regular 'haunts', 'associates', vehicles, employment, etc.; a separate 'vehicle index' in which entries by registration number refer to known users of vehicles, when last sighted, occupants etc. as well as details of colour, make and model, and a street index which would include details on persons seen frequenting particular premises, suspect businesses, offences which have occurred and so on. Additional indexes are frequently kept on 'coloureds', 'nicknames', 'females', and 'associates'.

On receiving any particular intelligence item, the DIO will enter it up under each appropriate index, carefully cross-referencing each entry to the others, so that any enquiry of one index will lead to the location of further information elsewhere in the system. Thus, for example, an officer of the crime patrol might report that a vehicle with the registration ABC 123 was seen being parked outside a particular house by a person 'X' who the officer believes may be 'of interest'. If this has not been done already, the Police National Computer at Hendon would be consulted and the name of the registered keeper of the vehicle established. The DIO might then add the following entries to his system. First, the relevant cards under the nominal index would be amended (or new cards started). The person sighted parking the car would have his card updated to show that he was using the car in question and that he is now frequenting this particular house, and, if appropriate, that he is now associating with the keeper of that car. If necessary, a card would be started on the owner of the car saying that he is the owner of a vehicle of interest to the police, giving his or her name and address (obtained from the Police National Computer) and stating him to be an associate of 'X'. Under the vehicles index, the registration number of the car and details of the owner and known user would be entered. Under the street index, the address of the now suspect premises would be entered with a note of the names of the two persons seen to frequent it. The DIO would then date and cross-reference each entry and forward a copy or abstract of the original report to central intelligence which is held at force headquarters.

We have already emphasized that only a minority of those named in the criminal intelligence indexes have any criminal record; however, it should also be noted that indexes are also kept on specific activities which do not necessarily follow the definitions of the criminal law. Thus, for example, in one station an 'indecencies' index was kept in which, we were told, were included the personal details of homosexuals on the grounds that 'they were a danger to themselves'. It is certainly one of the more alarming features of the system, as it has been allowed to develop, that the collators and DIOs, who usually hold the rank of constable, have been given so much scope to build up massive banks of intelligence which have been subject neither to outside scrutiny, nor, it seems, to serious internal review. This is no doubt in part a consequence of the piecemeal development of the system as it was first introduced under unit beat policing when 'supervision provided by sergeants and inspectors' was deemed adequate. Such are the changes in scale and purpose now, however, that serious consideration needs to be given to the problems of quality control and to criteria of relevance.

In the force we studied, the system of divisional intelligence is integrated through a central office of force intelligence at headquarters. There is, of course, a simple logic to having a fully centralized system. People of interest to the police do not stay within or limit their activities to any particular division. The significance of intelligence gleaned in one area of the city may thus be lost unless made available throughout the force. The problem of selection, however, is intensified as the criteria of what may be considered relevant are duly widened. Nobody knows at any point in the system what may or may not be of use to someone else so that it is only logical to include anything and everything, which is what in practice happens. An attempt is made at central intelligence to weed out intelligence that is 'too local' or 'too trivial' to keep on the central indexes, but such selection is made largely on grounds of efficiency alone. The system of manual indexing simply becomes too cumbersome and retrieval too slow.

The force intelligence system described here falls under the control of the CID. An embryonic system had existed in the early sixties, but the main expansion occurred with the rationalization of divisional intelligence during the late seventies and the introduction of the crime patrols. At present, it holds information on some 10 per cent of the population. However, it should be noted that this figure does not include additional intelligence held on nominal files at divisional and subdivisional level, so that the figure of 10 per cent may be substantially less than the total. As noted earlier, well in excess of 50 per cent of these persons do not have any criminal record.

We reiterate at this point that the subjects of criminal intelligence are not selected according to any particular 'qualification'. A detective inspector gave the following explanation:

We have to keep a close watch on people even though they're not convicted criminals . . . they *may* be involved. It's very difficult to define a criminal and of course we have to be very careful who we give our information to . . . it's purely for police use. We have to vet whatever comes in and decide if that person is *going to be* of interest to us. (Detective Inspector, Criminal Intelligence)

This statement clearly exhibits both the problems and the objects of criminal intelligence from the police point of view. It is impossible to know in advance who may or may not become involved in crime. In so far as the police are concerned with the prevention of crime, it therefore appears perfectly reasonable for them to be concerned with the prediction of likely criminals. Intelligence-gathering is thus defined not in relation to past crime and thus convicted criminals, but in relation to future crime and future conviction. Again this entails that the criteria of selection are extremely wide, amounting to nothing less than a biography of the individuals who might be of future interest:

> Every name we have here is in fact the life of the person as we have it. Take this man here. He was convicted in the sixties and all this information has been compiled since then. I can tell you who he was associating with in 1969, who he was living with and where he was living right up to the present day. We've got a record of all his known associates, previous addresses, cars he's used and all the cross-references. (Detective Inspector, Criminal Intelligence)

The product of the last ten years has thus been a tightly integrated system of intelligence collection, collation and analysis from sub-divisional through to force level. We have suggested that this might best be understood as an attempt to translate onto paper and, by so doing, make generally available the fund of local knowledge previously the property of the 'old style' policeman. Rationalization and centralization, however, have entailed that intelligence is collected on a more or less random basis as the criteria invoked by the locally based policeman, have been forgotten.

If the collection and analysis of intelligence has proceeded apace, the dissemination of the information is less well organized and, as such, it is said to be relatively under-used. At divisional level a daily intelligence sheet is circulated throughout the stations, as is the force intelligence sheet which is published three times a week. At subdivisional level the collator maintains a more informal contact with the officers of the different shifts.

The force intelligence sheet is almost journalistic in format. Running to perhaps three or four tightly printed pages, it might perhaps 'headline' information about and display a photograph of a well-known criminal from outside the force area, who has been seen at large and for whom a special watch should be kept. This might be followed by news of persons recently released from prison, usually giving their last-known addresses, what sort of offences they are known to commit, their associates, haunts etc. A short analysis of patterns and methods of crime particularly prevalent at the time, where they are likely to be committed and by whom, might then be followed by particular items on individuals, associates, vehicles and so on. An inter-force Police Gazette circulates the principal matters of interest within any particular force to all forces.

The intelligence sheets are usually read with some interest by the officers but, obviously, they can only touch on matters of immediate and pressing concern. The material held on the files remains largely a resource to be consulted by the operational officer, and, as such, the major obstacle in the way of developing intelligence for operational purposes has been its accessibility. Training courses emphasize the value and uses of the resource, and indeed one of the criteria now invoked for the purposes of annual career assessment is the officer's use of and contribution to criminal intelligence (see Appendix, para. 8). However, even so, it is a regular complaint made by DIOs that the PCs do not use the system to its best advantage.

At present, the difficulties of access have meant that the use of criminal intelligence is largely restricted to the investigation of crimes which have actually been committed. Names of suspects supplied by witnesses can be checked out and likely miscreants brought into the station for questioning. The most common use of intelligence is to structure interrogations, to suggest particular lines of questioning, and to break alibis. The significance of this should not be lost, however, as we shall argue later that the availability of criminal intelligence shifts the basis of criminal investigation towards detention and interrogation and away from alternative procedures based upon co-operation and consent.[3] At present, therefore, what has been termed the 'pre-emptive' potential of criminal intelligence, i.e. the surveillance of those 'likely' to commit crime in the future, has remained largely unrealized.

The computerization of local intelligence will remove the problems of access and allow its full effect upon police methods to be felt. At present the use made of intelligence is crude. It is decentralized, which leads to problems of communication; the divisional and subdivisional systems may be incompatible and idiosyncratic and often require the presence of the particular DIO to retrieve information; the manual system is slow and clumsy and as a result the pay-off, especially for the uniformed officer, is low. All this will change with computerization as officers are provided with virtually instant access, wherever they may be.

## The Computerization of Local Intelligence

The new 'crime and information' computers need to be carefully distinguished from the 'command and control' computers. Whereas the command and control computer is dedicated to the provision of information about police resources and the control of manpower, the crime and information computer is dedicated to the storage and retrieval of intelligence about the public.

Care should also be taken to note that these computers are locally based and controlled by individual forces, and that, as such, their function is very different from the national police data banks held, for example, in the Metropolitan force's 'C' Department computer and the Police National Computer (PNC) at Hendon. There are some similarities. The PNC, for example, in addition to holding information on vehicle ownership, stolen cars, etc., also maintains an index of wanted and missing persons, and an index of 'criminal names' listing the names of individuals suspected of 'more serious' crimes in different parts of the country.

The computerization of local intelligence is currently less developed and less widespread than computerized command and control. At present only five crime and information computers are operational – in the Cheshire, Metropolitan, Suffolk, Tayside and Thames Valley forces. A further nineteen forces are now developing or proposing to introduce the facility.

Of the five currently in use, most is known about the 'collator project' undertaken by the Thames Valley Police.[4] As its name suggests, the project has involved transferring all the data previously held on the old manual card index systems to computer, in order to facilitate easy access. By means of personal radio, the PC is now able to consult the VDU operator at the local station and be given immediately whatever information is held on any of the 160,000 persons (10 per cent of the area population) whose names appear on the index. This is expected to grow to some 280,000 (15 per cent) by 1986. In a series of detailed reports, Duncan Campbell, of the *New Statesman*, has shown that much of the intelligence held on the TVP computer is of the same quality as that gleaned by the crime patrols in 'R' Division. Campbell instances, as examples, hearsay comments to the effect that the subject 'fancies little boys', and records of 'offences' for which there was no criminal prosecution. Campbell has also established that the 'nominal index' is expanding at the rate of 120 new names *per weekday.*

In comparison to the Lothian and Borders Police Computer (LBPC), which was due to go 'live' during the early part of 1982, the Thames Valley computer is relatively unsophisticated. At a cost of £1.39m. and with an expected life of ten years, the LBPC will be the most powerful local crime and information computer yet in operation in this country. For that reason, we shall take the LBPC as the model for our discussion.

Data compilation and analysis for intelligence work is not the only function to which such computers can be put. Like command and control computers they frequently combine facilities for management and other operational purposes. The LBPC thus has additional features, such as a 'message switch', enabling rapid contact through a chain of visual display units in each station, a lost-and-found property index, an index of burglar alarms and key-holders. Table 3 shows the full facilities and the original projections of their likely use. The two indexes of particular interest in terms of intelligence and storage of personal data are the 'nominal' and 'crime reporting' indexes: the two largest files in the computer.

The LBPC employs a system known as 'free text retrieval' (FTR). FTR was described by the Lindop Committee on Data Protection in the following terms:

> There seems to be no way of regulating systems of this kind by reference to the structure or content of the information collected, or to the analytic processes, or to the form of output. To divine the purposes of keeping information in free textual form it would be necessary to ask questions about *each particular search* undertaken to discover its motivation . . . FTR will clearly present special problems of definition and control.[5]

# Table 3: Lothian and Borders Police Computer: Facilities and Projection

## Application Transaction Workloads

| APPLICATION | RECORD SIZE (chars) | FILE SIZE (records) | RETENTION PERIOD | FACILITY | CURRENT ANNUAL | PROJECTED ANNUAL | AVERAGE HOUR | PEAK HOUR | RESPONSE TIME |
|---|---|---|---|---|---|---|---|---|---|
| MESSAGE SWITCHING | 2,000 | 12,000 | 48 hours | Send Message | 43,152 | 258,912 | 30 | 234 | D |
| | | | | Display Message | 133,200 | 799,200 | 90 | 390 | A |
| CRIME REPORTING | 1,200 | 162,000 | 12 months | Create Record | 60,000 | 162,000 | 20 | 40 | B |
| | | | | Update Record | – | 200,000 | 23 | 60 | B |
| | | | | Interrogations | 17,500 | 50,000 | 6 | 12 | D |
| | | | | Unsolicited Messages Generated | – | 270,000 | 31 | 62 | D |
| LOST/FOUND PROPERTY | 250 | 30,000 | 12 months | Create Record (Lost) | 22,829 | 35,000 | 4 | 20 | B |
| | | | | Create Record (Found) | 26,000 | 45,000 | 5 | 15 | B |
| | | | | Interrogations | 64,000 | 80,000 | 9 | 18 | D |
| | | | | Unsolicited Messages Generated | – | 21,250 | 2.5 | 10 | D |

| | | | | | | | | | |
|---|---|---|---|---|---|---|---|---|---|
| NOMINAL INDEX | 1,000 | 50,000 | On-going | Create Record | — | 5,000 | 0.5 | 10 | B |
| | | | | Update Record | — | 100,000 | 12 | 48 | B |
| | | | | Interrogations | 26,000 | 200,000 | 24 | 34 | B,C |
| | | | | Unsolicited Messages Generated | — | 18,000 | 2 | 8 | D |
| PNC | — | — | On-going | All Transactions | 400,000 | 500,000 | 57 | 300 | C |
| SCRATCHPAD | 2,000 | 10,000 | On-going | All Transactions | — | 500,000 | 57 | 300 | A |
| PERSONNEL | 1,000 | 12,000 | On-going | All Transactions | 42,000 | 45,000 | 5 | 30 | B |
| FIREARM/SHOTGUNS | 500 | 17,000 | 12 months | All Transactions | 8,792 | 9,000 | 1 | 30 | B |
| KEY REFERENCES | 500 | 60,000 | On-going | All Transactions | 20,000 | 25,000 | 3 | 100 | A |
| BURGLAR ALARMS | 1,000 | 4,500 | On-going | All Transactions | 8,792 | 10,000 | 1.2 | 100 | A |
| MAJOR INCIDENTS | | | | | | | | | |
| REPORT FORMATS | | | | | | | | | |
| PROCESS REPORTS | | | | | | | | | |

**** INCLUDED IN SCRATCHPAD FILE SIZES AND TRANSACTION RATES ****

It is frequently said by the police and others that the computerization of data makes no real difference. After all, all the information is already down on paper somewhere, so what difference does it make if it is in a computer? The answer is, of course, an enormous difference.

In simple terms, FTR allows the user to store whatever and as much material as is desired without having to pre-code or classify the material, and limited only by the absolute capacity of the data bank. Thus, the need for a complex series of cross-referenced indexes as under the old manual system and less sophisticated computerized systems is done away with. So too is the need to sift, for example, crime reports and to abstract any specific items of interest. The computer does this for the user when and if required. Thus it is no longer necessary to 'collate' information in advance. Any specific item of information contained in crime reports, once the full text has been computerized, can be retrieved at the push of a button. The whole system is thus very simple to operate. All that is required is for the raw information to be typed directly into the data bank in 'free text' (i.e. without classification or encoding).

In place of the separate indexes as used under the old manual systems, the computer is programmed to relate the data to its own lexicon of key words. Thus, for example, in a passage of a document referring to a '*bald Englishman* with a *red dog*' the occurrence of the italicized words would be individually recorded in the lexicon alongside all other occurrences of the same words as they have appeared anywhere else in the data bank. To request information from the computer, the process is in effect reversed except that in addition to the original reference, *all* other occurrences of the same combination of words can also be retrieved. In effect, the user simply retrieves any reference to the subject of interest held anywhere in the raw data.

Obviously, the amount of information forthcoming depends upon the generality of the questions asked. In this way, the user can, if desired, simply 'browse' through the vast amount of information held by asking general questions. It is for this reason that Lindop said that to divine the purpose of keeping information in free textual form it would be necessary to ask questions about each particular search undertaken.

With these comments in mind, it is obvious that the only limit upon the use of the computer for intelligence purposes is the amount of the data kept. As we have seen, the crime report form is one of the sources of criminal intelligence most favoured by the collators and Divisional Intelligence Officers. Their computerization in FTR thus simplifies analysis and makes it more efficient so that very much more comprehensive use of data is possible. If we now consider exactly what is contained in a crime report form, we can get some indication of the potential uses of the system. Table 4 classifies under different heads the material contained in a crime report. It should be noted, however, that for the purposes of FTR such classification is unnecessary.

At present, crime reporting is a tedious job for the uniformed officer. Further, as many as six copies of the crime report will be circulated through the force for administrative use. Clearly, computerization will reduce the burden of paperwork immensely. Indeed, this is one of the selling points of the computer to officers within the force. In future, any constable will only need to ring through his report to a VDU operator at headquarters, who will type in the reports for the officers who will thus be released for 'operational' duties.

However, we should be clear about the nature of the crime report which is not only a record of the date, time, place, etc. of the alleged offence, but is a continuing record of the progress of the investigation, containing details of suspects and witnesses interviewed, persons arrested, detained and charged, as well as the comments and impressions of the different officers involved at different stages in the investigation. Clearly, such information is of immediate use to the actual investigation at the time. Just as important for the purposes of intelligence, however, is the availability of such information for subsequent analysis and use. Thus, for example, on the basis of information held in the crime reports, it will be possible to establish the number of times a named individual has been 'previously involved' in crime, either as a witness or a suspect, the number of times the person has been questioned by the police, the number of occasions he or she has been suspected, arrested, detained, charged etc. without prosecution being implemented.

## Table 4: Crime Reporting File: Analysis of Contents

| Division, Subdivision, Beat No.: | Complaint Received By: | Complaint Being Dealt With By: |
|---|---|---|
| Complaint Date:<br>Complaint Time:<br>Crime date:<br>Locus of crime:<br>SHHD/HO classification: | Modus Operandi:<br>**locus:** (free text)<br>**Props:** tools, weapons, vehicles, etc. (free text)<br>**Mode of entry:** (free text)<br>**Characteristics:** (free text) | |
| Complainant<br>**Surname:**<br>**Forename:**<br>**Date of Birth:**<br>**Address:** | Witnesses<br>**Surname:**<br>**Forename:**<br>**Date of Birth:**<br>**Address:** | Suspects<br>**Surname:**<br>**Forename:**<br>**Date of Birth:**<br>**Address:** |
| Aggrieved Person<br>**Surname:**<br>**Forename:**<br>**Date of Birth:**<br>**Address:**<br>**Statement:** (free text)<br>**Injuries:**<br>**Property:** (stolen damaged etc.) | Suspect vehicles<br>**Registration No:**<br>**Description:** | Persons arrested/detained<br>**Date:**<br>**Time:**<br>**Place:**<br>**Charge/No Charge:**<br>**Surname:**<br>**Forenames:**<br>**Address:**<br>**Statement:**<br>**Arresting Officer:** |
| Date of Detection<br>Remarks: (free text) | | |

It can be seen from Table 3 that at present the Lothian and Borders police deal annually with some 60,000 crime reports, that the projected capacity by 1990 is for some 162,000 and that the present number of interrogations of the data is expected to rise from 17,500 to 50,000 per annum. The important point to remember here, however, is that the information held on the crime reporting data base is not restricted to 'convicted, active criminals'.

Another data base is, however, restricted: the nominal file contains the personal information on 'active convicted criminals' which is presently held on a manual index by Lothian and Borders Department of Criminal Intelligence. It is emphasized by the Lothian and Borders force that 'unlike most other forces, we have given an undertaking to our local police committee that what we record is *factual information about convicted criminals*'. The undertaking, therefore, is that there will be no unsubstantiated gossip held on anyone, whether previously convicted or not. As a result, we were told that for purposes of computerization, only 18,000 of the 80,000 files currently held on central criminal intelligence (80,000 amounts to approximately ten per cent of the area population) would be computerized. It should be noted, however, that other forces, such as the Thames Valley, have not given such undertakings and that in any case the original manual index will in Lothian and Borders be maintained on an unrestricted basis.

The figures given in Table 3 are of interest for a number of reasons. First, they show the projected rate of growth of computerized criminal intelligence rising from a level of 18,000 to a maximum of 50,000 at a rate of 5,000 new files per annum. (It will be appreciated that this rise does not include the growth of the manual index.) It is projected that new items of intelligence and information will be fed into the data bank at the rate of 100,000 per annum. What is most significant is the projection on use: it is expected that the number of enquiries presently made of central criminal intelligence will rise from a present level of 26,000 per annum, to some 200,000 on computerization. As with the crime reports, the nominal index is accessed through free text. Table 5 shows the type of information held.

It is important to note that while the nominal index on first sight relates solely to the 'active and convicted criminal' FTR allows the user, as we saw above, to browse. The inclusion therefore of

# Table 5: Nominal File: Analysis of Contents

**Surname:**
**SCRO/CRO No.**
**Aliases/Nicknames:**
**Address:**
**Occupation:**

Reference No.
**Forename:** **Sex:**
**Local Photograph No:**
**Forename:** **Surname:**
**Previous Addresses:**
**Present employment:**

**Date of Birth:** **Place of Birth:**
**Collator area:**

**Present employer:**

Description
**Height:**
**Hair Colour:**
**Voice/Accent:**
**Manner:**

**Build:**
**Hair Style:**
**Distinguishing Features:**
(tattoos, scars, etc.)
**Gait:**

**Eye Colour/Peculiarities:**
**Facial Hair:**
**Habits:**

**Modus Operandi:**
**Locus:**
**Props:**
**Mode of Entry:**
**Characteristics:**

**Vehicles:**
**Registration Mark:**
**Colour:**
**Type:**
**Make:**

**Frequents:**
**Premises:**
**Addresses:**

**Associates:**
**Name:**
**Address:**
**Collator Area:**
**Ref. No:**

**Observation Reports:**
(free text)

**Reasons for Interest:**
(free text)

'associates' of convicted criminals in the nominal file gives some cause for concern, especially when used alongside and cross-referenced to the crime-reporting file.

With respect to the nominal file itself, although gossip and hearsay is to be excluded, free text is given for officers' comments and 'observation' reports (sightings). The exclusion of gossip thus pertains to second-hand information obtained from third parties, but does not exclude information directly obtained by officers from the person concerned.

It can now be seen that, with FTR, the crime report file and the nominal file makes available a vast amount of personal data on those who, however tangentially, have been involved in the criminal process: records of witnesses, suspects, detainees, arrestees, aggrieved persons, and vehicles are available on demand from the crime reports which may be supplemented by reference to the nominal index and vice versa.

At present, there is no statutory regulation of information data banks whether held by the police or industry. Despite the recommendations of the Lindop Committee and an assurance from the Home Secretary that it is the Government's intention to introduce legislation on the matter 'when an opportunity offers', there has been no attempt to do so as yet. Given the reservations of the Lindop Committee about the very possibility of subjecting the use of FTR to any meaningful scrutiny, given police reluctance to give evidence to that Committee about the use of the 'C' Department computer (which also utilizes FTR), and given the very nature of the resource itself, it seems very unlikely that an adequate system of monitoring the use of local computers by an independent agency will be introduced. Senior officers of the Lothian and Borders Police were aware of the problem and the personal responsibility they bear:

> To be quite frank about this there are unlimited possibilities for keeping track on all sorts of things – movements, anything. To some extent matters could be improved greatly. If they got an independent person to come round and examine the data file, with access and without too much warning preferably, that would go quite a way towards it. But I really think it's going to be extremely difficult. If we were twisted enough, I'm quite sure it's

not beyond our capabilities to hide whatever we wanted from someone we thought might try to look for it. It boils down to trust, really. Consensus policing, you know.

It appears that present thinking among senior officers sees the only effective control over the information held on the new computers to be the 'discipline of the force':

Of course, it doesn't take much common sense to realise that you could hoodwink an inspectorate. The only real thing that stops it is the fact that it's a disciplined service . . . We've given this undertaking that we won't be doing it, and as long as I'm here we won't.

Self-imposed controls in the Lothian and Borders Police have involved the undertaking that hearsay, gossip and rumour will not be entered on the computerized files, and the practice that before a new file can be opened on any particular person, a Detective Chief Inspector at force headquarters will vet the material and ensure that the individual concerned has a previous conviction and can be deemed 'active'. These restrictions apply only to specific entries in the nominal file, however, and not to the much larger crime report data base.

The development of personal data banks by state agencies has already provoked considerable criticism on grounds of the potential and actual invasion of privacy. There is concern as to the accuracy and reliability of information. The case of Jan Martin, an employee of the former television presenter, Michael Barrett, has been widely cited as a case in point. On the basis of information received from the Dutch police, the Metropolitan Police revealed to the firm Taylor Woodrow that the lady in question was suspected of having terrorist connections. Taylor Woodrow duly refused Michael Barrett and his team entry into their factory, informing Mr Barrett of their reasons. Through Ms Martin's father, a former Detective Chief Superintendent at New Scotland Yard, the source of this information was established and shown to be wholly inaccurate.[6]

There are worries not only about abuse but concerning the security of information. There have been a number of cases in which the resources of the PNC and the Thames Valley Police Computer have been misused for personal gain by both serving and ex-police officers and where outside enquiry agents have been given access to information held on police computers.[7]

Nor should political implications be forgotten: it has been pointed out that there could be widespread resistance to computerization of such information were it realized that such data might be employed for the purposes of intelligence and surveillance. It has been suggested, for example, that the use of the PNC constitutes a significant step in the direction of covert policing. Duncan Campbell instances the relationship between the PNC and the DVLC at Swansea, whereby changes of address of vehicle owners notified to Swansea – a requirement at law – are immediately made available to the PNC. Patricia Hewitt of the National Council for Civil Liberties (NCCL), has written that it is 'almost inconceivable that Parliament would have enacted a law requiring all citizens to notify a change of address to the police. But such a requirement has now been introduced for most adults without any legislation whatsoever.'[8]

There are worries, in addition, about future uses concerning the surveillance of political activists and minority groups, and even the survival of democratic freedom of association and expression – not because of any threat of actual oppression but in consequence of the 'chilling' effect of such data and consequent reluctance of individuals to participate in the democratic process and to 'become involved'. Specific instances of the use of criminal intelligence to vet jurors has only added to such concern. There can be no doubt that such anxieties are relevant to the nature of policing as much as they are to broader issues of political freedom.

## Conclusions: The Shifting Balance in Police Work

In all its aspects, the rationalization of the police forces – specialization, centralization and computerization – has been undertaken with one end in view, namely, to increase output per man-hour and thereby the relative strength of the police numbers, based on the simple philosophy that more police makes for better policing. At the same time, the actual number of police officers has virtually doubled since the war. The changes which have been made to achieve these ends have already secured a substantial change in the quality of policing, and not necessarily for the better. 'Fire-brigade' policing, which came about as a less than fortunate and unintended outcome of unit beat policing has, in some forces, been institutionalized in computerized command and control systems. In the name of technological efficiency these have served only to legitimate depersonalized and insensitive police regimes. A very similar line of development can be observed in the development of local intelligence. The role of the collator under unit beat policing has been revolutionized. Local intelligence has undergone the sequence of specialization, centralization and now finally computerization, and the change of emphasis is clear.

Nobody can dispute that information from the public is essential to police work. The police simply cannot operate without it. However, information can be obtained in very different ways. At one end of the spectrum it can be given voluntarily. This might properly be termed policing by consent. At the other end it can be obtained by threat, coercion or torture, which provides one model of a police state. Between these two extremes, however, are other points on the continuum. Information can be bought by the police – as with the use of paid 'squeaks', informants and 'supergrasses'. Witnesses can be compelled at law to give evidence (in one draft of the Criminal Justice (Scotland) Bill the police were to have been given the power to detain not only suspects, but witnesses). Alternatively, information or 'intelligence' can be collected covertly but passively, as described in this chapter, or more active involvement of the police can be encouraged as, for example, in the use of *agents provocateurs*. There are, no doubt, other methods which could be fitted into this scheme. The point is, however, that the manner in which information is obtained is as critical as, if not more important than, the mere possession of the information. The way in which the information is obtained shows more clearly than any other index the relationship between police and public at any time. The developments described represent a substantial step away from policing by consent – a movement, if it remains unchecked, that will become ever more pronounced.

In practical terms, it may be felt that a shift in the relationship between police and public is a small price to pay for the more effective detection and prevention of crime. After all, certainty of detection and prosecution is said to be the best deterrent. But the efficient detection of crime requires active participation and co-operation by the public often in actually detaining offenders – and information necessary for detection is usually situationally specific – it can only be provided by those present at the time and place the offence was actually committed. Thus the police can rarely claim the full credit for the detection and arrest of offenders, except for certain 'self-reporting' offences, such as 'drunk and incapable', and for 'police initiated' arrests, of which traffic offences are the most commonplace.

There has been a substantial amount of research on this point, one of the most recent studies being that of Dr Michael Chatterton at the University of Manchester, whose findings we reproduce here.[9]

Chatterton's study was of a force in the north of England. He analysed official records to determine the extent to which members of the public were actively involved and participated in police arrests. He found that the majority of arrests (67 per cent) were actually 'initiated' by the public. Thus, for example, in 18 per cent of cases the prisoner was actually detained by the victim or

**Table 6: Sources of information and types of investigation leading to arrests:** distribution of arrests for crime showing the branch of the arresting officer and the source of information and type of investigation leading to the arrest of the prisoner.

| Mode of detection | CID | | Uniform | | Total | % |
|---|---|---|---|---|---|---|
| | No. | % | No. | % | | |
| Named | 155 | 25 | 50 | 7 | 205 | 15 |
| Search | 10 | 2 | 85 | 12 | 95 | 7 |
| Enquiries | 126 | 20 | 28 | 4 | 154 | 11 |
| Implicated | 91 | 14 | 51 | 7 | 142 | 10 |
| Fingerprints | 24 | 4 | – | – | 24 | 2 |
| Other unit | 71 | 11 | 19 | 2 | 90 | 7 |
| Radio call | 10 | 2 | 74 | 10 | 84 | 6 |
| Police-initiated | 47 | 7 | 272 | 38 | 319 | 24 |
| Detained | 95 | 15 | 143 | 20 | 238 | 18 |
| Total | 629 | 100 | 722 | 100 | 1,351 | 100 |

witnesses before the police arrived (the 'detained' category above), 15 per cent of offenders had been positively identified by a witness at the time the police arrived ('named') and a further 11 per cent during subsequent investigation ('enquiries'). A further 6 per cent of arrests were made immediately on arrival at the scene of the crime following a call from the public ('radio call') and another 7 per cent on a search of the surrounding area on the basis of a description furnished by a witness. A further 10 per cent of arrests were made following information from persons taken into custody ('implicated').

In all these instances it will be seen that the information is situation-specific and quite particular in content. Such arrests we may say are initiated by the public upon whom the police are dependent. 'Police-initiated' arrests Chatterton defines as 'those cases where the arresting officer was not following up a complaint or request from a member of the public, for example a radio call or crime complaint, but had initiated his involvement in the incident or encounter with the prisoner himself'. (The examples of drunkenness, traffic offences etc. were given earlier.) In Chatterton's study such arrests accounted for only 7 per cent of those made by the CID – it should be borne in mind in the context of our comments that criminal intelligence is seen primarily as a CID resource – and for 38 per cent of arrests by uniform branch officers. Forensic evidence accounted for only 2 per cent of arrests, while the remaining 7 per cent could not be analysed in terms of police or public initiation as they were made following requests received for other units.

What such studies show is the singular importance of public involvement in police work even as it is currently organized. However, it should be noted that within force areas and within divisions variations will be found. In the unit area described in the last chapter, where it was readily acknowledged by the officers employed there that their relations with the public were very poor, the clear-up rate of reported crime was less than one-half of the national average. Indeed the lack of public co-operation, as we saw, was frequently put forward as the main reason for bending the rules and for relying on interrogation as a major tool in the investigation of offences. In such circumstances it is at least plausible to suggest that these practices will reinforce distrust, reduce the likelihood of co-operation, and so increase the pressure to adopt alternative methods.

One of the main arguments against the general use of crime information computers then is that the kind of information they hold is not sufficiently specific to be of use in detection and arrest. We shall return to this point presently. Before we do so, however, we should be careful not to attribute the rise of the new technology simply to difficulties in police/community relations. This would be to put the cart before the horse, for to a great extent such developments provoke rather than are provoked by lack of co-operation. There are other factors at work, which are internal rather than external to the police. One of these is police culture itself.

We have already noted the 'practical policeman's' ideal of a 'good capture' and the prestige and satisfaction derived from it. In itself this is not particularly surprising, but in a very important sense the 'capture-culture' and its notion of 'real police work' runs counter to a philosophy of policing by consent.

A 'good capture' is too loose a notion to define precisely. It is probably best to consider it in terms of the resources employed by and the resourcefulness of the arresting officer. Thus an arrest which has relied upon police initiative and resources, upon compiling evidence and painstaking detective work is regarded as a better capture than one where the prisoner was detained or named directly by a member of the public or implicated by another prisoner. Crudely, we might say that the less use is made of outside resources, the 'better' the capture.

The premium placed on the 'good capture' is reflected at all levels of the force. This was constantly brought home in observations and comments made during the research period. Older and more senior officers, now 'driving a desk' in headquarters frequently regret their separation from 'real police work'. A young PC expressed both surprise and satisfaction at the reaction of very senior officers at headquarters after he had delivered a particularly 'good prisoner' to the CID:

> It was amazing. To be honest it was sheer luck that I got the guy, I was just in the right place at the right time – and it was my last day in plain clothes! . . . Anyway I walked into the main office and there was the Deputy Chief sitting with all the big bosses

celebrating . . . and I was really dirty and scruffy! So one of them says 'here he is!' and one of them pours out this glass of whisky. Straight up. I was the bloody hero. Me and all the bosses, it was great. I got back to the station and breathed booze all over the Chief Inspector . . . and there was nothing he could say!' (PC, 5 years' experience)

It is also worth noting that for senior officers the 'good capture' is not only an important part of their culture, it is also a justification for expenditure upon increasingly expensive technology and equipment and a particularly public demonstration of the need for and value of the 'professional force' which they head and upon which their own social status rests.

It should also be observed that the very idea of professionalism within the force itself reinforces the separation of police and public in the conception of police work as undertaken by an independent 'expert' body. Indeed, for the 'professional' – be it the professional lawyer, doctor or policeman – the need to rely upon outside, lay or amateur opinion or resources is a mark of failure and a challenge to the status of the job itself. Increasingly, within senior police circles, the idea predominates of a professional force, in control of its own resources with expert or 'scientific' knowledge in the field, upon which the public should rely. This is a very different idea to that of a force which relies upon the public. Again, the pressure to deny the dependence of the police upon the public is self-evident as is the attraction of sophisticated technology as a mark of expertise.

Such observations on the nature of police culture perhaps deserve to be argued in greater detail. However, as they stand, they suffice to demonstrate that the culture within which computerization has already been received, encourages a particular use and emphasis. When placed alongside the unquestioned assumption that the solution to the problems of contemporary policing is to be found in more and better-equipped police officers and the corresponding withdrawal of the police from the community consequent upon centralization and rationalization, it can be seen that a series of factors – cultural, organizational and technological – are almost conspiring to divert the course of consensual policing.

It has been argued that the computerization of intelligence is part of a wider movement in favour of police-initiated activity – sometimes termed 'pro-active policing' – in which relations of mutual dependence are redefined to stress the independence and expertise of the force. But perhaps this is not such a bad thing if the information collected allows those wrongly suspected of crime to be readily eliminated from police enquiries and those subsequently proved guilty of offences to be readily apprehended?

We have suggested, however, that most of the intelligence held will be of too general a nature to be of relevance to specific offences. We have seen in some detail the methods employed and the nature of the material collected by the crime patrols and we have doubted the accuracy and value of what is frequently no better than unsupported general gossip and hearsay. In addition, we noted earlier that the rivalries and the desire for a good capture more often than not result in the more pertinent information being withheld by individual officers. More significantly, however, it has been pointed out that the scale and centralized organization of criminal intelligence necessarily widens the criteria of relevance: the officer in receipt of information cannot know whether it is of relevance to someone else in the force, with the result that everything and anything is included.

At a different level, and more important, is the necessary emphasis placed in pre-emptive policing strategies upon the prediction of crime and, more particularly, upon those persons considered likely to commit crime. For these purposes, all knowledge is relevant in so far as the more information that is held on a person the greater the likelihood of successful prediction. In the past, practical limits have been imposed by the lack of capacity of the old manual systems and the practical use of criminal intelligence for the officer on the street was restricted. The infinitely greater capacity of the new computerized systems and their accessibility would appear to change all that.

Of course, the whole of society will not come under surveillance as a result of these innovations. What will happen in practice is that, as now – but to a much greater extent – police activity will be directed towards certain sectors of the population. The inhabitants of working-class areas of the cities and towns, where the rate of reported crime is the highest, will come under even greater scrutiny. In such circumstances, the effects of the new technology and the rationalization of policing upon police practice become critical: if certain areas of a city are subjected to a higher level of more aggressive policing than others, the probability of resentment, with all its attendant problems, is so much the higher. This is all the more likely if policing itself, in terms of the detection and prevention of crime, is less efficient.

The strategy of pre-emptive policing relies upon the assumption that those convicted of crime are likely to commit crimes again, and that therefore the police are under an obligation to keep themselves informed about their activities even though they have not actually committed any further offence. As Tony Bunyan has pointed out, the development of the specialist CID squads and intelligence-gathering operations – the regional crime squads, the National Drugs Intelligence Unit and the introduction of the Police National Computer – demonstrate the growth of this form of policing at the national level throughout the seventies.[10] The general application of pre-emptive policing at the local level, however, is far less developed. Predictably the associated tactics and practices, facilitated by the availability of the new intelligence resources, will encourage a more aggressive style of policing.

Criminal intelligence serves to provide the investigating officer not only with a series of potential suspects, but also with the questions he should ask. Thus the computer provides a list of all persons previously suspected, detained, arrested or charged with similar offences in the past (whether or not they have been convicted at law) but it also tells the officer exactly how many unresolved crimes of the same sort are outstanding and which correspond to the details held on particular individuals. From the point of view of the operational police officer the efficient and rational option in such circumstances is to detain potential suspects for questioning. As we shall see, this has required changes in the law, but, for example, the police in Scotland have already been given precisely this power under section 2 of the Criminal Justice (Scotland) Act 1980. Likewise, in both England and Scotland, the law on the admissibility of evidence obtained by confession has been progressively relaxed, and it appears from research presently being carried out by the Scottish Home and Health Department that already increasing use is being made of detention and interrogation as a means of obtaining evidence.

The intrinsic danger of such procedures is that they will be perceived and, indeed, practised as a mode of persecution rather than prosecution, and that the role of the police will change. Our own evidence suggests that a change in the character of policing is already occurring. In addition to the crime patrols, there is already a tendency among some area constables to obtain information from rather unexpected quarters. Thus, one area man we spoke to referred to his work as follows:

> We go down to the schools a lot. You get a hell of a lot of information from the kids. They get wise to us once they're about seven or eight, but they still like to boast about what their big brothers or their dads have been up to so we get a lot off the teachers.

The use of intelligence for pre-emptive policing clearly requires that the intelligence itself is kept up-to-date. As it was put to us, it could prove very embarrassing to stop a vehicle listed as 'suspect' on the PNC only to find that the new owner was the wife of the local MP. In this respect, it is predictable that the work of squads such as the crime patrols will become of increasing rather than diminishing importance, as the number of nominal files increases and the need to update them grows. At the level of the streets it is likely that for this purpose the use of 'stop checks' – again facilitated under recent legislation – will increase and with it charges and allegations of police harassment.

The picture we have presented here is necessarily speculative. As such we may be accused of exaggerating the probability of trouble. We have seen, however, that in terms of organization there are a series of reinforcing tendencies at play which have turned the police away from the public and militate against community involvement in law enforcement. We have pointed to the potential consequences. There is an undeniable danger that public reaction to the shift in police methods and strategies, to the rationalization and centralization of police tasks, and to police culture and the new technology may combine to reinforce perceptions of the police and their function as separate from and independent of the communities within which they work. The danger is no less on the part of the police as it is on the part of the public.

We suggested in the previous chapter that the current emphasis upon, and manpower committed to, programmes of community involvement is inadequate. We are less than convinced that even the more ambitious projects of 'community policing' are sufficient to provide an effective counterbalance to the developments we have described. The combination of 'reactive', 'fire-brigade' policing and 'pre-emptive' police methods as institutionalized in new forms of organization and technology are likely to prove a far stronger force than has been recognized in the formulation of community-policing strategies. Furthermore, it should not be forgotten that, while for the purposes of study, reactive and pre-emptive policing have been taken separately here, in practice, the two are by no means mutually exclusive. In the major cities of Britain – Glasgow, Liverpool, Birmingham, London – there has been massive public expenditure on both crime and information and command and control systems. When such innovations are considered alongside the problems of an adequate machinery for internal and external control of police practices, analysed in the next chapter and the developments in the law, described in Chapter 5, it will be seen that grounds for pessimism are not wholly unfounded.

We conclude this chapter with a caveat to our comments. While both command and control and crime information systems have potential dangers and, in the present context of their use, signal a qualitative change in the direction of policing, we are not suggesting that all computer-aided policing is necessarily and in itself a bad thing. Clearly there are justifiable uses and the technology itself does not entail the consequences we have outlined. A major murder enquiry can obviously be facilitated by the specific use of computers for the analysis of information. We pointed out in the last chapter that a rapid response to an emergency call is highly desirable. There is clearly a place for such resources and it would be as ridiculous to assert that the problems facing contemporary policing are to be resolved by their withdrawal as to suggest that they are to be resolved by their introduction. The point to be made is that a style of policing already present is further encouraged by the avail ability of the new technology. If it is not to dominate policing in the next decade, changes in the organization and methods of police work are essential. Rewriting the law will be of no effect unless accompanied by concrete reforms of this kind. Through changes in organization and practice backed up and reinforced by changes in the law, the new technology must be subordinated to the needs of the community, and by so doing the emphasis upon mutual dependence and policing by consent must be re-established.

## Further Reading

Bunyan, T., *The Political Police in Britain*, Quartet, London, 1977.

Campbell, D., 'Society under Surveillance', in P. Hain (ed.), *Policing the Police*, vol. 2, John Calder, London, 1980.

Chatterton, M., 'Police in Social Control', in J. F. S. King (ed.), *Control Without Custody*, Cambridge University Press, Cambridge, 1976.

Mawby, R., *Policing the City*, Saxon House, London, 1979.

Pope, D. W. and Weiner, N. L., *Modern Policing*, Croom Helm, London, 1981.

Pounder, C. and Anderson, S., *The Police Use of Computers*, Technical Authors Group, Edinburgh, 1981.

# 4

# The Local Politics of Accountability

The last twenty years have seen the most substantial and far-reaching changes in the political structure of the British police forces since Sir Robert Peel introduced the Metropolitan Police Act in 1829. Since the early sixties, in the place of a loosely co-ordinated association of small, locally based police forces, there has been a concerted move towards what is now a tightly integrated, national network of highly professionalized, autonomous police bureaucracies.

In 1962, when the last Royal Commission on the Police reported, there were 158 local police forces in Britain. By 1972, this figure had been cut by two-thirds. Thus, by 1982, excluding the Metropolitan and the City of London Police, there were forty-one forces left in England and Wales and eight in Scotland. Approximately half the population of Scotland is now policed by one force (Strathclyde: population 2.4 million) and there is continuing pressure to reduce the number of forces still further.

These vast new bureaucracies now dominate the shape and direction of British policing. Excluding the Metropolitan Police, in 1962 eight forces policed populations in excess of one million, only one of which – Birmingham – was an urban force. Today there are twenty-three urban forces and four of these – Greater Manchester, West Midlands, West Yorkshire and Strathclyde – each police over two million people. In the Metropolitan Police area, the population is in excess of seven millions. Thus, approximately one-third of the population of Britain is policed by five forces. In such circumstances, reference to 'local police forces' accountable to the 'community' is no longer realistic.

The same demands for rationalization and greater efficiency which saw the emergence of 'fire-brigade' and pre-emptive policing led – more directly this time – to the creation of the new 'superforces'. A further series of problems has been provoked which aggravate those encountered at street level. Put bluntly, the new police bureaucracies are too remote, both from the public and from the officers at street level. The power of Chief Constables has increased as their numbers have diminished, yet there has been no meaningful attempt to make that power accountable at the local level. Policy formation has thus become divorced from local populations: internally, the sheer weight and size of the forces has thrown up critical difficulties of management and control; at the same time internal problems of discipline and complaints from the public have become increasingly contentious.

Any system for regulating police activity has to deal with two major problems: first, how to reconcile acceptable democratic participation with effective policing and, second, how to ensure that agreed force policy is implemented on the street. Preoccupation with the control of Chief Constables, though attending to the first of these problems, tends to divert attention from the need to ensure effective control within police forces.

These two issues cannot be treated separately. Any consideration of external accountability and policy review requires analysis of the internal organization that either permits or obstructs the implementation of preferred policies. It is pointless to demand that Chief Constables be accountable unless they have effective control at ground level. In this context, it is necessary to look both at the formal systems of accountability and complaints and also at the internal politics of police organizations.

## Local Accountability

A police service, immune from the ideological pressures of any single political party, provides the surest and only guarantee of the people's individual freedom . . . I firmly believe that there is a long-term political strategy to destroy the proven structures of the police and turn them into an exclusive agency of a one-party state.[1]

Such statements as the above, from James Anderton, Chief Constable of Greater Manchester, show how necessary it is to distinguish between the *accountability* and the *control* of the police. Although the two may fuse together in practice and in debate, there is an important difference in theory: accountability is liability to account for a decision after it has been taken; control, on the other hand, exists where influence is exerted in making a decision. To demand control over Chief Constables is, therefore, to ask for a say in making policing decisions; to propose that Chief Constables be accountable is to emphasize their freedom to decide operational matters but to impose on them an obligation to justify those decisions afterwards.

Modern Chief Constables are accountable to Police Authorities, the weak successors to the watch committees of the nineteenth century. The latter were able to exercise considerable control over policing policies and, backed up by powers to dismiss chief officers, they could, and often did, call for weekly reports. In addition, they were able to lay down policies to be followed by Chief Officers (an example is given by Geoffrey Marshall[2] in which the Head Constable of Liverpool in the 1890s, Sir William Nott-Bower, was instructed by the watch committee to proceed against brothels without delay).

By 1960 the tide had turned against the watch committee. The previous year, the Home Secretary had backed the Chief Constable of Nottingham, Captain Popkess, against his Police Authority and the idea was growing that no longer were Chief Constables merely 'executive officers' of the watch committees.[3] When the Royal Commission on the Police reported in 1962 it looked in detail at accountability and argued that Chief Constables should be accountable to no one for enforcement policies. Having said that, however, the Commission went on to ask whether there should be no control 'in the formulation and application of . . . policies in matters which concern the public interest'.[4] It concluded:

it cannot in our view be said that the duties of the kind we describe require the complete immunity from the external influence that is generally acknowledged to be necessary in regard to the enforcement of law in particular cases. . . It appears to us . . . that the Chief Constable should therefore be subject to more effective supervision than the present arrangements appear to recognize. (paras. 91–2).

When the 1964 Police Act followed the Commission report, it largely failed to give effect to any such desires to increase local supervision. Its principal accomplishment was to set up new Police Authorities as committees of local councils. These were given the responsibility for maintaining 'an adequate and efficient police force for their area' but to do this they relied on limited powers and a peculiar constitution in which two-thirds of their members were nominated by local councils and the other third were chosen from the magistrates. To this day, the Authority approves the police budget (subject to full council consent); appoints the Chief Constable, his deputy and the assistant chief constables (watch committees appointed all officers); sets the size of the force (with the Home Secretary's approval); deals with complaints against the most senior officers; provides buildings and equipment; and has reserve powers to call on the Chief Constable to retire and (though receiving annual reports) to call for a report on any matter related to policing in its area from the Chief Constable.

In a number of respects the Police Authorities' powers of supervision have been less effective than they might have been. Budgetary approval, for instance, is not required for expenditure in compliance with Home Office regulations on pay, which, as Hewitt notes,[5] accounted in Merseyside in 1979/80 for 73 per cent of the whole police budget. Nor is approval required for expenditure directly financed by the Home Office, such as the Thames Valley Databank; local supervision moreover, was made more difficult by the amalgamation of forces. Geoffrey Marshall has commented:

There has inevitably been a wider gap between the elected members and their constituents on the one hand and the new police authorities on the other. For one thing there is no longer any genuine financial accountability. Annual estimates may be forwarded by joint authorities to the constituent councils but I doubt if many councils have made use of them either as a vehicle for commenting on general levels of expenditure or for debating matters of police administration . . . Nor, so far as I know, has it been a general practice to make agenda and minutes of the combined police authority available to individual councils or councillors in time for them to request action by their representatives on the joint authority.[6]

As the Police Authorities have been weakened, so the Chief Constables have consolidated their positions, ACPO has grown both in terms of policy formation and as an effective national pressure group. At the same time central supervision by the Home Office has increased. Nor is it easy for local authorities effectively to exert their power by calling for reports on local policing: section 12(3) of the 1964 Act provides that if it appears to the Chief Constable that such a report would contain information that, in the public interest ought not to be disclosed or 'is not needed for the discharge of the functions of the police authority', he may refer a report request to the Home Secretary.

Some have found more disturbing than their limited powers the Police Authorities' failure over the years to use even these to the full: the Labour Party's criminal justice group has now attempted to encourage Authority members to make better use of their powers.[7] A survey in 1976 revealed that seven Police Authorities *never* asked for reports from their Chief Constables and twenty-four did so infrequently.[8] The same study indicated that about half of the police committees of local councils in England and Wales either did not report to their council or else marked their reports 'for information only'.

Such a meek approach on the part of Police Authorities is perhaps indicative of their cumulative demoralization. One person, however, who could not be said to have been daunted is Margaret Simey of the Merseyside Police Authority, well known in recent years for her differences of opinion with Chief Constable Kenneth Oxford. Jack Straw MP in the memorandum on his ill-fated Police Authorities (Powers) Bill of 1979 reproduced a letter from Lady Simey saying:

Over the years, the role of the authority has been consistently redefined in terms favourable to an increase in police power. Democratic scrutiny of this public service has been reduced to an unacceptable minimum . . . Policing has become a purely professional responsibility. Its serious social and political implications are to an increasing extent, being taken over by the police to the exclusion of the elected member.

She further asserted that the question whether or not the full council might debate Police Authority minutes was determined not by the council but by the county solicitor without appeal.

Margaret Simey has, however, placed emphasis on extending the use made of present Police Authority powers as opposed to increasing these powers; others would argue that much can be done to increase democratic influences over policing. Certainly, there is evidence that, if they so desire, Chief Constables are in a position to exclude much of their activities from Police Authority scrutiny and to diminish the Authority's status. Thus, when in 1979 the West Yorkshire Police Authority called for a report on the Chief Constable's financing of a publicity campaign to catch the Ripper (instigated without consultation with the Authority) the report was disclosed to the press before it was given to the Authority. When, more recently, members of the Merseyside Authority asked Kenneth Oxford for details on the police enquiry into the death in custody of Jimmy Kelly, the Chief Constable refused to add to the press statement he had already made.

In London, where the Police Authority is the Home Secretary, the position is perhaps worse since exchanges between Home Secretary and the Metropolitan Police Commissioner are at no point submitted to public scrutiny. The authority for our largest police force, and (especially in security and public order matters) the one involved in the most contentious of policing issues, is the subject of public discussion and accountability only in the context of parliamentary questions and debate. Here, Home Secretaries have been eager to sidestep questions by labelling them as involving operational matters for the Commissioner's decision alone.

In recent years, efforts have been made to reform the system so

as to provide more effective local accountability but little progress
has been made. In 1979 Labour MP Jack Straw introduced a
Private Member's Bill to provide for the kind of policy control that,
he said, was envisaged by the 1962 Royal Commission on the
Police. His Police Authorities (Powers) Bill would have given
Police Authorities powers to determine 'general policing policies'
for their areas. Chief Constables would have been bound to act in
accordance with these policies but would have been entitled to
delay action or refer disputes to the Secretary of State. The
Authorities would, in addition, have been given the power to
appoint chief superintendents and superintendents.

The Conservative Government did not endorse the Straw Bill
and it failed to become law. Nevertheless it stimulated debate,
some of which was hostile: the President of ACPO, Alan
Goodison, saw it as the thin end of the wedge, warning 'once you
allow the political influence to play any part at all . . . you are
changing the complete nature of policing in this country'. Others,
however, wanted such changes. The Labour Party at its Brighton
Conference in 1981 passed resolutions not only to disband special
patrol groups and set up an independent police complaints system
but also to give local police committees greater powers. Alex Lyon
MP, a former Home Office Minister of State, warned that the only
people who could decide on the policy of the police towards a
community were the local councillors: these, he said were the only
hope for riot-torn places like Toxteth.

How popular such ideas were to be with the Police Federation
was indicated by the editor of their monthly magazine, Tony Judge
who said that the Brighton proposals could mean only 'naked
political interference and that it would destroy the operational
independence of the police service'.[9] He argued that he was not
against democratic control – which already existed with the Police
Authorities – but he said 'No' to political interference. In similar
vein, a *Times* leader in May 1981 criticized the London Labour
Party's manifesto proposal to create a London Police Authority,
saying that this would endanger the police's already precarious
credit as a body outside party politics.

It seems there are two problems with proposals on accountability. First, the extent to which it is in practice possible to exert
increased democratic control over policing policies without

running over into strictly operational matters. Second, the question (inadequately drawn out in reports of the 1981 Brighton Conference) whether those arguing for more democratic control make any such distinction between operational and 'wider policy' matters. On the first issue it seems that, as Jack Straw's modest Bill assumed, it is possible to control 'general policing policies' without assuming all-pervasive control: one can, for example, envisage Authority policy-making on issues such as whether there should be more beat policemen, whether pornography should be intensively policed or whether community policing should be adopted, but it seems feasible to deny to the Authority the power to direct operations by statements such as 'do not protect this march' or 'always have a constable at X street at closing time'. A system could be set up whereby Chief Constables might appeal such issues either to a designated court or tribunal or to the Home Secretary.

The second question – which type of control is sought – is one (for the Labour Party especially) that requires very careful definition: to seek control over general policies such as the overall use of support groups and surveillance may be one thing but to seek to influence the policing of individual events or offences may be another (in both practical and electoral terms).

If something of a party political impasse has been reached in terms of formal accountability (one that is not resolved by the Royal Commission's silence on the subject) then there may be another way forward. This involves bridging the gap between review by the Police Authority and the system of informal consultation that goes on between some forces and the public. Proposals on consultation at the local level have been championed in recent years by John Alderson as part and parcel of his community policing scheme.[10] In Devon and Cornwall there exist Police Authorities, as elsewhere, but in addition there are community policing consultative groups. Police officers also attend and observe debates at council meetings. When he gave evidence to Lord Scarman in 1981[11] Alderson argued that his form of informal consultative arrangement had to be put on a statutory footing. At local government level, he said, the Police Authorities should be required to set up district community police councils and in localized urban areas neighbourhood community police councils. (The function of the latter would be carried out rurally by existing parish councils.) Since Alderson is of the view that extended control over the police by a wholly elected body creates a dangerous potential for political control (and this is why he rejects more powerful Police Authorities)[12] his scheme for community police councils attempts to avoid undue party bias by dividing membership into thirds with each third nominated by the Police Authority, the County or Metropolitan Council and voluntary bodies respectively.

The job of Alderson's community police councils would be 'to receive information about crime and police problems within the area and to represent the public interest'.[13] They would be empowered to ask questions concerning the policing of the area and to make representations to the Police Authority; they would receive and take on resolutions from neighbourhood police councils or parish councils and would be entitled to send an observer to Police Authority meetings. In London there would be a Metropolitan Police Council for the Metropolitan District with members appointed by the Secretary of State, the London Boroughs and the GLC in respective thirds. Each borough would have a borough community police council on similar arrangements as would apply in the provinces. In a further endeavour to broaden the political base of community policing Alderson advocated that at central government level there should be set up an advisory department for community policing sponsored by the Home Office, and Departments of Health and Social Security, Education and Science and Environment.

The view of the Metropolitan Police was very different. Wilfred Gibson, Assistant Commissioner in charge of uniformed operations, branded Alderson's ideas as impractical. He said that the proposed central government advisory department would not work because of the number of other departments concerned; as for the new community police councils, he did not see that they filled any gap that was uncatered for by normal consultative methods.

After the Brixton disturbances, however, Lord Scarman was concerned that a key stage in the riots had been the breakdown of voluntary consultative relationships between the police and community representatives. His report showed that not only had intensive SPG operations similar to 'Swamp '81' been conducted without disclosing these to community leaders, but in the case of

'Swamp '81' not even the home beat officers in the district had been informed in advance.[14] As for the use of public liaison branches, Scarman acknowledged that many forces already possessed these but, he said:

> A number of those who have given evidence to the Inquiry, however, see these Branches as a mere public relations exercise. They instance the reluctance, amounting in many cases to outright refusal, of senior police officers to discuss operational questions with leaders of the local community. (para 5.55)

Nor did Scarman subscribe to the view that all contact involved 'political interference', he argued:

> Community involvement in the policy and operations of policing is perfectly feasible without undermining the independence of the police or destroying the secrecy of those operations against crime which have to be kept secret. (para. 5.56)

The conclusion followed:

> Accountability is, I have no doubt, the key to successful consultation and socially responsive policing. Exclusive reliance on 'voluntary' consultative machinery will not do, as the Brixton story illustrates. It must be backed by law. (para 5.57)

Scarman thus agreed with Alderson that at present there was no sufficient link between accountability and consultation – it was 'tenuous to vanishing point' in London. He recorded that three defects in the accountability system had been suggested to him: magistrates were present on police committees; these committees had limited powers in relation to the appointment of senior officers; and there was no duty on police committees to set up consultative machinery.

The answer, he said, was not to change the formal powers of Police Authorities but was for them to assume a more active role in expressing community views to the police. If a statutory duty was placed on the Authorities to establish liaison committees then this, Scarman said, would encourage more vigorous action on their part

– a voluntary system was no use as it would break down under stress. He recommended the imposition of such a duty at law and, like Alderson, advocated that in London statutory consultation should operate at the borough level but that outside the Metropolis it should work at police divisional or subdividisional levels. (para 5.65).

In the debate following Scarman, John Alderson, not surprisingly, was to call the proposal on statutory consultation the 'single most important recommendation made'. Other chief police officers continued to oppose such formal arrangements. ACPO had two very effective arguments: democratic control was opposed on the grounds of being 'political' but apolitical consultation was too undemocratic! Mr Alan Goodison, Chief Constable of Leicestershire, told the House of Commons Race Relations and Immigration sub-committee shortly after Scarman was published:

> It is all very well to say liaison committees should be set up; but who is going to comprise the community representatives? There are community leaders who are not community leaders. They do not represent the people at grass-roots level in the way they think they do . . . We have got to identify the minority group members of the right type who are prepared to help us.[15]

William Whitelaw, the Home Secretary, told the Commons on 10 December 1981 that he 'did not rule out' a statutory framework if his consultations pointed firmly in that direction but he then said that the 'first step is to discuss this nationally with representatives of Police Authorities and chief officers'. It seems likely that ACPO will try to persuade any government to keep the voluntary system that Lord Scarman criticized so heavily. For his part John Alderson has already stated publicly that Scarman has been 'mugged' by the Government on the issue of statutory consultation.[16]

## Conclusions on Accountability

There are good reasons for having a two-tier system of oversight with statutory consultative councils on a local level and with Police Authorities for each force. In devising councils and authorities however, the spectre to be avoided is that of party politicians instructing the police on operational details. With this in mind we advocate the retention of Police Authorities but with certain changes in their powers and constitutions. Their membership should be comprised of those elected to local councils (as is the case in Scotland) and there should be an end to the appointment of magistrates (it is particularly undesirable that the individuals who try persons brought by the police to court should also sit on the Police Authority). The Authority should have power to lay down 'policy guidance' for Chief Constables and should have strengthened powers to call for reports from them.

A further function of the Authorities would be to consider the views of local community police councils which they would have statutory duties to set up at both divisional and subdivisional levels of the force. We would not follow John Alderson, however, in de-politicizing these councils and structuring their composition to ensure the representation of voluntary organizations etc. To rig their composition in any way would most likely provoke more difficulties than it would be worth. (Who would be eligible as a voluntary organization? Who would select worthwhile bodies to consult – the police? Would this avoid political bias anyway?)

The consultative councils would be wholly elected – on the lines of Scottish community councils or rural parish councils in England and Wales. However, the police must be obliged by statute to engage in reasonable consultation if the object is to go beyond mere public relations. To this end, provision – again at law – must be made for the representation of different ranks at council meetings. Thus, from a local unit station, as described in Chapter 2, police representation would include chief inspector, inspector, sergeant and at least one constable. This would give a two-tier elected system of consultation and review. Those about to shout 'political interference' should be reassured on considering that, should the prosecution function be taken from the police and given to an independent Crown prosecutor, as the Royal Commission has recommended, then the dangers of political control are lessened. Second, the dangers of political bias by Police Authorities have perhaps been exaggerated; many may have forgotten that the 1962 Royal Commission on the Police dismissed such dangers saying: 'We understand these misgivings, but experience in Scotland and in the English and Welsh boroughs suggest they are groundless.'[17] In recent years Scotland has seen many a political outcry but few against elected Police Authorities.

Chief Constables might object to the use of policy guidance but we would envisage protection against the encroachment of the Authority into operational matters. A provision as found in the Straw Bill would allow Chief Constables to delay action or refer to the Home Secretary in defined circumstances. It should be remembered also that the courts as a matter of law will not allow 'guidance' that is so peremptory or specific that it amounts to 'direction'[18] and they would therefore protect chief officers from undue interference. In doing so they would not allow guidance to prevail over the Chief Constable's general duty to enforce the law and, seen in such a light, the guidance system constitutes a modest proposal indeed. Nor would an increased power to call for reports – as found in the Straw Bill – change matters drastically; it would simply place a heavier onus on chief officers to justify in writing and within a limited time any decision to refuse to report to the Police Authority. This seems only reasonable for there is no point in having a system of oversight that is only too easily by-passed by Chief Constables keeping information of a sensitive nature from their Authorities.

As for the statutory consultative councils, Lord Scarman appears correct in arguing that to place them on a legal footing would allow them more easily to withstand periods of contention as occurred in Brixton in 1981. On the 'party-political' point it should be borne in mind that, on a local basis, local issues have a tendency to prevail over party politics, that any bias may well be cancelled out by another at the Authority level and that in any case such bodies are not directive, only consultative. In further response to Alderson-style structuring of consultative councils it might also be said that the wholly elective system, as well as being less problematic than alternatives, may be expected to be used by the intelligent electorate to produce a reasonable system of representation for voluntary organizations, church groups etc.

## Complaints against the Police

Public confidence and trust in the police depends to an important degree on the belief that complaints will be dealt with fairly and efficiently. It was only in recent years, however, that any change was made from the system in which the police both investigated themselves and also decided what action to take on complaints. The 1976 Police Act, which came into force in June 1977, set up the Police Complaints Board (PCB) not to investigate the police but to play a limited role following investigation. Such a move followed intense negotiation and bargaining behind the scenes.[19] The Police Federation and the Superintendents resisted reform and chief officers went for the least change by arguing for *ex post facto* review in which an independent person would look at investigation papers after an enquiry was over – they objected to the setting up of the PCB as an interference with the Chief Constable's disciplinary powers.

The Police Federation was persuaded to accept the PCB by the Home Office's conceding important points: officers were to receive copies of complaints and the Federation was to be allowed to use its funds to prosecute those making allegedly false and malicious complaints.[20] When the Act was passed the Federation announced that it would 'sue where necessary' to discourage malicious complaints – but how many complaints with just causes would be deterred was not mentioned.

For his part, Sir Robert Mark (Commissioner, 1972–7) was not happy at all. He said that he would not operate the new system and retired from the force early. Like others he had wanted *ex post facto* review and objected to the PCB's powers of involvement in discipline and investigation. He argued that the new complaints system introduced by the 1976 Act (with provision *inter alia* for tribunals to be set up by the PCB) would not have allowed him to 'weed-out' corrupt officers as he had done in the years up to 1977: clever and corrupt officers would escape the formal net, he said, whereas informal action could more effectively induce them to resign. (Derek Humphry has argued, however, that though such an argument may have much truth in it in a corrupt London force it ignores the need for a complaints system elsewhere that will be seen as open and impartial in run-of-the-mill complaints.)[21]

How then does the new system work? When a person complains then police stations must record all details of the complaint and its processing. Deputy Chief Constables are responsible for complaints and enquiries into them must be carried out by the police as soon as possible after recording (if the PCB does not receive a copy of the papers in a case within four months then reasons must be given for the delay). The Police Act 1964 still governs recording and states that if there is the suggestion in a complaint of an offence against Police (Discipline) Regulations then this must be investigated by an officer who is at least a Superintendent (in the Metropolitan Police a Chief Inspector or above) from a different division of the force (subdivision in the Metropolis). More serious complaints may be investigated by officers from other forces but it has been said by the PCB[22] that Deputy Chief Constables have not always given enough attention to the appointment of external investigators.

When the investigation report is completed it goes to the Deputy Chief Constable who must pass it on to the Director of Public Prosecutions if it discloses evidence of a criminal offence. If the DPP does not prosecute, or if no evidence of a criminal offence is contained, the Deputy Chief Constable must decide whether or not to take disciplinary action. If disciplinary proceedings are taken the matter is decided by the Chief Constable; where none are taken or the issue is contested, the Deputy Chief Constable must send the PCB a copy of the report (in other cases the PCB receives the report at the outcome of the case). Only at this late stage is the PCB in a position to demand further investigation, recommend disciplinary action to be taken or order the setting up of a disciplinary tribunal.

The PCB thus has no power to conduct investigations into complaints; it cannot take action on complaints sent directly to it apart from sending them to the chief officer of police. Nor has the PCB powers to deal with questions of criminal proceedings against police officers following complaints. In its 1977 Report it said:

the Police Complaints Board have no positive part to play in the handling of a complaint until it has been recorded and investigated by the police and until it has been referred, if necessary to the Director of Public Prosecutions. The Board cannot question the decision of the Director on criminal proceedings. Where the Deputy Chief Constable decides to prefer disciplinary charges, the Board have no power to vary these charges: in such a case they are solely concerned, where the charges are denied, to decide whether or not the charges should be heard before a disciplinary tribunal . . . It is not the Board's function, however, to give a judgement on the merits of a complaint or to say, for example, whether or not the police officer or the complainant was at fault; and the Board cannot deal with questions of compensation or redress.[23]

The figures indicate the size of the PCB's influence: in 1980 out of 14,984 complaints dealt with, it made recommendations for disciplinary charges in only eighteen cases. The 1976 Act was supposed to revive public confidence in the impartiality of investigations but no great rise in public confidence seemed evident. In its first year the PCB stated that the number of cases forwarded to it from local police forces was 'much lower than might have been expected'; not only that but a survey published in the *Sunday Times*[24] showed that cases were taking longer to process than formerly, more cases were being withdrawn, and fewer complaints were being substantiated.

The greater withdrawal rate was perhaps due to the new procedure (laid down by Home Office circular) in which all complaints were recorded no matter how trivial; previously a complainant would have had an opportunity to withdraw following discussion with a senior officer before recording the complaint. Another factor, in both withdrawal and in deterring complaints flowed from those concessions made to the Police Federation. The leaflet issued at police stations 'Police and the Public: Complaints against the Police' was hardly encouraging. It pointed out that officers would receive copies of complaints and (more threateningly) warned that complaints deemed false and malicious might lead to a police officer taking legal action for defamation against the complainant.

Lord Scarman, for one, was certain that the 1976 Act had not reassured the public:

The evidence . . . has convinced me that there is a widespread and dangerous lack of public confidence in the existing system for handling complaints against the police. By and large people do not trust the police to investigate the police. This may not be fair to the police: but unless there is a strengthening of the independent non-police element in the system, public confidence will continue to be lacking.[25]

One defect in the present system is plain: whether or not the PCB is involved at a later stage, the initial investigation of a complaint is conducted by the police and, as Lord Scarman said, whether vigorous or not such a system is distrusted by the public. In such investigations as that following the death of Jimmy Kelly in Merseyside, allegations of selective police interviewing have not increased confidence[26] and the PCB itself has stated that interviews of police witnesses are not always as rigorous as they might have been.[27] A second avenue of discontent concerns the *efficiency* of complaints rather than any bias – they are said to be slow, cumbersome and tend to aggravate rather than resolve contention. Not only that, but Lord Scarman (see para 7.15) was told how complaints are directed against individual officers and do not cater for objections to general force policy.

Perhaps responsible for more dissatisfaction than anything else in the complaints system is the 'double jeopardy' rule – in principle the rule that a person should not be tried twice for the same offence. Patricia Hewitt describes[28] how in 1975–6 the Home Office agreed with the Police Federation that officers would not be disciplined on evidence that the DPP had found insufficient for a criminal charge.[29] In practice this means that, since the DPP bears in mind the difficulties of securing convictions against police officers,[30] there is both a low chance of prosecution and a barrier to disciplinary action. A DPP decision not to prosecute has the effect of acquitting an officer of a disciplinary offence.[31]

Understandably low public confidence has meant that people tend to view complaining as a waste of time (Lord Scarman talks of a 'widespread reluctance' to complain [para 7.14]). It was this public distrust rather than any finding of partiality that started moves to reform the complaints system. In 1980[32] the PCB itself recommended that an independent team of police officers on secondment should be set up answerable to an independent lawyer or judge and given the task of investigating any serious allegation of assault by a police officer. This suggestion was considered by a Home Office working party under Lord Plowden, the PCB chairman, but was rejected: a predictable response given overwhelming police and prosecution representation on the working party.[33]

The working party's own proposal came soon after the Royal Commission report of January 1981 had skipped over the topic of complaints in two paragraphs; the working party proposed to extend arrangements under which officers from different forces should be used for investigations and to use the chairman of the PCB or his deputy to oversee the investigation of the most serious complaints.

There was little in this package to please anyone – the police would still investigate themselves and in supervising serious cases the PCB representative was to be 'assisted' by a senior police officer. Media pressure pointed towards more radical reform. In the summer of 1981 *The Times* disclosed an unpublished Home Office Research Unit report that alleged serious defects in the internal investigation of alleged police assaults, the riots further emphasized dissatisfaction and William Whitelaw, the Home Secretary, agreed to review the complaints system again.[34] A working group of the Police Advisory Board, chaired by the Home Office Minister, Lord Belstead, was set up to deliberate.

In late 1981, with the Scarman Report looming on the horizon, Alf Dubs MP presented a ten-minute Bill to Parliament to reform police complaints. He pressed for an independent police ombudsman with his or her own staff and noted that in the preceding three weeks no less than three Chief Constables, including James Anderton of Manchester, had spoken in favour of the independent investigation of complaints. (It was almost as if the police had been given sight of William Whitelaw's advance copy of Scarman.) The Police Federation, which had long opposed independent investigation, announced on 8 November a dramatic turnabout; James Jardine said not that an 'independent element' should be introduced but that complaints should be handed over 'lock stock and barrel' to a new independent investigating body. He said that the complaints issue had dragged on for too long and was harming the relationship between the police and the public. There was, however, to be no surrender of officers' interests; as a *quid pro quo* Jardine demanded increased civil rights for officers (including legal representation) throughout investigations by such an independent body – rights that would make discipline more difficult to apply than at present.

Senior officers disagreed. On behalf of ACPO Mr Barry Pain of Kent criticized the Federation proposal as unworkable saying 'it seems to ignore completely the disciplinary relationship between Chief Constable and his force. Neither do we believe it would meet current objections to the existing scheme.'[35] By now the debate was heating up; a week later the *Observer* asked 'Are Our Police Still Wonderful?'[36] and published an *Observer*/NOP poll showing, *inter alia*, that almost one person in four had decreased confidence in the police in recent years.

To a ready public Lord Scarman presented his report on 25 November 1981. As we have seen he found the existing complaints system unconvincing but saw practical difficulties in the way of a wholly independent investigation service – it might cost £9m a year. His 'radical' proposal was for such a service to investigate not just serious but all complaints. If this was found impractical he advocated, as second choice, the Home Office working party's system of a lay supervisor assisted by investigation officers from another force, but subject to two added requirements: in serious cases there should be a duty, not a discretion, to involve officers from other forces and the independent supervisor should be the Chairman of the PCB or his nominee. He was to be involved in the investigation and have powers to direct it.[37] In addition, Lord Scarman suggested a statutory conciliation procedure whereby an officer of inspector rank could be nominated in each station to offer conciliation as an alternative to the formal recording and processing of every single complaint. As for the 'double-jeopardy' rule he urged flexibility so that non-prosecution should not thwart appropriate disciplinary action.

## Conclusions on Complaints

Any governmental action on complaints is likely to depend on the conclusions of the Home Affairs Select Committee that is now deliberating but which seems liable to follow a conservative Home Office line.[38] The arguments considered here incline strongly towards Lord Scarman's 'radical' proposal, a process that strongly resembles that suggested in evidence to him by the NCCL. It is to be hoped that the NCCL's notion – that the investigation team might comprise officers seconded not merely from the police forces but from such other units as the Customs and Excise and Inland Revenue – might be given due attention as a way to overcome the practical difficulties Lord Scarman envisaged. Any arrangement that involves a wider base from which to draw officers must, furthermore, have advantages in terms of public confidence.

Such independent prosecuting teams should be empowered not merely to act in ordinary cases but also in those where a complaint of police malpractice in relation to a trial is made between a person's conviction in court and the subsequent appeal. The organization, 'Justice', has long fought against the police refusing to investigate such complaints on the basis of their being *sub judice* until the appeal is decided (when it is too late). Although the Home Secretary did respond to the Justice campaign by issuing a circular to chiefs of police in April 1977 urging a flexible approach to such investigations this kind of administrative action is insufficient. Any independent investigation should be given statutory powers to investigate such matters, and where there is any chance that such investigations might have bearings on appeals, these should be given high priority.

In conclusion, a central difficulty in all complaints systems should not be ignored. The Scarman proposals involve a procedure in which a police inspector would meet those who complain at the police station and would 'seek to conciliate' (para 7.24). Cynics would fear that this procedure could be used to discourage the recording of complaints. Coupled with the use of leaflets that threaten legal action on the basis of false and malicious complaints there are perhaps grounds for such fears. In implementing such proposals, therefore, thought has to be given to defining more closely the rights of officers to sue complainants and to redrafting the Home Office leaflets on complaints to remove what Derek Humphry has called 'menacing' wording.[39] Involvement of the independent investigator in the preliminary assessment of complaints would help matters here as would Lord Scarman's proposal (para 7.25) that complaints should be lodgeable at Police Authorities, consultative or liaison committees, Citizens Advice Bureaux as well as at police stations. This, if placed on a statutory footing, would allow more cool-headed mediation and would constitute a major contribution towards an accessible and open complaints system.

## The Power of the Chief Constable

The changes we propose in relation to local accountability and the complaints system will have no effect unless substantial efforts are also made to reduce the size and structure of forces and to change the system of organizational control exercised within the new police bureaucracies. If formal systems of accountability and complaint are merely appended to present organizations, the effect will be marginal.

Much of the current debate on policing and police accountability is informed by the narrow view that since, over the last two decades, the power of the Chief Constable has grown along with the size of the forces at their disposal, all that needs be done is to subject the police chiefs to greater outside control and influence. Alternatively, it is said that Chief Constables should take their decisions as they think fit, for they are the only persons qualified to do so. Both positions are inadequate. They impute too great a power to senior officers, and fail to take into account the basis of that power. A Chief Constable's ability to determine policy is conditioned by the nature of the organization and the system of control instituted within it. In the modern police force, the nature of that organization and control is quite specific and severely limits the options available to policy-makers.

For example, were it thought desirable to redeploy officers and put them 'back on the beat', reorganization at all levels of the force would be required. First, the number of officers made available for patrol work would have to be increased. This, other things being equal, would require a reduction in the number of constables allocated to specialist squads and units. The process of rationalization through specialization would have to be reversed. This in turn would entail a review of policy priorities. (What kind of work should be emphasized? How many officers should there be on general patrol duties? How many in the drugs squad? How many in fraud? etc.) More fundamentally, career structure, mobility and promotions would have to be redefined and new criteria for purposes of assessment would have to be established. (How is the aptitude and general efficiency of an officer to be gauged? What criteria introduced for purposes of promotion? What is the role and function of the senior officer?) New problems of supervision and training would be encountered. (How much freedom of action and decision-making should be given to the PC? How would general duties be defined? When is a cup of tea a skive and when is it good police work?)

As we shall see, these problems would not be resolved simply by employing more officers to work the beat. The real difficulty, however, is that the implementation of such policies would undermine the very basis of power and control exercised by the Chief Constable and senior officers. Put bluntly, certain policies are ruled out of order from the outset. Any policy that would return power of decision-making to the individual officer on the streets is a negation of the present system of organization and control, which, over the past twenty years, has been explicitly directed to limiting the operational autonomy of the PC. Despite official emphasis upon the individual *responsibility* of the PC, senior officers are now in the position of exercising substantial *control* over the collective force. This is the result of a series of internal reforms. In particular, changes in supervision and discipline, in career structure and mobility, and in job specification and specialization have combined to reduce the scope, diversity and capacity of decision-making at street level.

The emphasis in control has shifted from negative limitation to positive direction, that is, from the situation in which the officer is simply told what must not be done and then left to get on with the job, to one in which the officer is instructed on what must be done in each and every circumstance. Thus, standing orders are now detailed to the finest degree, providing full instructions on how to handle incidents ranging from an aircraft disaster, to the procedure to be followed on stopping a motorist for speeding, and even detailing when police hats will be worn. Every post within the force – the area PC, the operations room PC, the administrative sergeant, the training sergeant, etc. etc. – has a precise breakdown of responsibilities and regular functions to be fulfilled (see Appendix).

In the early days of the police this kind of precision was not

realistic, simply because it was impossible to maintain the continuous contact and communication with officers on the street
which would have made it worthwhile. The extent of supervision
and control was therefore limited, the system working on the basis
of negative limitation and regular inspection at fixed points, supplemented by a tradition of military discipline.[40] Communication,
originally by whistle and rattle, was made marginally more sophisticated by the use of telephones in the police boxes, but it was not
until the introduction of personal radios in the sixties that the
transformation of control within the force was made possible.

For most officers the 'papa' radio is at once an advantage and a
disadvantage. It can be a life-line as well as a stranglehold. The
opportunities for skiving are substantially reduced, but at the same
time a call for assistance will be answered immediately. Older
officers frequently suggest that the radios have reduced the young
officer's initiative and the need for applied common sense. It is also
said that the 'atmosphere' of the job has changed. In the following
conversation a young PC disputes the suggestion of two older
officers that there is a lack of discipline in today's force compared
to twenty-five years ago:

*First PC (aged 23)*: You're saying there is a lack of discipline in
the force – now? I totally disagree with you.
*Second PC*: All over. In the schools, the home, everywhere.
*First PC*: But not in the police force ? I mean what went on in the
force years ago doesn't happen now. It's nothing like it used to
be . . . we're clean living now!
*Second PC*: How many years' service have you got? Four? Five?
*First PC*: I know. I'm just saying what I've heard . . . the stories
you've told me and all the others.
*Second PC*: All right. They had more . . . freedom.
*Sergeant*: They got up to more dodges then.
*Second PC*: Yes, they had more spirit. Young policemen had a
lot more spirit and there was a lot more *esprit de corps*.
*First PC*: Come on! You can't claim on the one hand they had
more spirit and got up to more dodges than we do, and still say
they were more disciplined!
*Sergeant*: The difference was they didn't have the personal
radios then. So it was good for the job in one way, and it was

maybe bad in another. They had to use their initiative much more – you couldn't just wireless in and ask what to do – but then on the other hand the senior officers never knew what you were up to. Once you'd seen your sergeant that was it.

*Second PC*: It was a happier job then that's for sure. You got a lot more job satisfaction than you get now. You weren't tied the same way as you are now.

*Sergeant*: The job's entirely different now. They're not allowed to use their discretion the same. They're governed a lot more.

The introduction of computerized systems of command and control, as the name suggests, will further tighten control and limit the power of the individual PC (see above, pp. 51–7), and indeed, with the development of sophisticated control systems a change in the supervisory role of senior constables and sergeants in relation to recruits and young PCs is already apparent. Training is now a specialized job, and there is no longer the same emphasis placed upon the role of the older PC 'showing the recruit the beat'. Older PCs regret the change:

You were there to supervise, to show him how to do the job. If you weren't too busy, you'd maybe go into headquarters and show him what went on in CID, take him into criminal records, to the courts . . . give him a general picture of what was going on. They don't get that nowadays . . . for a start headquarters is too far away now, then you've got all the calls, there's not enough time, the laws are so complex . . . the job's just so different. (PC, 20 years' service)

The nature of supervision has altered accordingly, direct control has replaced basic training in street ways and means. More and more, the job of the supervisory officer is reduced to ensuring that the constable is doing what he is *meant* to be doing – in the right place, at the right time and according to the book.

To some extent these developments have come about as a result of the shortage of recruits during the sixties and early seventies. This has meant that many forces are now over-subscribed with young officers, a fact of which many more experienced PCs are only too painfully aware:

Nowadays it's recruits trying to tell recruits how to do the job. And between the lot of them they've no idea. They're told to read it up and go by the book. So when they get out on the streets, either they do nothing – they'll sit in the car next to you, staring at the sky as if they're there to stop speeding jumbos – or else they're getting stuck into everything and everybody in sight, getting into bother and putting out calls for assistance. (PC, 15 years' service)

However, the shortage of experienced officers to pass on the job is unlikely to be resolved solely by changes in recruitment policy. We noted earlier that the job of the patrol officer had changed, and that beat work had been de-skilled and devalued. The range of duties and the responsibilities of the PC as laid down in standing orders are both more narrow and more tightly prescribed. The patrol officer is increasingly a pawn to be moved about the city streets at the command of senior officers. In his book *Organisational Aspects of Police Behaviour*, J. Mervyn Jones (a serving police officer) writes:

In earlier times, the uniformed patrol constable was the generalist officer capable of dealing with a whole variety of police problems including, for example, traffic accidents, serious crime, juvenile delinquency problems etc. Nowadays many of these problems have become the specific areas of competence of a multiplicity of specialisms and sub-specialisms. As a result the beat role has come to be identified with less interesting and challenging work than that of the specialised departments. It is perfectly natural, therefore, that keen patrol constables find the abandonment of uniformed duties, in favour of specialisation, a more desirable proposition.[41]

Thus Jones presents evidence to show that there is a natural movement of experienced officers away from the beat, so much so that in the force Jones studied over 90 per cent of officers on foot patrol were found to be young and inexperienced. Such findings, he rightly points out, directly contradict the 'official line' which suggests that the job of the 'beat bobby' is the most important and highly regarded in the service. If anything, the opposite is true:

The only effective sanction in the police service, outside dismissal or requirement to resign, is the threat of return to beat work. Far from being the most important part of the police service, the beat, for many, is its gaol.[42]

Specialization and the devaluation of beat work thus creates a new sanction and with it a new system of control through the career structure. Beat work has been devalued so much that it is now seen as mundane, routine and utterly boring. While this must also have an effect on the way in which that job is done, it clearly subjects police constables to pressure to conform, to keep in place and to 'keep in with the bosses'. A young officer here describes his reaction towards a return to the beat:

I know it's going to happen eventually. Unless I try for promotion, I'll have to go back on the beat. But I'm dreading it, I really am. It's just so quiet compared to the cars. You're walking about in the cold and wet . . . ohhh! It's got nothing going for it compared to this. That's if you're not afraid of hard work. Especially up the town . . . it's terrible. You can be very busy at times, but on the night shift and the early shift you're walking around doing nothing. It has got its good points though. You'll meet more people than on the cars, do a bit of community involvement – even if it's just drinking tea with shopkeepers. But at least they know your name which is good. But then there was one sergeant we had who'd give you a row even for that. (PC, 5 years' service)

Young officers clearly resent the level of supervision encountered in this kind of work. Every job has a standard response laid out in standing orders, many of which seem out of touch with reality, either the product of tradition or of the pen-pushers at force headquarters. Two young officers (twenty-two and twenty-three years old) recalled their introduction to the beat:

*First PC*: We used to have a sergeant who, if he caught you anywhere having a cup of tea, you were bollocked. It's crazy as far as I'm concerned.
*Second PC*: I mean everybody does it and all the bosses know it

goes on, but if they catch you they go mad.

*First PC*: It's just crazy. Some of their ideas are just stupid. When I first worked the town, on the night shift from ten till eleven you were coupled up with your neighbouring beat man. After that you were back on your own. I questioned it: 'Surely the ten till eleven bit was designed for when the pubs shut earlier . . . they're not even out at eleven now.' 'Oh no . . . that's how it's always been. That's what divisional orders say.' I mean anybody can see that's stupid. They did change it eventually.

*Second PC*: You know what they say about it being a young force and how that's no good. Well some of the things you look at, from my point of view, seem to show a hell of a lack of imagination. All these people joined after the war and they're going back to those times. They've still got the same standing orders they had in 1939, 1940. They've just lost contact with the streets.

*First PC*: I mean you look at headquarters. The only real contact we have with headquarters is the CID, but other than that the only contact is getting a new uniform, getting petrol, or getting a cup of coffee in the canteen. Anything else – the planning department, the chief's office, whatever – as far as I'm concerned they don't exist. I never hear from them, they never hear from me. I don't know what the hell they do. Obviously they do something, but I don't know what it is.

*Second PC*: I have a lot of contact with people who work at HQ. I play rugby and cricket with them, you know. And some of them are way, way behind. They've been there for five or six years and they've completely forgotten what the hell's going on outside. It's just an office job to them now.

*First PC*: I mean they haven't any right to say how we do the job. They really haven't. They don't know what's going on. I mean there's no ill feeling. If that's what they want they're welcome to it. But it's just terrible that all the decisions are made from there – regarding policy, standing orders, hundreds of forms and petty rules.

*Second PC*: You don't get any preparation for it. You do your two weeks' summation course at headquarters, which is rubbish. In fact I so much regretted joining the job during those first two weeks, I just about packed it in on the spot. Then you did eight

weeks at the college, which quite a lot of people enjoyed, but
when you go out on the street it's completely different. Theory is
that you go out with an experienced man, but the first guy I went
out with was a probationary constable. You're not prepared. I
was dead worried. I mean I'm still not sure of my powers . . .
There's one guy I know – he got completely confused with what
he was trying to do – he charged a bloke with defamation of
character! I mean there's no such charge but he thought he done
it all right. Someone had called some woman all the names under
the sun. As far as he was concerned he'd heard it on television,
this phrase 'defamation of character', so he thought it was okay.
He got a lot of shit for that . . . But it could have been any of us.
*First PC*: There's quite a lot of young guys just stick by the book
now just to stay out of trouble. I mean there's certain PCs that
just go by the book totally. I mean, they'll charge people with
anything, just to impress the bosses and further their careers. It
does work like that, definitely. But I can't work like that. If you
go by the book you're that officious, it's no good. Mind you,
we're lucky really. We've got a good Chief Superintendent who
can see through the guffies that do this . . . well I think he can
anyway. The older PCs say he can. But a lot of bosses really like
it: 'by the book, down the line' all the time. It depends who your
boss is. Mind you, as far as I'm concerned I'm quite happy where
I am, doing what I'm doing.

As these changes have come about, so the nature of discipline
within the force has altered. The old style of military discipline has
given way to greater informality. As each new cog in the machine
has been fitted into place, so the emphasis upon what is euphe-
mistically called 'teamwork' has grown. Certainly the discipline
code still has a role, and older officers still put a high value on 'bull'
and the 'short back and sides' – but increasingly less so. In most
forces more informal 'counselling sessions' are held – at least once a
year for the PCs and every three months for recruits – at which the
officer's record is assessed, 'career chances' discussed and overall
performance evaluated. A very high value is placed on ambition
and a desire to get on and up in the force.

Alongside the counselling service, job satisfaction is now a problem which has to be dealt with, and personnel and welfare depart-

ments have grown up in many forces. It is important, however, that both faces of such innovations are recognized. The officers clearly prefer the 'soft approach' but at the same time there is no doubt that 'man-management' has a central disciplinary function. The reward for good behaviour is either promotion, or, more likely, sideways movement away fom the beat into one of the specialisms. Inability to 'fit in' is punished by a return to uniformed patrol or a 'sideways push' into one of the more repetitive and less desirable specialisms.

In the light of such changes and, looked at from the bottom, the official criteria of what makes a good policeman have changed. It is the source of some bitterness. The emphasis upon the specialisms, upon special training and paper qualifications, contradicts the expectations of many of the officers themselves. There is extreme and widespread cynicism, especially among the older officers, who, over the last ten or fifteen years have experienced the job and control over their own work slipping away:

> The people they're actually employing at the moment aren't your ordinary guys – Joe Soap and his brother, general blokes. It used to be that anybody could join the police. Not any more. What the police force is geared for now is graduates, college boys, kids with all the exams. And I'll tell you, if they want a police force like that, they're going to have to get the fucking army in – the 'professionals' with their martial law – 'cos these guys just cannot do the job. You should be getting blokes out there on the street who can work on 90 per cent common sense and 10 per cent the law. Fellas like that know when there's something wrong and they can handle it, even if they don't know exactly what it is. They can't say whether it's the Coal National-ization Act 1946 – they've never heard of it. But they know it's wrong, so they fix the guy first and then come back to the station and start looking at the books. They can't quote it all verbatim . . . but all these college boys are coming in and studying their books – quoting this and quoting that – but they don't know why they are doing it. If only the police would go back to the old idea of the bobby joining the force to do an ordinary job . . . OK, you've got to have some bright sparks to get promoted and be the Chief Constables and the rest. But there's only one Chief

Constable in this force and two and a half thousand men. So your chances of getting there are pretty fucking slim! (PC, age 34)


The picture of control within the modern police bureaucracies is thus one in which the police constable is subject to a series of interrelated managerial, occupational and operational restraints. To the extent that such controls are effective, so the power of the Chief Constable and senior officers is increased. However, this very power is based upon the form of organization and related strategies adopted – thus we have seen the correspondence between management systems of command and control and 'fire-brigade' policing. In such conditions a move away from 'fire-brigade' policing would demand fundamental organizational changes which in turn affect the roots of the Chief Constable's power. The extent of that power, however, must not be exaggerated: we must now balance the account and look at the countervailing pressures at work.


## The Countervailing Power of the Local Station

As for these bleepers – it's like anything else they've given us. They've given us personal radios, they've given us radios in the cars and now these computers. But you name it there's ways round them all. If I want to disappear off the face of the earth for a while – I'll disappear. Regardless of all their buttons, radios or whatever else they think up – I'll disappear. And they'll never, ever stop a cop doing that. (Police Constable)

The private language of the police is replete with derogatory references to the anonymous policy-makers at headquarters: 'Disneyland' – this disnae work, that disnae work . . . 'olympic torches' – they never go out; and possibly the most telling 'mushroom men' – keep them in the dark, feed them shit and they're happy. But of course not everybody is included. There are those senior officers who are remembered as 'good practical policemen', who, when they 'come back out' to the divisions are well respected. Such officers still recognize the ground rules which make an otherwise inefficient system work – at least for the officers. They tolerate certain abuses and transgressions, know the unspoken limits beyond which the practical PCs will never go but within which they are safe, and they know when not to pull rank. They recognize that 'out there' in the divisions and local stations there exists another set of rules – for keeping out of trouble in their work and with the law.

Police officers – especially the PCs – have a constant eye open for bother: not only on the streets but also 'in the job'.[43] The strict authority and control from above can never be ignored. The limits of what can and cannot be done are set, but within these limits – as with any system of rules – there is always room for manoeuvre. Officers find the 'practical' ways of doing the things required of them, and carve out their own space so as to do that which they think should be done.

The informal practices and purposes pursued frequently bring the officers at street level into conflict with the formal rules and regulations, so that the power at the top is renegotiated at the bottom, but within definite limits.

If officers get into trouble, whether it is with the discipline code and force orders or with the law, it is usually held by their colleagues that they have only themselves to blame and that they must not drag anyone else down with them. When the rule book is brought out, everybody in the immediate area is at risk. Nobody bears too close an inspection and it is all too easy to become contaminated. For this reason there are rules about how to break the rules. These must be learnt by the young probationer and followed carefully. Done properly, this can provide the basis for trust and acceptance; failure may be a reason for segregation and exclusion.

Where the law is unclear or the event obscure, practical routines are available for managing incidents as well as for self-protection. Some are high risk, but are tolerated both inside and outside the force, others are more private.

Domestic disputes are typical. Few officers relish a call to a fight between husband and wife. Emotions and the law are too confused. Different strategies are employed. A drunken husband will be taken for a ride and given a long walk home with the instruction 'cool down and sober up'. No charges follow. Alternatively, where there are signs of violence, but no witnesses, the husband may be put out of the house, and a breach of the peace deliberately provoked. If on the other hand it is judged that the matter can be managed on the spot, again quite deliberately, an officious tone may be adopted in order to reunite the husband and wife – against the police. Such strategies are relatively high risk. The law is stretched, often broken, and the discipline code is blatantly flouted. Sometimes it all goes horribly wrong.

Young officers are schooled in these routines and must learn how to avoid trouble. In the following passage a PC describes the arrival of a new probationer at the station:

> The first day he came here the whole station was in uproar. Almost straight away he twice had the head stuck on him and within two weeks he was in hospital. He'll make a good cop when he learns to speak to people and just say 'come on, don't be silly'; but at the moment his first words are 'if you don't move, I'll take your head off'. He'll learn . . . he'll have to.

The probationer had yet to learn when violence was legitimate, and when it was not (see p. 50). He has since been taken in hand. Indeed the 'training' is often quite explicit. On one occasion, witnessed at first hand, an illicit late night drink in one of the local pubs had become a little bit more than that. Several officers as well as members of the public were present; all was quiet on the streets. A call came through on the radio, and a young officer volunteered to take a police vehicle and attend what appeared to be a minor (non-criminal) incident. He would, he said, return for his partner (and the researcher) later. He received a severe rebuke from a more senior officer: 'And what happens if you get a "treble nine" call and your mate's left here in the shit? Cover yourself. If he gets done, you'll get it as well, remember.'

The rule that officers should cover themselves against trouble in the job follows them onto the street. It may cause some ill-feeling. Thus, for example, in no circumstances will the wise PC allow a driver away – even a friend – if there is any smell of alcohol. What would happen if there was an accident further up the road, and the driver could legitimately claim that he had been allowed to continue? On such occasions officers must go by the book for their own self-protection.

Other areas are more open to debate. For example, there are different attitudes to the degree of violence legitimately used. For some officers force is always very much a last resort but some are quite happy to 'go boxing', and for others 'self-protection' (in both senses) requires the use of the baton. As one officer explained it:

> I'll always use my stick rather than punch somebody. If I punch somebody there's a good chance I'll end up being charged for assault. But if you use your stick (a) you're protecting yourself, (b) you don't get sore hands, and (c) all you need to do is put in a memo afterwards and you're covered. (Police Constable)

Different officers have different styles of working. Individual differences are tolerated and accepted so long as nobody oversteps the mark. But those officers who cover themselves in glory at the expense of the rules – 'you don't drop somebody else in it by poaching on their patch' – are excluded, as are the 'uniform carriers' who cover themselves by keeping strictly to the book and staying out of harm's way: 'they're unreliable if you're in a corner'. A 'practical policeman', on the other hand, who knows and follows the rules, can trust and will be trusted by his colleagues. Thus, where 'rule-bending' is collectively regarded as necessary and legitimate, close colleagues will provide cover for each other, without requiring detailed explanation. As one officer put it 'you'll never be short of a second witness'. Much the same is expected of senior officers.[44]

Many studies have revealed the process of negotiation that goes on between the ranks. Constables expect their immediate senior officers – sergeants, inspectors, chief inspectors – to be satisfied with their work and performance on the streets so long as the ground rules are complied with, trouble is avoided and the job gets done. In return they expect cover for any 'necessary transgressions' and a 'sleeping dogs' approach to be adopted. A sergeant here explains the daily workings of the system and his own position within it:

> *Sergeant*: I don't have much difficulty. I've got a good team, they all work for each other and this makes it a lot easier for me.

Basically my job is making sure we don't go over the score. As you'll appreciate some of them can; I like to keep a rein on it . . . but not too strict, that's impossible. Making sure the young lads are pointed in the right direction.
*Question*: Do you find that you have divided loyalties between the men and the bosses?
*Sergeant*: The sergeant's always in that position. But I make no bones about it – my loyalties are to the men. But I also have to carry out instructions from above and see that they are complied with.
*Question*: What happens if you disagree with them?
*Sergeant*: I'll discuss it with the bosses, but if they say so it has to be that way. But I reckon I'm on good enough terms with the inspector and the chief inspector to say when something's a load of crap. But some of the bosses at divisional headquarters I just don't bother with . . . I know I'm not going to get anywhere. But at the end of the day, it's down in black and white, it has to be done and the boys'll do it.
*Question*: How much do you cover for each other?
*Sergeant*: Oh . . . up to and including the chief inspector. I mean if I cock something up the inspector'll say 'What's this?' and that's an end to it. If one of the boys makes a mess, they'll either sort it out themselves or I'll do it. We all cover for each other. For example, not so long ago two of the boys were standing by at a stolen car. So they thought 'the car's not going anywhere, we'll clear off and do a couple of jobs'. Anyway they came back and all the wheels had been stolen off it. We managed to cover that one. The chief inspector dealt with that one himself. . . . We very rarely have to hand out any bollockings. The system's such that if somebody does make a mistake the shift'll make such a piss-artist of him that he'll never do it again.

Constables thus place a very high value on a 'good shift' and 'good senior officers' who know 'what it's like on the street'. They are able to negotiate with these officers, to ameliorate the system and, in part at least, have some say in their conditions of work. This can be extremely important:

We reckon we're the élite, the top team down here. Particularly this shift, but we've worked at it. We can't pick the men they send down here, but we're lucky with our bosses. Normally we'll get a word with the sergeant when we hear of moves coming off, and let him know who we want and who we don't want. He'll work on the inspector and chief inspector, and then normally we'll get something along the lines we're looking for. Mind you, it's not meant to work like that. Not at all. In some stations it's bloody dreadful. (Constable)

Trouble has a variety of sources: colleagues, senior officers, the public and not infrequently the law. Very often the legal rules are perceived as an obstacle not only to justice but more obviously to the satisfactory performance of the job. In the research force, however, there was rarely any suggestion that their powers were insufficient or too limited. There were complaints that the law was unclear, that the officers 'didn't know where they stood' and there was great bitterness with time wasted – both with paperwork, and most of all in attending court. The major difficulties encountered with the law were those associated with bad public relations and feelings towards the police, in particular those encountered as a result of witnesses refusing to give evidence. Again methods were employed, which by definition were in breach of the discipline code and often the law. Such strategies rely on privacy and the advantage of a better working knowledge of criminal procedure. It should be emphasized, however, that there are still limits to what can be done. Suspects are not 'fitted up'. Pressure may be brought to bear on someone by suggestion (to obtain a confession) but only where the officer is very sure of his ground. Otherwise the risk is too high and the wise officer will 'wait until the next time'.

We shall return to the problems of the law in the next chapter. The following comments and conversations are included to reflect some of the officers' own feelings on the subjects raised in this section. We have been careful to select statements which are widely held within the research force and which in our own experience *and the opinion of the officers we spoke to* are representative of a cross-section.

*Superintendent (Complaints Dept., Force HQ)*: Our chief worry is that we're getting attitude complaints . . . complaints that they're arrogant, verbally aggressive towards respectable members of the public who've done something wrong . . . I mean if you ask me if I think an eighteen-and-a-half-year-old, who's never worked anywhere else before joining the police, is capable of handling an irate member of the public – say a respectable businessman who has been caught committing a traffic offence – the answer is: *not many of them can.*

. . . Youth is arrogant now. Youth generally are arrogant, a lack of feeling towards others, insensitive. And we've got to recruit from them. Yet they're a better educated bunch than we've ever had . . . paper educated.

*First PC (age 22)*: Complaints arc at the back of your mind all the time – 'cos it happens a heck of a lot. You worry at the time, but . . .

*Second PC (age 22)*: Our motto is 'always do the right thing even if it might not be the right thing according to the book'. Trouble is the public don't always see it like that. But most of the complaints you get working day to day are pretty minor. You're maybe half an hour late for a call and they'll say 'where the hell have you been hiding?' So you tell them, and they don't like it. But that's just total ignorance on the public's part. They don't know what the pressure's like . . . Then you get the regular complainers – no matter what you do they'll say you stole money off them or whatever. But you can usually just forget about them 'cos they've no evidence at all. It's just another crappy complaint.

*PC (Operations Room)*: This complaint thing is always in the back of the younger cops' minds. I blame the civil liberties lot. I mean it's actually got to such an extent now that we can actually turn round and laugh about it. If we see one of the inspectors from the Complaints Department in here we laugh. 'Oh, aye. Who's he going for this time?' We know full well that it's just going to be a lot of crap from start to finish.

*Second PC*: The only time you worry is if you've really done something wrong and it's blatantly obvious that you've done something wrong. It's never happened to me.

*Superintendent*: I'm not saying our officers are angels . . . anything but. I'm not saying that the amount of force might not have been slightly excessive. But it's very difficult in a situation like that, where perhaps there's just one person to two officers, where somewhere along the line he may get thumped. We're in exactly the same position as if we were investigating a complaint between two members of the public and we can't find anyone who saw anything.

*PC*: An independent complaints board? What do they know about getting evidence? Against us? We're the experts!

*Superintendent* (*Complaints Dept.*): I'd be absolutely delighted if some independent organization handled complaints. But I must stress the word independent. I wouldn't want it riddled with civil libertarians. They're no more representative of society than the police. But it still wouldn't be a better system. If an outside body came in, *I* would stand on *my* rights. As it is very few of our officers stand on their rights and normally we get a detailed statement from them. If an outside body came in I *would* stand on my rights. I could not see any reason whatsoever for giving them any more co-operation than they were entitled to by law. And it would be very difficult for the organization. They could complain until doomsday before they'd get the co-operation from the men that we get.

*First PC*: You can always rely on the public's ignorance of the law. I don't mean arresting for nothing . . . but you can always rely on them not knowing exactly. Like sometimes we go into people's houses, and we've no right to be there, and if they did complain and it was followed up properly, something could be done. But it's been done like that for the last fifty years and no one's been caught on it . . . But then there's a few times you feel like kicking a door in 'cos you *know* there's someone in there, but you can't do that. That's *too* risky . . .
But every situation, once you've got a bit of experience, you can manage. You know what you can't do, what you're not allowed to do and what you can get away with.
*Second PC*: If you're not too sure – say it's a new law – you try to work the thing out another way. Like a dom-dis: get the bloke

out of the house and do him for a breach.

*First PC*: If it's something really complicated – like a Rent Act or something – you'll say 'I'm going to charge you under the Rent Act' and just make up some crappy charge meanwhile. You'll say 'other charges may be preferred in place of this one'. So you charge the guy on the spot, come back to the station and either look it up yourself or ask the sergeant. If it's OK, stick at that. If not go back and see him. You can always charge them with something at the time.

*PC*: The majority of calls I get, it's families fighting each other. And they'll always say 'I wanna charge that bastard'. But I always advise them: 'look, I'll come back and see you tomorrow. If you want to go up to court and give evidence against your brother, I'll take your complaint then.' But that's not how you're *meant* to do it, not the *right* way. You should do it straight away. But it's a waste of paper. Six months later on the day of the court they'll be the best of pals.

*Sergeant*: You hear all these stories about the Met and how they're always fitting people up . . . I don't think it happens here at all. I've never seen it. Nor the corruption . . . I've never been offered a decent bribe – in twenty years! OK, you'll get round evidence in court sometimes. I mean you'll never be short of a second witness . . . You sometimes see them afterwards and they'll say 'you lied' . . . But then they did, didn't they? After all he really did it!

*Sergeant*: The law's fine in theory. You're not meant to put on the pressure in an interrogation. But – maybe this sounds hard – but if a person's innocent and you put pressure on and he's nothing to tell you, it's blatantly obvious.
*Question*: What difference would it make if all interrogations had to be taped?
*Sergeant*: There's ways round everything!
*PC*: It wouldn't make any difference to what we do. You'd interrogate your prisoner first – in the car, anywhere. Find out what he's going to say and then bring him in. I mean say you got a boy in for an HB [house-breaking], you'd interrogate him, may-

be a bit of the strong-arm tactics, you know? Then eventually he coughs. That's when you formally caution him and switch on the tape.

*Question*: Do you have to pressurize people a lot?

*Sergeant*: The hardened ones you have to, yes.

*PC*: It's the type of guy you get. You can get a young kid in here who at the mere sight of an angry cop immediately bursts into tears: 'I'm sorry! I didn't mean to do it.' But you can go on for hours – literally – with some of them, and however much pressure you put on they don't say anything.

*Sergeant*: The laws of evidence don't allow for being on the street. If you go on being Mr Nice Guy all the time, you're not going to get anywhere. The fella's just going to look at you and think to himself: 'He's a soft touch, I'm home and dry.' You have to put the pressure on. It's different up the town. With the run-of-the-mill shoplifter, petty crime, you'll get away with just pulling them in. The fright of just being caught by the police is enough. But with the hardened criminal you got to alter your tactics.

*PC*: They know. They can size up a policeman just as much as we can sus out what kind of a person they are. They can tell 'he's not going to try anything with me', you know? Maybe a young cop . . .

*Sergeant*: The old 'hard guy, soft guy' trick's still the best. But likes of – [refers to well-known family of local thieves] once they know you have them, they'll come across. But if they think they've got the upper hand, then you'll get nothing.

*PC*: If you know how to sus your prisoner out, you can tell whether you're wasting your breath or not. They you can try the strong-arm tactics, the easy approach, anything.

*Question*: Do you have one person that plays the role of the hard man all the time?

*Sergeant*: (laughs) You've met him!

*PC*: But you find a lot of policemen, when they arrest someone it's *their* prisoner. I don't like anybody muscling in and beating up any prisoner of mine. It's my neck that's on the line if a complaint should come along. It's my decision.

*Question*: So is the law on admissibility ever honoured in the breach?

*Sergeant*: What goes down on paper and what actually happens are usually two different things. I'm not saying the facts are different. We don't fit people up. But the methods are different. What we put down on paper has to comply with the law.

*Question*: So how often do you use statements in court which strictly speaking are inadmissible?

*Sergeant*: Quite often. I mean I think you've seen yourself we're usually struggling for evidence . . . witnesses won't come forward. But, say we have one witness or enough circumstantial evidence and we can get the accused to give a statement under caution, then we reckon we're home and dry. I mean, we'll put that in and hope they'll plead guilty.

*PC*: This is what they're after you for all the time in court . . . what led up to him saying he did it.

*Question*: It must be quite easy to get caught out?

*Sergeant*: A good lawyer could have a field day, yes.

*PC*: You've just got to know your story before you go in. If you don't you're a fool, you've just not done your homework. Before I go to court, I'll always dig out the report a good week beforehand and read over it two or three times until I know exactly what my statement consists of. I don't go into court without knowing exactly what's in my report, so that report has got to be right when you put it in.

## Conclusions

It would be misleading to suggest that the officer on the beat has unlimited freedom. Chief Constables and senior officers within the present system do exert substantial and pervasive control. As such, it may be argued that they should simply be made directly accountable to the public. Such control, however, is of a specific kind. It is essential to recognize the direct connection between the internal organization of the modern police bureaucracies and the implementation of 'fire-brigade' and pre-emptive styles of policing.

The foundation of both has been the process of rationalization and specialization within forces. It is for this reason that, unless organizational changes are made, reforms to the present system of accountability and complaints will make little real difference to the way in which the streets are policed. Strengthening scrutiny and control may indeed have the reverse effect to that intended and make the present system worse by intensifying the distrust of officers both towards their own colleagues and the public. So long as the primary motives to circumvent trouble, and the law remain, the officers' response to the idea of external controls (that they will not co-operate) will be realized. The situation would thus be compounded and the spiral of confrontation given a further twist.

So what can be done? In organizational terms there is a need for reduction in the size of forces. Resistance to change within the bureaucracies – despite the fact that they are less than ten years old – is probably sufficient to ensure that this will not happen quickly. Alternatively a substantial devolution of power within the present system is necessary. In terms of police styles also, major changes have to be made. We discuss proposals on both subjects in Chapter 9 after considering how controls may operate within alternatives to the 'fire-brigade' or the pre-emptive police systems. Before that is done, however, we need to look at that other, most formal, limitation on police activity, the law. If internal controls have been tightened, it will be seen that external control by the law has been relaxed.

## Further Reading

Baldwin, J. and McConville, M., *Negotiated Justice*, Martin Robertson, Oxford, 1977.

Bordua, D. J., *The Police: Six Sociological Essays,* Wiley, New York, 1966.

Cain, M., *Society and the Policeman's Role*, Routledge & Kegan Paul, London, 1973.

Hain, P., Humphry, D. and Rose-Smith, B., *Policing the Police*, vol 1, John Calder, London, 1979

Lundman, R. J., *Police Behaviour*, Oxford University Press, Oxford, 1980.

Manning, P., *Police Work*, MIT Press, Cambridge, Mass., 1977.

Marshall, G., *Police and Government,* Methuen, London, 1965.

McClure, J., *Spike Island*, Macmillan, London, 1980.

Reiner, R., *The Blue-Coated Worker*, Cambridge University Press, Cambridge, 1978.

Skolnick, J., *Justice Without Trial,* Wiley, New York, 1966.

Wilson, J. Q., *Varieties of Police Behavior*, Harvard University Press, Cambridge, Mass., 1968.

# 5

# The Police and the Law

The last two chapters show how various factors can act to limit the significance of law in controlling police behaviour. What the law does state is nevertheless important to the police and to those considering reforms in criminal procedure. Here we look at developments in the law in recent years and, in doing so, draw attention to the manner in which such shifts have mirrored certain changes in our policing system. Although we posit no conspiracy whereby judges attune the law to new emphases in policing there are parallels that should be drawn. Thus for instance, as police organizations have centralized operational control so we see that the law is predicated on individual rather than collective responsibility and incorporates the fiction that officers are islands unto themselves. The concept of policing under the rule of law accordingly favours a view of the constable as acting in a political vacuum. Similarly, just as police forces are increasingly catering for a system of police-initiated conviction (e.g. by computerization and confronting the public) so we see that the law seems conveniently to be accommodating this change in emphasis.[1]

Readers are warned that any discussion of the law on police powers will seem unsatisfactory. This is because the law is a mess. We attempt to show how law and lawyers have typically responded to the question of controlling police activity, but it will soon be noticed that clear principles have not prevailed. We aim to show some of the ways in which the law has become confused and some of the reasons why.

Since we distinguish clearly between what the law says the police may do and what is actually done, this chapter deals first with the *theory* (or strict law) on powers and then looks at those powers in *practice*. The account will deal principally with English and Welsh law, but for purposes of comparison, Scots law will be touched upon where this differs significantly.[2] We consider the law as it was at the start of 1980, that is as the Royal Commission on Criminal Procedure was sitting and before the Criminal Justice (Scotland) Act 1980. The issues raised by the Commission and the new Act are dealt with in subsequent chapters.

## Police Powers in Theory

The traditional view is that the High Street bobby is no more nor less than an ordinary citizen: 'A policeman, in the view of the common law, is only a person paid to perform, as a matter of duty, acts which if he were so minded he might have done voluntarily.'[3] We have to note, however, that constables now have a whole range of statutory powers that ordinary citizens do not enjoy.[4] They are, on the other hand, subject to a statutory scheme of discipline by senior officers.

These officers are headed by a Chief Constable (Commissioner in London) who is responsible for enforcing the law and for the discipline of his force. The chief officer is alone responsible for the manner in which officers are investigated and prosecuted:

in all these things he is not the servant of anyone, save of the law itself. No Minister of the Crown can tell him . . . that he must or must not, prosecute this man or that one. Nor can any police authority tell him so.[5]

Each police force is based on a local authority area (there are forty-three forces in England and Wales, eight in Scotland) and oversight of the force rests with a statutory body, the Police Authority, usually a committee of the local authority.[6] The Police Authority, so often criticized as toothless, relies on powers to appoint and dismiss chief officers; it determines the size of the force and expenditure and receives an annual report from the chief officers.

Overall responsibility for policing in England and Wales rests with the Home Secretary by virtue of the Police Act 1964. A principal function of the minister is to make regulations on the police service to govern such matters as conditions of entry, promotion and discipline. A chief officer may be required to submit a report to the Home Secretary on any matter connected with policing his area; in addition the Home Secretary may hold an enquiry into such matters. Guidance on the criminal law, on procedure and on police practice is issued by means of Home Office Circulars.

Whereas in England the police force engages in prosecution this is not the case in Scotland where an independent official, the Lord Advocate is solely responsible for all prosecutions. In this task he is aided by his Advocates Depute and by the procurator-fiscal service who, on receiving reports from the police, take the decision whether to prosecute or not and who appear in court to carry out prosecutions.

As far as the ordinary citizen is concerned he or she still enjoys powers of arrest[7] though these are not accompanied by powers of detention or charge. The private prosecution is still possible but it may be subject to the Attorney General's or Director of Public Prosecution's powers and is considerably restricted.[8]

When a policeman takes action against a person, then whatever is done should be justifiable in law. How the law sets limits to police powers can best be described by looking at four sorts of activity that people will most readily identify as police operations: arrest, detention, questioning, and stop, search and seizure.

### (a) *Arrest*

Knowing when arrest occurs is difficult enough for lawyers, worse for police officers and sometimes unfathomable for suspects. The law emphasizes a constable's individual responsibility for arrest but offers little help to persons who may have to make split-second decisions on an act's legality. Arrest has been said to consist in:

the seizure and touching of a person's body with a view to his restraint; words may, however, amount to an arrest if, in the circumstances of the case, they are calculated to bring and do bring to a person's notice that he is under compulsion and he therefore submits to the compulsion.[9]

Further reading of the law tends to obscure rather than clarify the issue. Though it is clear that arrest can only be lawful if in the exercise of asserted authority[10] the question whether a person has actually been arrested has been said to depend not on the legal propriety of any action but on whether a person has *in fact* been deprived of liberty.[11] The issues came to a head but were left unresolved in 1977 in the case of *R v. Brown.*[12] Officers, without suspicion relating to a particular offence, signalled a vehicle to halt. Michael Brown, the driver, stopped, and then unexpectedly ran off. An officer rugby-tackled and forcibly detained him. Lord Justice Shaw warned that though in a sense Mr Brown might be said to be arrested if restrained by a police officer, this might not be an actual arrest and the officer might have to answer in court for such action.[13] Typically, responsibility in the case fell on the individual officer.

The Court of Appeal supported the conviction in the Brown case but did not distinguish clearly between arrest and detention. They failed to lay down the criteria necessary for *lawful*, as opposed to *factual* arrest. This decision has been widely criticized.[14] In effect the court connived at the police officers' detaining Mr Brown without arrest 'for so long as might be necessary to confirm their general suspicions or to show them to be unfounded'.[15] The court shut its eyes for the convenience of the officers involved in the case at hand.

In Scotland the judges have done no better. In a famous case[16] David Swankie recklessly overtook a car one November evening and forced it off the road, onto the verge. Unfortunately this was a police car. The officers, when they caught up with Mr Swankie, suspected him of having been drinking. They took his car keys and, waiting with him, called for uniformed assistance to breathalyse him. Although the Sheriff in that case conceded that any attempt to leave would have been prevented he found that David Swankie had not been formally arrested, but simply detained. The Appeal Court agreed with the Sheriff.

In another regularly quoted Scots case[17] a Mr Muir was standing with others on a street corner one summer Sunday in Hamilton when a sergeant and constable charged him aggressively with the strange offence of having bought a drink in the County Hotel that morning 'by falsely representing himself to be a bona-fide traveller'. Mr Muir thought they were joking, denied the accusation and offered to meet the police at the hotel that evening to challenge the identification. Instead he was immediately 'marched-off' through the streets to the hotel. When he brought an action for illegal apprehension Lord Salvesen accepted that he had only gone with the officers through fear of the consequences of his refusal to do so. Nevertheless it was found that, in the absence of 'actual force', there had been no 'apprehension' (i.e. arrest) at all.

After such cases, it was difficult by 1980 to state exactly what constituted arrest. The law had failed to define relevant issues; it had thrust responsibility upon unguided police officers but the judiciary had tended to come to their aid when contention had arisen. (We return below to consider whether the police in law do have a power of detention short of arrest.)

A lawful arrest may be made with or without a warrant. It might be thought that the principle behind the warrant system is that such a serious action as arrest must be justified by the police in advance to an independent person (except in urgent cases) but if such a principle existed it has been severely eroded.[18]

*Without warrant.* Power exists[19] to arrest without warrant in relation to the wide group of offences (or attempted offences) for which a first offender might be sentenced to five years' imprisonment ('arrestable offences').[20]

As well as these provisions many statutes confer powers of arrest without warrant for particular offences even though the maximum penalty involved is less than five years' imprisonment (e.g. s.11 of the Prevention of Offences Act 1951 and s.5 of the Sexual Offences Act 1967).[21] In some other cases the power of arrest is exercisable only if the name and address of the suspected offender cannot be ascertained to the satisfaction of the police officer or if the danger of absconding is suspected: e.g. Children and Young Persons Act 1933, s.13(1)(a), Firearms Act 1968 s.50(3), Misuse of Drugs Act 1971 s.24, Prevention of Crime Act 1953 s.1(3).[22]

*Under warrant.* A number of statutes, principally the

Magistrates' Courts Act 1980,[23] empower magistrates to issue warrants to arrest following their being informed that a person is suspected of an offence. The warrant orders that the person in question be arrested and brought before a magistrates' court.

Standard procedure is for a police officer to 'lay an information' before the magistrate who then has final say on whether or not to issue a warrant. The warrant is either endorsed for bail, in which case the police must release the accused to appear before the magistrates' court as specified or, if unendorsed, bail is not authorized and the police must bring the accused before a named magistrate's court immediately.

*Executing an Arrest.* As we have seen in cases like Brown and Swankie, arrest need not necessarily involve an act of physical seizure. It must, however, be made clear to the person involved that he is arrested and he must be made aware of the grounds of arrest. In 1947, in what was a classic statement of the law, Viscount Simon set down five points designed to protect the arrested person's interests:

> (1) on arresting without warrant a policeman must normally inform the person of the grounds of arrest; (2) failure to do this may make the officer liable for false imprisonment; (3) the requirement to so inform lapses if the circumstances indicate that grounds of arrest must be known already; (4) no technical or precise language has to be used to give reasons for arrest, and (5) the arrested person cannot complain of lack of such information if he has made it impossible to inform him (e.g. by running away).[24]

Given the law's failure to *define* arrest, these protections are however of limited value.

Whether under warrant or not, an officer may, in effecting an arrest, use 'such force as is reasonable in the circumstances'[25] and it seems that the courts will, in considering reasonableness, 'take into account all the attendant circumstances'.[26] Again, judges are left to cut the judicial cloth according to the expediency of the individual case.

(b) *Detention*

Apart from that form of temporary detention connived at in the Brown case[27] the broad rule is that a person's liberty should be taken away only in the course of a lawful arrest. There is no power at law for a person to be detained or held while evidence to create reasonable cause to arrest is collected.[28] In short, there is no lawful power to detain merely for the purpose of questioning. This was decided in a case[29] in which two schoolboys were calling at houses on Stoke Newington Common to tell fellow team-members about a school rugby match. Two police officers on the basis of only *general* suspicion asked what they were up to and caught hold of one. The boys fought to escape and were charged with police assault. It was decided in court, however, that they were not guilty of assault in resisting arrest since the officers had no powers to detain for questioning.

On the other hand, it has been held, in, for example, *Donnelly v Jackman*,[30] that an officer acts lawfully in touching a person's shoulder in order to stop him for the purpose of questioning. The basis for this view was a statement by Lord Parker C. J. in *Rice v Connolly*[31] that

it is part of the obligations and duties of a police constable to take all steps which appear to him to be necessary for keeping the peace, for preventing crime or for protecting property from criminal injury.

A broad view of this statement would completely undermine restrictions on powers to detain on suspicion. It seems best to interpret it narrowly: as another concession to the particular case in hand, another instance of judicial connivance at a minor police transgression.[32]

Even if there are sufficient grounds to arrest there can be no detention for questioning short of arrest. The proper process of arrest must be used. Thus, in one case in 1973,[33] a man, Derek Inwood, was out when police called at his house looking for stolen goods. Inwood went voluntarily to the police station but after an hour or so of interview he got up to leave. Officers barred his way and there was a fight ending with Inwood rushing out of the door dragging a policeman, who was holding onto his coat. On appeal, the court quashed a conviction for assaulting the police, rejecting the idea that arrest arose automatically in such cases.[34] It was decided that whether the police had properly informed Mr Inwood that he had been arrested was a question of fact for the jury. It was not the law that notification of an intention to bring charges meant that actual arrest was taking place.

In addition to detention before or as an alternative to generous powers of arrest there occurs detention *between* arrest and charge. Whereas Scots Law treats arrest and charge as one process subject to the same legal tests,[35] English law drives a wedge between them. By distinguishing between the *grounds for arresting* and the *basis for charging* a person it is possible to state both that a person may not be detained or arrested solely for questioning and also that detention for questioning may follow arrest.

Lord Devlin explained the difference between 'reasonable cause' to *arrest* and a *prima facie* case sufficient to *charge*:[36] 'Reasonable cause' to arrest involved a lower standard than information sufficient to charge and thus to make a *prima facie* case in court. Suspicion (or 'reasonable cause') and *prima facie* proof differed in terms of their value as evidence; thus:

> Suspicion arises at or near the starting point of an investigation of which the obtaining of *prima facie* proof consists of admissible evidence. Suspicion can take into account matters that could not be put in evidence at all.

This view not only means that grounds for arrest will not necessarily justify a charge but, as the Royal Commission of 1981 put it:

> Accordingly, the period of detention may be used to dispel or confirm that reasonable suspicion by questioning the suspect or seeking further material evidence with his assistance. This has not always been the law or practice but now seems to be well established as one of the primary purposes of detention upon arrest.[37]

What is perhaps more worrying about Lord Devlin's judgment is that it seems to make it impossible to prove wrongful arrest. If 'reasonable cause' could 'take into account matters that could not be put into evidence at all' the arrest on 'hunch' may in practice prove virtually unchallengeable.

Assuming that arrest has been lawfully exercised the next issue of pressing interest to a suspect will be the length of time he or she may be detained pending charge, appearance in court or release. If arrested under warrant, a person must be taken before the court that issued the warrant immediately unless the warrant is endorsed for bail. In the case of persons arrested without warrant there are five possible outcomes.

First, they may be released without charge if there is insufficient evidence to justify prosecution.[38] Second, they may be released, the question of prosecution being still under consideration. Third, they may be released on bail to attend at a specified police station if the enquiries into the offence cannot be completed forthwith. Fourth, they may be released on bail to appear before a magistrates' court. Fifth, they may be held in custody.[39]

If a person is kept in custody after arrest a police officer of inspector's rank or above (or the officer in charge of the station) may enquire into the case and, unless the offence involved is a 'serious' one, grant bail.[40] If it will not be practicable to bring a person before a magistrate within twenty-four hours such enquiry *must* be made.

Where persons are held in custody they 'shall be brought before a magistrates' court as soon as practicable'.[41] In relation to the above provisions the terms 'serious offence' and 'as soon as practicable' are not defined; nor are details given of what shall constitute a 'proper reason' for not releasing a person. A large degree of police discretion is conferred.

## (c) *Questioning and the Right of Silence*

Police officers investigating a crime clearly feel it helpful to ask questions of various persons ranging from those who volunteer information to those who are charged with an offence. Not only that, but as we have seen, the modern police organization puts a disproportionate premium on evidence generated within the police station. A balance has to be effected between these (perceived) investigative interests and the rights of individuals not to be prejudiced by the use of unfair methods of questioning.

In the early part of this century guidance of an extra-legal nature was provided when, in 1912, the first set of Judges' Rules was issued. These made it clear that arrested suspects might be questioned by the police provided that they had first been cautioned. The present rules were issued to the police in 1964 after approval by all Queen's Bench Judges. Appended to these is a set of Administrative Directions to the Police which were drawn up by the Home Office and also approved by the judiciary.

The Rules state that they do not affect certain principles of law; for example: that police officers cannot other than by arrest compel a person to come or to remain in a police station; that persons must be able to consult solicitors at all stages of investigation (provided there is no hindrance to investigation) and that it is a condition of admissibility of any evidence resulting from questions that it be given voluntarily.

The Rules themselves provide that a police officer may question an individual whether or not that person is in custody but 'so long as he has not been charged with the offence or informed that he may be prosecuted for it'. (Rule I) Under Rule II an officer, as soon as he or she has evidence giving reasonable grounds for suspicion, shall caution the suspect before asking more questions. If a statement is then made a record should be made of the time and place and the persons present.

When a person is charged with an offence (or informed that he may be prosecuted) Rule III provides that a caution be given and states that at this stage 'it is only in exceptional cases that questions relating to the offence should be put to the accused person. If such questions are asked a further caution is to be administered.' The Administrative Directions on Interrogation and the Taking of Statements give further details on the conduct of interrogation and its recording, dealing with such issues as the comfort and refreshment of the person, supply of charges and facilities for defence. On the latter point it is provided:

*a*   A person in custody should be supplied on request with writing materials.

Provided that no hindrance is reasonably likely to be caused to the processes of investigation or the administration of justice:

  *i*   he should be allowed to speak on the telephone to his
        solicitor or to his friends;
  *ii*  his letters should be sent by post or otherwise with the least
        possible delay;
  *iii* telegrams should be sent at once, at his own expense.
*b*  Persons in custody should not only be informed orally of the
     rights and facilities available to them, but in addition notices
     describing them should be displayed at convenient and con-
     spicuous places at police stations and the attention of persons in
     custody should be drawn to these notices.

It is clear that the Rules in themselves have no legal force[42] and
that breaches of the Rules do not automatically invalidate evidence.[43] The introductory note to the Rules merely states that
nonconformity 'may render answers and statements liable to be
excluded from evidence'. It is to the case-law therefore that we
must look.

*Questioning and the admissibility of evidence.* A suspect is not
compelled by law to answer police questions. Lord Chief Justice
Parker said in *Rice v. Connolly*[44] that the whole basis of the
common law was 'the right of the individual to refuse to answer
questions put to him by persons in authority . . .' Or as Lord
Diplock has put it: 'no one can be required to be his own
betrayer'.[45] On the police's part, however, neither Judges' Rules
nor law states that questioning must cease on arrest or on a person's
refusal to answer. Protection for the individual against undue
pressure or influence has, therefore, come to rest on the 'voluntariness' test and on the exclusion of evidence that has been wrongfully
obtained.

The principle of voluntariness is given force in extensive and
confused case law. Statements and confessions have been ruled
inadmissible where they have resulted from (sometimes mild)
inducements or exhortations by those in authority (including police
officers, fathers and social workers).[46] Voluntariness since the
1960s has also been said to imply the absence of oppression, which
Sachs, J. said in *R v. Priestley*:[47]

imports something which tends to sap, and has sapped, that free
will which must exist before a confession is voluntary . . . They

include such things as the length of time of any individual period of questioning, the length of time intervening between periods of questioning, whether the accused person had been given proper refreshment or not, and the characteristics of the person who makes the statement. What may be oppressive as regards a child, an invalid or an old man or somebody inexperienced in the ways of this world may turn out not to be oppressive when one finds that the accused person is of a tough character and an experienced man of the world.

In contrast with a number of earlier decisions on exhortation and oppression an indication of how far police activity might be carried inside the law was given by the case of *R v. Praeger*[48] in which questioning the accused intermittently in custody from 9.15 a.m. to 11.30 p.m. was not considered oppressive. Nor is the state of the accused always decisive: in *R v. Isequilla*[49] two armed policemen pounced on a suspected armed robber in a car. The man started weeping and became hysterical and confessed. His statement was held admissible in spite of arguments that it was unreliable. Lord Widgery stated that the officers had acted properly and that exclusion of evidence must always involve some improper or unjustified act by the authorities. He added that: 'such considerations as fatigue, lack of sleep, emotional strain cannot be efficacious to deprive a confession of its quality of voluntariness'.

Going beyond oppression, practices involving torture (either physical or psychological) clearly render a statement involuntary. Under present law a judge, on finding a statement to be 'involuntary', shall automatically exclude it from evidence put to the jury. As the Royal Commission of 1981 stated:

> The rationale behind the present law is that evidence of certain kinds is or may be so unreliable as to preclude its being heard by the jury.[50]

If, however, evidence is obtained unfairly, or in breach of the Judges' Rules yet is not involuntary on the above test, exclusion is not automatic. In such instances the judge has a discretion to admit the evidence or not.[51]

Scottish courts have for many years been more protective of the person who is questioned in custody. The position there rests on common law and there is no Scots equivalent of the Judges' Rules. The traditional view in Scots law, as set out in the Chalmers decision,[52] was that police enquiries should be divided into three stages (stages corresponding to those assumed by Judges' Rules I, II and III in England but long abandoned in English case law). They are: (1) before the police have reasonable cause to suspect a particular person; (2) after they have reasonable cause to suspect but are not in a position to charge; (3) after charge.

At stage 1 the police might question without caution, no one has a legal duty to assist them but any statements are admissible in evidence. At stage 3 any police questioning apart from that used to clear up ambiguity is unfair. At stage 2 the position was described in Chalmers in terms that contrast sharply with the English notion that the period between arrest and charge can be used for the purpose of obtaining prejudicial information from the accused. Lord Justice-General Cooper said in a classic judgment[53] that it was not the police's function to obtain a confession or incriminating statements from suspects. When suspicion centred upon a person he warned:

> further interrogation of that person becomes very dangerous; and, if carried too far, e.g. to the point of extracting a confession by what amounts to cross-examination, the evidence of that confession will almost certainly be excluded.

Nor was Lord Cooper happy with the way the police were conducting investigations, he added:

> I view with some uneasiness the situation . . . in which a suspect is neither apprehended nor charged but is simply 'asked' to accompany two police officers to a police office to be there questioned . . . However convenient the modern practice may be, it must normally create a situation very unfavourable to the suspect. In the eyes of every ordinary citizen the venue is a sinister one. When he stands alone in such a place confronted by several police officers . . . the dice are loaded against him.

Although Chalmers has not been overruled, Scottish judges in recent years have weakened its authority by showing a willingness to admit evidence in circumstances similar to those involved in the above English cases.[54] Chalmers does nevertheless survive with its 'cross-examination' test and its procedure of hearing argument on admissibility in the jury's absence (the 'trial within the trial').[55] It is a case that many English liberal lawyers view with envy.

*Exercise of the right of silence.* If a suspect stands on his common law right to say nothing in response to questions it might be assumed that no prejudicial inferences may be drawn. Such an assumption is not, however, borne out by the law. In respect of failure to answer questions before a caution has been administered it has been indicated that, although a person is not bound to say anything, failure to do so when an answer 'could reasonably be expected' may provide some evidence in support of an accusation.[56]

The police may therefore lead evidence on a suspect's silence when questioned or confronted with information. It is then up to the jury to decide whether the suspect's response, action, conduct or demeanour amounts to acceptance of the points made.[57]

Once a person has been cautioned and told that he need not say anything then 'the law is that it must be unsafe to use his silence against him for any purpose whatsoever'.[58] Such a view accords with the rule that an accused cannot be compelled to give evidence at his or her trial and that the prosecution may not comment on any failure to do so.

In contrast to the freedom of the jury to draw inferences from a suspect's silence the kind of comments a judge may make on silence in response to questioning before trial have been restricted in many cases.[59] The Court of Appeal has stated that it constitutes a misdirection to invite the jury to form an 'adverse opinion' against an accused because of his or her pre-trial silence but this may not be the case in respect of silence at the trial itself:

No accused can be compelled to speak before, or for that matter, at his trial. But it is another thing to say that if he chooses to exercise his right of silence, that must not be the subject of any comment adverse to the accused. A judge is entitled to comment on his failure to give evidence. As the law now stands, he must not comment adversely on the accused's failure to make a statement.[60]

In the same case Viscount Dilhorne said:

> As the law now stands, although it may appear obvious to the
> jury in the exercise of their common sense that an innocent man
> would speak and not be silent, they must be told that they must
> not draw the inference of guilt from his silence.

Thus, in relation to silence on charge or questioning by persons in
authority, the rule is that whatever weight is given to this by a jury,
a judge may not invite the drawing of adverse inferences nor can
silence be put forward as corroboration of any other evidence.[61]

### (d)  *Stop, Search and Seizure*

*Stop*. At present there is no general power in Britain allowing
the police to stop or search individuals and any unauthorized
search may constitute an assault rendering the offender liable to
civil action. There are, however, two sets of instances in which
persons may be stopped and searched: where there is specific
statutory authority, and, in limited circumstances, following arrest.
As might be anticipated the exceptions to the general rule are
extensive.

A number of statutes concerned with a wide range of matters
(e.g. badgers, firearms, drugs, terrorism and birds)[62] empower the
police to stop and search on reasonable cause to suspect a person of
a statutory offence. In addition, local provisions such as section 66
of the Metropolitan Police Act 1839 give similar powers in relation
to stolen goods. Traffic legislation gives powers to stop motor
vehicles, for example to examine the vehicle mechanically (no
prior suspicion is required) and section 159 of the Road Traffic Act
1972 gives a *uniformed* constable a general power to stop vehicles.

*Search*. Following arrest, *Halsbury's Laws of England* states:

> There is no general common law right to search a person who has
> been arrested, but such a person may be searched if there are
> reasonable grounds for believing (1) that he has on his person
> any weapon with which he might do himself or others an injury
> or any implement with which he might effect an escape, or (2)
> that he has in his possession evidence which is material to the

offence with which he is charged.[63]

It is clear, however, that the right to search depends on *actual* arrest having occurred rather than there being a *right* to arrest in the circumstances.[64]

In the case of premises and property as opposed to persons there is no police power of search without permission.[65] Entry without lawful authority constitutes a trespass rendering the offender liable to civil action. As in the case of persons, however, there are a number of statutory powers of entry to public officials.[66]

Following arrest, the power to search property is unclearly stated. A constable, however, appears to be empowered to search 'areas under the immediate control of the prisoner',[67] covering at least the room in which arrest occurs. If arrest occurs outside the premises in question then search, to be lawful, must relate to the same offence as the arrest.

Search warrants may be issued by a magistrate under a number of statutory provisions and the warrant must be in the possession of the executing officer.[68]

Power to issue warrants to enter and search may be issued by senior police officers under a number of statutes[69] (e.g. the Explosives Act 1875 s.73 in which the authority is a constable of superintendent rank or over). A further power of entry is given in the rule that a constable may enter in order to effect a warrant of arrest where he has reasonable cause to believe that the wanted person is on the premises.[70]

There is no general power to enter to arrest without warrant but subsection 2(6) of the Criminal Law Act 1967 (section 2 of which provides for arrest without warrant in certain conditions), states:

> For the purpose of arresting a person under any power conferred by this section a constable may enter (if need be, by force) and search any place where that person is or where the constable, with reasonable cause, suspects him to be.

In cases of urgency the common law gives further powers of entry (or at least the courts have connived at these). In the main these relate to three sets of circumstances: (i) to deal with or prevent breaches of the peace; (ii) in pursuit of an escaped prisoner; (iii) to

save life, limb or to prevent serious damage to property.[71]
*Seizure.*

> Where the police enter a person's house by virtue of a warrant,
> or arrest a man lawfully, with or without warrant, it is settled law
> that the police are entitled to take any goods which they find in
> his possession or in his house which they reasonably believe to be
> material evidence in relation to the crime for which he is arrested
> or for which they enter. If in the course of their search they come
> on any other goods which show him to be implicated in some
> other crime, they may take them provided they act reasonably
> and detain them no longer than is necessary.[72]

Although a search warrant may not authorize 'fishing' for evidence unrelated to the offence in question, the case of *Chic
Fashions (West Wales) Ltd v. Jones*[73] indicated that in searching for
stolen goods a constable did have some freedom. Chic were re-
tailers of clothes in Cardiff and Llanelli. The police had a tip that
some stolen brands of clothes were being sold in the Cardiff shop.
With a warrant to search for clothes of the 'Ian Peters' brand they
swooped on all Chic shops and the proprietors' home. Though they
found no 'Ian Peters' clothes they took sixty-five garments of other
brands believed to have been stolen. The court decided that in
looking for stolen articles, officers might seize goods unmentioned
on the warrant provided that they believed on reasonable grounds
that they had been stolen or were material evidence on a charge of
stealing or receiving.

Again, this case broadened the law, as did *Ghani v. Jones*[74] in
which the Court of Appeal, though affirming the rule against
arbitrary search, stated that, without arrest or charge, property
might be seized if the police had reasonable grounds for believing
(*a*) that the offence was serious; (*b*) that the article was either the
fruit of the crime, the instrument of committal or material
evidence; (*c*) the person possessing the article had himself
committed the crime or was implicated or accessory to the crime or
that refusal to hand over the article was quite unreasonable.

## Police Powers in Practice

The above review concerns the law; it does not outline the manner in which police actually operate. The powers assumed by constables may bear little relationship to any description offered by the courts or textbooks. A distinction has arisen, as the above cases indicate, between the rules that courts *say* the police must operate and the rules that they *allow* the police to operate.

With respect to arrest, detention, questioning and search, the practical position is similar in Scotland, England and Wales; there has been a retreat of law. L. H. Leigh has stated that a 'tendency has developed to construe the rules liberally in order to allow scope for police inquiries'.[75] It is arguable, however, that rather than having been 'construed liberally' the rules in this area have been confused, subjected to exception or else ignored. The law has not been stated clearly but has been used to veil police powers.[76] In the Michael Brown[77] case the court conspicuously avoided stating the legal grounds of difference between detention and arrest in order to ensure conviction. *Hussien v. Chong Fook Kam*[78] extended police discretion and stretched the notion of 'reasonable cause to suspect' so that it became almost unchallengeable.

Such decisions have exemplified an increasing reluctance on the part of the judiciary to subject police powers to law rather than discretion. Whereas in Scotland's Chalmers case Lord Cooper saw the exclusionary rule as a tool with which to control police interrogation, later Scottish courts moved to a position in which the judge's duty has been directed towards controlling the quality of evidence.[79] Similarly in England emphasis used to be placed on controlling the police[80] but this has moved, especially in the area of search and seizure, so that in a recent House of Lords case, *R v. Sang*[81] Lord Diplock said that it was no part of a judge's function to discipline the police or prosecution in respect of the manner in which evidence was produced. If it was obtained illegally, he said, there was a remedy in civil law; if it breached rules of police conduct that was an issue of internal discipline. Except for admissions, confessions and evidence obtained from the accused, the judge, he said, had no discretion to refuse to admit relevant evidence on the ground that it was obtained by improper or unfair means. The court, it was emphasized, was not concerned with how evidence was obtained.[82]

Scottish courts, when they have acknowledged the issues on questioning openly, have moved to a position in which the interests of individuals and of the police investigation have to be 'balanced'.[83] Where this has not become an issue, evidence has been admitted after long periods of detention and questioning.[84] In the case of other powers, for example search, case law has proved flexible enough to allow search without warrant in cases of 'urgency' and the test of urgency has in some instances remained conveniently subjective and in the hands of the police.[85]

### 'Helping the Police with Their Enquiries'

As we have seen, in neither Scotland before 1980 nor in the south was or is there a police power to detain persons for the purposes of questioning. In England there has to be valid arrest, in Scotland arrest and charge. In spite of this state of the law the police in both jurisdictions have for years have asked citizens to 'help with their enquiries'. They have detained individuals for questioning in police stations and have on occasions used force to prevent 'volunteers' from leaving. In some instances (for example, the case of Inwood)[86] such forcible restraint has been held to be unreasonable and unlawful, but on other occasions such a process has been held to constitute lawful arrest.[87]

That the police engage in a process of extending their powers by straying beyond the bounds of law is no longer a contentious statement. The Thomson Committee[88] said of the Scottish law:

> It must recognize the realities of the situation, and *take account of those police practices which are accepted as fair by the public including criminals although they may be technically illegal or at least of doubtful legality.* It must avoid the situation which many police officers claim exists at present in which strict adherence to the rules would so hamper their efficiency and so reduce the detection rate as to subject them to severe criticism. (para. 2.03)

and

We believe that the police at present are able to carry out their functions only because some persons whom they detain without warrant fail, through ignorance or fear of authority to exercise their rights. (para. 3.11)

In England similar practices are adopted by the police to extend their powers. Nor, it seems, does the existence of the Judges' Rules act as an effective restraint. When Sir Henry Fisher investigated the Confait case in 1977[89] he found that the Rules had been breached in that instance by police interviewing persons of limited intelligence without the presence of parent or guardian, by their failing to inform suspects of their rights to communicate with solicitors or friends, and by their prompting suspects during the taking of a statement.

More worrying were Sir Henry's general findings. Other rules, he said, were misunderstood or 'not given their proper effect'.[90] In particular, he found that Administrative Direction 4 (on interviewing young persons only in the presence of parents or guardians) did not seem to be known to all the lawyers or police involved in his enquiry. Of the provision stating that those in custody should be informed of their rights to telephone solicitors or friends and to consult privately with solicitors, he found:

The existence of Administrative Direction 7 was unknown to counsel and to senior police officers who gave evidence before me. In the Metropolitan Police District it is not observed.[91]

The Royal Commission of 1981 was told by the police that officers:

frequently have to lay themselves open to the risk of civil action by stopping and searching in circumstances where they have no power to do so but where equally they will be criticized for failing to act.[92]

In para. 3.75, on arrest the Commission stated:

The evidence submitted to us supports the view of the Police Complaints Board, expressed in their triennial report, that police officers are so involved with the process of arrest and detention that they fail at times to understand the sense of alarm and dismay felt by some of those who suffer such treatment.

And on detention:

> people often go voluntarily to the police station to help the
> police in the investigation of crime and there may sometimes be
> a doubt about whether they are free to leave. (para. 3.97)

In their evidence to the Royal Commission the National Council
for Civil Liberties described what they saw as the two major problems in 'helping police with their enquiries':

> The first problem is that in many cases the police will say words
> to the effect of 'we're going down to the police station now'. The
> person concerned assumes that he has no choice, that he has
> been arrested and accompanies the officer. Where that 'Arrest'
> is later challenged the officer will maintain that there was no
> arrest but that the period in the police station was undergone
> voluntarily. The second problem concerns those people who
> have voluntarily gone to the police but who would be arrested if
> they tried to leave, or who do not ask to leave because they are
> given to understand they would not be allowed to. In practice
> 'helping police with their enquiries' as a form of detention does
> exist.[93]

It is instructive that the Metropolitan Police went to the Royal
Commission and not only admitted that their legal powers were
routinely exceeded but actually used this as an argument for
increasing these powers. This raises questions as to whether the
police are above the law at present, and whether judicial controls
may be relied upon in this area.

In looking at discrepancies between law and practice there are
different approaches. One is to argue that the courts already allow
the police a free hand and that changes in the law to rationalize
current practices will not change matters.[94] After all, it is said, the
police can do what they want within the law already.

Another approach states that judicial connivance at certain
police practices (for example, use of the 'holding charge'; compulsory 'helping the police with their enquiries') does not give legal
authority to otherwise illegal activity. Informal procedures may be
tolerated by courts but that does not alter, for example, the rule in

Chalmers stating that detention requires arrest and charge. To argue that such activity is within the law is an extreme form of rule scepticism; it amounts to legal defeatism that, by conceding that what the police are allowed to 'get away with' is therefore legal, has the effect of placing the police beyond judicial review and beyond the law.

There is another distinction to be made, namely between extra-legal activity that is connived at and activity that is sanctioned by law. 'Helping the police with their enquiries' now occurs in a context wherein the police exercise a certain care knowing that the courts and juries will tolerate this provided that (as in *R v. Inwood*) things do not go too far. To legalize such practices would not only sanction them on a larger scale but would remove that limiting context.

## Conclusions

There is a stark contrast between law and practice. In law there is no power to detain for questioning; there is no compulsion to give evidence; there is no general power of stop and search; there is no common law power to search arrested persons. In practice people do 'help with enquiries'; they are questioned; they do give evidence and are stopped and searched under various degrees of compulsion. Judicial flexibility has corresponded to both police needs in particular cases and the reorientation of the force towards the police collecting their own evidence rather than relying on public co-operation and information. As we describe in Chapters 1 and 7 the police themselves have encouraged the drift away from policing by consent by asking for greater powers.

It should be emphasized, however, that the police are not above the law in spite of the fact that they have strained at its frontiers. Judicial controls have moved from the traditionally clear position to one in which judges have allowed the law first to grow vague and then to retreat from the areas of arrest, detention, questioning and search. More can be expected. Instead of granting added discretions to the police, the courts must apply more precise rules of law to the circumstances of the case. Police powers must be balanced with definite protections for individuals and, where breaches of the law occur, the judiciary should enforce the law by excluding from trials evidence that is derived from such breaches.

It will be argued by some that there is little to be gained, and much lost in terms of detection by more rigorous adherence to principle. The difference, however, is not simply the conviction or not of one individual; it reflects the kind of policing we are to foster in this country. There are two major arguments for protecting the liberties of the individual. The first concerns justice. It is right that individuals should be tried on reliable evidence. In so far as sanction is given to police action that goes beyond the principles of law then evidence becomes less reliable – this was seen in the Confait case and in Sir Henry Fisher's subsequent recommendations – the danger increases that society may suffer by convicting the *wrong* person and allowing the guilty to escape that way.

The second argument concerns the kind of policing we desire. As police powers and discretions increase without improved systems of review so the courts move away from principle to expediency and, in turn, we drift into policing by compulsion and away from that based on co-operation. The less rigorously the courts protect individuals from overzealous police action the less likely it is that an individual will offer help or information to the police. (If I tell them about the man I saw breaking the window will they detain me for questioning?) The Royal Commission's research has found that:

> The success of the police in the detection of crime depends for the most part on how much useful information the public is able to give the police about the circumstances of the offence.[95]

Any loss in goodwill arising from the exercise of police powers will thus prove expensive in terms of lost police efficiency in detection. The prevalence of law over discretion can only improve relationships between the police and public and the role of the judiciary in this respect is important. If the debate on powers that follows the Royal Commission Report achieves anything it is to be hoped that it will at least prompt the courts to abandon the current process of mystification and to reassert the role of the judiciary in controlling activity that goes beyond the law.

## Further Reading

Blake, N., *The Police, the Law and the People*, Haldane Society, London, 1980.

Bowden, T., *Beyond the Limits of the Law*, Penguin, Harmondsworth, 1978.

Boyle, K., Hadden, T. and Hillyard, P., *Law and State: The Case of Northern Ireland*, Martin Robertson, Oxford, 1975.

Cox, B., *Civil Liberties in Britain*, Penguin, Harmondsworth, 1975.

Justice, *Pre-trial Criminal Procedure*, Justice, London, 1979.

Leigh, L. H., *Police Powers in England and Wales*, Butterworths, London, 1975.

McBarnet, D. J., *Conviction: Law, State and the Construction of Justice*, Macmillan, London, 1981.

# 6

# Reforming the Law or Legalizing Abuse?

If by the late seventies the reality of police work had become far divorced from the law on police powers, there was something else more worrying: in addition to the legal there was a political limbo. Debates on police powers had become fruitless exchanges from entrenched positions and nobody seemed to be looking at what was happening to police officers or to suspects on the ground. As a result the police could rightly complain that their powers were vague and by the same token libertarians could say that rights and freedoms were poorly defined.

How was the position to be remedied? It might have been obvious to some that what was needed was an approach that looked at the daily realities of policing not only from the point of view of the officer but also from that of those involved with the police. In addition, it might have been clear that reformers would ask what kind of police force and policing it was desired to encourage. As we shall see, however, this was not the line that was adopted. What the recent politics of policing has produced has been a different and narrower perspective.

Recently Britain has experienced two major attempts to devise laws governing police powers – the Criminal Justice (Scotland) Act of 1980 and the Royal Commission on Criminal Procedure 1981. In this chapter we look at what has happened in Scotland and in the next at what the Royal Commission proposed for England and Wales. As the debate on police powers continues it is increasingly clear that there are valuable lessons to be learned from the passage of the Scottish legislation. These lessons apply in looking not merely at how the law can deal with police action but also in understanding the politics of the legislative process and the way that public debates on police power are conducted.

## Behind the Politics in Scotland: The Movement to Reform

What the Criminal Justice (Scotland) Act of 1980 did was to introduce, among much else, sweeping new powers for the police to stop, search and detain 'suspects' without arrest, charge or formal caution. It provides that suspects may be held for up to six hours' interrogation without access to legal advice and without necessarily being able to inform a relative or third party of their whereabouts. During detention the police are empowered to fingerprint, search and body search suspects; in addition identity parades may be held. In short the legislation can be said to have legalized then existing procedures whereby members of the public were said to be 'helping the police with their enquiries'.

The origins of this legislation are complex and to be found in a period of gestation that lasted at least twelve years. This process was notable not so much for the role of politicians as that played by the legal profession.

The documented history of the Criminal Justice Bill can be seen to begin as far back as 1968 when the Scottish Law Commission published its inauspicious *Second Programme of Law Reform*.[1] Under Item No. 13 – Criminal Procedure the following comment can be found:

> There is evidence . . . of apprehension in members of the public as well as in the legal profession that among the reasons for the current increase in crime is the fact that our criminal procedure places unnecessary obstacles in the way of ascertaining the truth, with the effect of allowing guilty persons to escape conviction.

Little else was said – Item No. 13 ran only to half a printed page.

However, the Commission concluded by recommending that:

> Scottish criminal procedure be examined by a Departmental
> Committee under terms of reference wide enough to enable
> them to examine fundamental principles, such as, for example,
> the doctrine of self-incrimination, pre-trial examination of
> accused persons, and the availability to accused persons of state-
> ments by Crown witnesses.

One year later it became apparent that there was a potentially
very powerful lobby at work. In its Fourth Annual Report for the
year ending 15 June 1969 the Commission stated:

> In our Second Programme, which was approved on 25 June 1968
> we proposed that Scottish procedure should be examined by a
> Departmental Committee, *largely in consequence of represen-
> tations made to us by one of Her Majesty's Commissioners of
> Justiciary.* We had hoped that this Committee would have been
> appointed by now but, despite pressure from us, this has not yet
> been done.[2]

There is, then, some evidence that the initiative on police powers
came from senior members of the legal profession, and was
couched in terms of concern at the manner in which rules of
evidence were seen to be hampering the efficiency of prosecutions.

To be more specific, this concern was directed at the fundamental principle laid down in the case of *Chalmers v. HM
Advocate* in 1954 which had given a very strict interpretation to the
exclusionary rule[3] (see Chapter 5). Lord Cooper's judgment was to
come under progressively stronger attack or 're-interpretation' in
the period immediately leading up to the Law Commission Report,
and gradually the exclusionary rule was to be displaced by the
so-called 'test of fairness' in a string of cases in the late sixties.[4]
Thus Lord Strachan pronounced in *Miln v. Cullen* in 1967:

> the mere fact that a suspected person is asked a question by a
> police officer before being cautioned is not in itself unfairness.
> The whole circumstances must be taken into account, and the
> test in every case is whether in the particular set of circumstances

there has been unfairness on the part of the police.

Such reformulations of the law on admissibility in the period in question display not only the radical nature of the changes urged in legal terms, and not only the strength of the lobby behind the Law Commission's recommendations, but also clearly show a significant shift in relation to judicial attitudes towards the police and police interrogation. Thus, whereas in 1954 Lord Cooper had been 'uneasy' about the questioning of a suspect in the 'sinister venue' of the police station where the dice were loaded against him or her, by 1968 the tone had completely changed. Thus in the case of *Thompson v. HM Advocate* Lord Wheatley directed the jury as follows:

> if the police in the course of a very difficult and serious investigation have got to keep asking questions and probing and probing and probing then as long as they are doing that fairly having regard to their task and duty . . . then of course anything that they can elicit is normally competent and acceptable evidence.

Further confirmation of the new approach is readily available. For example, in September 1969 Mr A. M. Johnston QC, a member of the Law Commission who was later to sit on the Thomson Committee and after that to become a High Court judge, delivered a paper to the Law Society of Scotland under the title 'Has an Accused Person too many Rights?'[5] Admitting with remarkable modesty (thereby assuming the mantle of common sense) to being 'a tyro in this field' with 'no personal experience of police investigation', Mr Johnston asked whether the accused was not overprotected. He proposed that both suspects and those charged with an offence should, in the presence of their law agent, be subjected to questioning by the police. The interrogation envisaged was to be full cross-examination by the police with a 'view to obtaining information'. Mr Johnston said 'the presumption of innocence and the burden of proof rules seem to me to have no compelling relevance in this context . . why should the citizen's obligation to assist the police terminate abruptly when he becomes an accused person?' He commented 'surely the horrifying increase in crime during the last twenty years justifies the reintroduction of exam-

ination in some form or another of an accused person who appears
to the police to be withholding relevant information'. Though
seeing the problem principally in terms of legal evidence Mr
Johnston cautioned that there were situations 'in which common
sense is preferable to a pure legal concept'. He concluded by
'offering no apology' to those who saw his comments as 'naïve,
unrealistic, even inaccurate'. He was an 'innocent abroad in the
criminal law'. Writing the paper had, however, convinced him that
it was his 'statutory duty' immediately to study the matter in
depth.[6] Four months later he was appointed to the Thomson
Committee.

## Depoliticization: The Thomson Committee

We have pointed to the case law and the debate occasioned in the
late sixties not solely to stress the difficulties in terms of the law, but
because it was a time of crucial transformation. Pressures extrinsic
to the system of formal legality – the 'horrifying rise in crime', the
belief that too many 'criminals' were being acquitted, 'common
sense' – gave sway to greater judicial support for the police and a
belief that increased police powers would lead to a greater efficiency of the criminal justice system even if achieved at the expense
of the rights of the individual. When in January 1970 a High Court
judge, Lord Thomson, was asked to head a committee to look at
criminal procedure such 'common sense' was taken for granted and
naturally informed the approach of the Committee:

> It is necessary that [the law] should be so framed as to allow the
> police to perform legally whatever functions in the investigation
> and prevention of crime the public regard as proper. We believe
> that the police at present are able to carry out their functions
> only because some persons whom they detain without warrant
> fail, through ignorance or fear of authority, to exercise their
> rights . . . *At worst such legalisation of police practices as we
> propose will place the articulate and knowledgeable citizen in the
> same position as that presently occupied by the ignorant and
> inarticulate citizen.* As people become increasingly aware of their
> rights the present tacit co-operation which makes it possible for

the police to function may not continue, and the police may find themselves in a position to do only what they are specifically authorised to do by law.[7]

The dominance of this taken-for-granted 'prosecution view' of the questions at issue is not surprising given the composition of the Committee. Of its thirteen members, it included two judges, a sheriff, a JP, a professor of criminal law, a criminal lawyer, and a QC as well as a Chief Constable and the Chairman of the Scottish Police Federation. Hardly balancing such representation, the Committee's secretariat was provided by the Crown Office and included the man who, in 1974, left to become Crown Agent – the civil service head of the prosecution service in Scotland.

The significance of the Report that finally appeared in 1975 was not so much the nature and content of its assumptions, but the manner in which it translated these assumptions exclusively into an issue of technical law, thereby removing the issue from the level of everyday political discourse. Thus it was that the basic questions on interrogation and detention of suspects faced by Thomson in relation to police powers were presented as stemming directly from the problem of the admissibility of evidence and specific 'uncertainties' in the law. Their recommendations both in relation to powers of detention and in relation to interrogation were approached from this same direction. New powers of detention were required because evidence obtained by questioning after arrest *might* have been inadmissible (para. 7.12). The problem became a technical one of rule formulation. Rules prescribing the limits of police interrogation of suspects were necessary to ensure that the interrogation was conducted 'fairly', that is, to ensure that the fairness test – adopted by Thomson in preference to the rule in Chalmers – was met and that the evidence elicited was admissible.

What we saw in operation in Thomson then was an extremely narrow legalism, with the result that virtually no consideration at all was given to broader perspectives, beyond very infrequent and, where present, dismissive asides. Thus the social-psychological processes of interrogation which Lord Cooper saw to be of such significance were referred to briefly but discounted. The question of sanctions against the police and the rights and remedies of the individual was given even shorter shrift:

The sanctions against unlawful arrest or detention are prosecutions for assault or disciplinary proceedings against the constable but these are not within the control of the citizen. His only remedy is an action for damages. There are very few reported cases of such actions, and not many unreported ones. This may be due to the rarity of unlawful arrest, to difficulties of proof, or to the fact that a person with a criminal record is unlikely to receive more than derisory damages, particularly if he has been convicted of the offence for which he was arrested. We do not suggest any change. (para. 3.32).

Little, if any, consideration was given to alternative means of ensuring the control and accountability of the police, for example, through the introduction of an independent police complaints board. It was perhaps an irony that the Committee should have commented that 'an exclusionary rule is the only effective weapon possessed by the courts to control police interrogation' (para. 7.02).

Issues of civil liberties, and community relations with the police scarcely merited a mention. Neither fell within the frame of reference of the Committee, although they clearly came within its remit: 'to report whether, having regard to the prevention of crime on the one hand and to the need to fairness to accused persons on the other, any changes in law and practice are required' (para. 1.01).

It may be objected to our claim that social considerations and the rights of the individual were passed over by the Thomson Committee, that in fact the Committee included in its proposals a series of concrete protections for the individual suspect. These included the tape-recording of all interrogations; provisions that the suspect should be formally cautioned; and that he should be provided with the 'earliest possible opportunity to admit or deny having made any such statement or to challenge it on the grounds that it was inaccurate or unfairly obtained' at a judicial examination (ch. 8 passim). It was also recommended, in relation to detention, that the time of detention should be recorded by the senior station officer, that detention should cease as soon as there existed grounds for arrest, and that if the detainee so requests, information 'shall' be sent to his solicitor and to a friend or relative (para. 3.27).

While the value of such measures (at least in certain circumstances) cannot be written off, we would reiterate that the dominant question was not one of the protection of the individual and
his liberty, but how best to secure good legal evidence. Nor in view
of the Committee's rejection of the exclusionary rule in favour of
the recently developed fairness test, can it be claimed that
Thomson was unduly concerned about police malpractices.
Indeed Professor Gerald Gordon, a member of the Committee
was to write subsequently – and with some concern – that: 'in
the absence of any guidelines for juries beyond "fairness" there
is a risk that undesirable police practices will be encouraged,
or at least condoned, as means justified by ends . . .' In the days of
Chalmers a policeman might have been limited in his questioning
techniques, but: 'today he will always be well advised to chance his
arm . . . because of the strong likelihood that any relevant
evidence will be admitted'.[8]

An inversion had occurred. In so far as individual rights were of
consequence it was only in terms of a means to secure an end –
admissible evidence and the greater efficiency of the prosecution
system – rather than as objectives in their own right. Paradoxically,
it was this inversion which resulted in the ultimate omission from
the legislation of these very 'protections' that Thomson had made
the preconditions of change. For, in the re-translation into the
political discourse of the House of Commons what had become in
Thomson an unquestioned and an unquestionable trust in the
police was to render all such protections unnecessary.

## The Labour Bill of 1978

The effect of Thomson was to depoliticize proposals which had
started life as a political – albeit 'common sense' – response to a
perceived crisis in law and order. This resulted in a limitation in the
form and content of the ensuing debate in the House of Commons.
The Labour Bill was seen very much as a 'lawyers' Bill' of little
party political significance. Certainly there was no question of
broader policy implications for Scotland or for the rest of the
country.

When the issues reached the House of Commons the questions

were posed explicitly in terms of efficiency. Thus on 12 December
1978 Mr Ronald King-Murray, the Lord Advocate, introduced the
Bill to the Scottish Grand Committee in the following terms:

> There are three main ways in which to tackle crime; long term
> prevention, principally through education and by involving
> parents and the community in fostering socially responsible
> attitudes among young people; short term prevention, through
> improving police efficiency and morale and encouraging a
> preventive role; and third by ensuring that the criminal justice
> system is geared to deal fairly and effectively with those who are
> charged with crimes.
>     It is at the third method of dealing with crime – ensuring that
> the criminal justice system is geared to cope with those charged
> with crime – that the Bill is principally aimed.[9]

Of course in practice such distinctions are illusory. The three
'methods' to which the Lord Advocate referred are substantially
interrelated. To regard them as distinct was once again to demonstrate the risks inherent in treating the legal, the political and the
social as separate spheres and to ignore the fundamental inter-
relation of prosecution, policing and community. Be that as it may,
an altogether different, 'common sense' conception of 'fairness'
was now at work: the 'protections' included in Thomson were
omitted, although the rhetoric of individual liberty was never far
away. Thus Mr King-Murray summarized the police powers of
detention as placing 'good police practices on a sound legal footing,
defining both police powers and the citizen's rights in this very
sensitive area' (col. 5).
    In considering the principle of the Bill, only two MPs (both
Labour) objected that the citizen's rights were only 'defined' by
taking them away. Mr Donald Dewar, an experienced criminal
lawyer and member for Glasgow Garscadden, stated that the
power to detain for questioning would 'kill and bury' the Chalmers
doctrine as set out by Lord Cooper. He referred to the powers as
'an invitation to the police to put pressure on a suspect' and a
'dangerous inclusion in the Bill' (col. 31). While opposed in
principle to these powers, hc insisted upon the inclusion of the
Thomson protections. Mr Norman Buchan was perhaps more

forthright. He rejected the notion that 'because the police feel that they have to take certain measures to cope with the problems we should therefore legalise those measures: that since the police have felt they must use irregular methods to deal with the problem we should regularise them' (col. 45). This, he said, would be to erode fundamental liberties, the more so because the Thomson safeguards had been omitted. There was a danger that relationships between young people and the police would break down as had happened with the use of the 'sus' laws in the inner cities.

The Labour front bench however was to remain unsympathetic to such attempts to broaden the debate. In his concluding statement in Committee Mr Harry Ewing, the Under-Secretary of State for Scotland, replied to such criticisms:

> Even if the Thomson proposals on tape-recorded evidence, judicial examination, powers of detention and stop and search powers were accurate, it does not mean that the package is indivisible. We can easily – this has been the case in so many aspects of policy – take parts from a package and come up with a good legislative proposal. My view is that this is what happened in putting together the drafting of this Bill.[10]

By now the specifically legal problem of admissibility with which Thomson had been so concerned, had dropped out of sight. Thus in relation to the powers of street detention and detention for questioning Mr Ewing continued:

> Both these aspects of questioning are at present part of current police practice and the purpose of the clause is to regularise what happens now. The clause does not make changes in the present law relating to the admissibility at his or her trial of answers given by a suspect in response to police questions. (col. 110).

By this time we should note that since Thomson had reported, the Scottish judiciary had continued to relax the rule in Chalmers, so much so that in 1970 in the case of Hartley[11] a confession to murder was held admissible after a youth of seventeen, who had attended a special school, had been held in 'custody' for twelve hours overnight, without sleep, and without parental or legal advice. In such circumstances it would not appear unrealistic to suggest that the only remaining control upon the police remains that 'essential fund of common sense, training and experience which every police officer is deemed to possess in some measure, and without exercise of which he may find himself in trouble with his superior officers'.[12]

The law relating to admissibility was crying out for clarification, yet this aspect of the law was made exempt from change. The issue had been posed as simply one of 'regularization' and the Bill had been accepted, even by its parliamentary critics, as 'a non-party cross-political measure' up to the point where it fell with the calling of a General Election.[13]

## The Conservative Bill of 1979

On 5 May 1979, just two days after the Scottish electorate had firmly voted Labour, the *Edinburgh Evening News* carried a full-page interview with the newly appointed Conservative Solicitor-General for Scotland, Mr Nicholas Fairbairn QC.[14] Under the banner headline HOW THE TORIES PLAN TO BEAT THE THUGS: 'The war against crime is on . . . this is how the Government is going to fight', the opening paragraph read as follows:

> A tough new Criminal Justice Bill for Scotland was promised in the Queen's Speech by Prime Minister Mrs Margaret Thatcher. The new measures which will put Scotland in the front line in the Tories' big blitz against crime will include new stop and search powers for the police, controversial proposals to abolish the need for the police to caution a suspect and the defining of vandalism as a specific crime.[15]

The article gave a clear indication both of the general direction of Conservative thinking on law and order, and of the particular moves being considered to secure their new policies. Much was confirmed in the Criminal Justice (Scotland) Bill, published that December and which was to become law at the end of 1980.

The new Bill (comprising some eighty clauses and eight schedules) proved very much larger than its Labour predecessor. It included the promised short, sharp shock provisions, provision for the payment of compensation by offenders, the introduction of limited prohibition intended to criminalize the consumption of alcohol at football matches, as well as miscellaneous provisions such as one to permit the trial in absence of the accused in the event of such misconduct that 'in view of the court a proper trial cannot take place unless he is removed'. The clauses on police powers however were substantially the same as those contained in the Labour forerunner.

## a   Street Detention

Where constables had 'reasonable grounds for suspecting' that a person had committed or was committing any offence they might detain that person for as long as was necessary to verify the suspect's identity and to ask him 'for an explanation of the circumstances which have given rise to the constable's suspicion'. The constable was empowered to use reasonable force to secure these ends. There was no requirement for a caution to be given, nor had suspects to be told of their right to remain silent. The constable had, however, to inform the suspect 'of his suspicion' and 'of the general nature of the offence which he suspects has been or is being committed'. (Initially the constable was to have had powers to detain witnesses and 'any other person . . . who the constable believes has information relating to the offence' but this was dropped at Committee Stage in the House of Lords.)

In principle, these provisions were identical to those of the Labour Bill. The only difference of any significance being that under the Labour Bill exercise of the power was to have been restricted to 'any public place' whereas under the Conservative Bill the power could be exercised 'in any place where the constable is entitled to be'; in certain circumstances this could include dance halls and private homes, which amounted to a considerable extension.

## b   Compulsory Detention for Questioning

Under clause 2 of the Bill the police were empowered to use reasonable force to detain any person where there were reasonable grounds to suspect he had committed or was committing an offence punishable by imprisonment. The detainee could be taken to and held in a police station or 'other premises' for up to six hours' interrogation, during which time he might also be stripped, searched, body searched and fingerprinted. A formal record was to be kept of the time place and purpose of the detention even though no criminal charges had to be brought.

The position of a detainee under these provisions was weakened substantially and fewer rights were accorded than under arrest. The constable had to inform the detainee of his suspicion and of the 'general nature of the offence which he suspects has been or is being committed'. This compared unfavourably with the law on arrest where immediately upon arrest the suspect had to be charged with a specific offence and formally cautioned.

Again in substance these provisions replicated those of the earlier Bill, the major differences being that in the Labour Bill the period of detention was to have been limited to four hours and the taking of fingerprints was expressly excluded. One major addition to the Conservative Bill, however, was a provision allowing the re-detention of suspects for successive periods of six hours 'on the authority of a justice on cause shown'. No such clause had been included in the Labour Bill and indeed Malcolm Rifkind, Under-Secretary of State for Scotland and one of the Ministers charged with steering the new Bill through the Commons had introduced an amendment to the Labour Bill specifically to exclude the possibility of re-detention. It is worth quoting the Minister's former words:

The only concern prompting the tabling of this amendment is that, in the Bill as it presently stands, there appears to be no reason why the police, having released someone at the end of the four-hour period, could not five minutes later re-detain him under the same provisions for a further four hours. I hesitate to make comparisons with other countries, but, for example, the notorious ninety-day detention law in South Africa worked in this fashion.[16]

Ironically, almost exactly one year after the same sentiments were heard again, this time from Lord McCluskey during the Second Reading debate in the House of Lords:

I direct attention particularly to Clause 2(3). This is a wholly bad provision. I detect shades of South Africa here, and indeed of the police state, in allowing successive periods of detention on a mere magistrate's warrant.[17]

The sub-clause was subsequently withdrawn.

## c Stop and Search for Offensive Weapons

This was an entirely new measure introduced by the Conservatives. The police were empowered to detain for the purpose of search any person reasonably suspected of carrying an offensive weapon in public.[18] Doubt was consistently expressed throughout the debates as to the efficacy of such a measure. It was frequently pointed out that on occasion the head or the boot could be as offensive as a knife and that the definition of an offensive weapon would necessarily be quite arbitrary. Concern was expressed lest the power be used for random and mass searching of young people (which, to be an effective deterrent, it would have to be) with consequent danger to relations between the police and younger members of society. Dangers of harassment were pointed out. Although Mr Rifkind gave an undertaking that random searches would not be permitted, the Government refused to allow an amendment to that effect.

## d The Judicial Examination

This again was a Conservative innovation. A quasi-inquisitorial judicial examination before trial, called by the prosecution, was to be introduced to allow the accused to comment on any extra-judicial statement or confession he is alleged to have made.[19] (This stood to be very much a double-edged sword, if indeed it is of any advantage to the accused at all.) Initially the clause read that it should be 'permissible for the prosecutor or for the judge presiding at the trial to comment upon any failure by the accused to answer at examination; and they may also comment upon any inconsistency between what was said by him at examination and what is said by him (or on his behalf) at his trial'. Only the prosecutor would be allowed to question the accused, cross-examination by defence counsel was not provided for. On amendment however, in

nse to the claim that such provision was one-sidedly in favour
e prosecution, the defence was allowed to put questions to the
accused but only where ambiguity had arisen.[20]

## The Career of the Tory Proposals

It would be too simple to account for the 1979 Bill solely in terms of
a moral panic over law and order. Undoubtedly the Government
and supporters of the Bill played on this theme – 'the most
important civil liberty is the right to walk the streets in safety' was
an almost constant refrain – yet the rhetoric appeared to have little
purchase. Within the media only the *Guardian* and the *Sunday
Post* provided the Government with any comfort. The major
Scottish dailies – the *Scotsman* and the *Daily Record* – kept up a
sustained flow of critical articles and editorial comment on the Bill.
Possibly the most damning comment appeared in *The Times*
editorial of 14 April 1980 under the heading 'The Wrong Scottish
Precedent'.

The general lack of press support for the Government here
indicates the weakness in this instance of an explanation of the
passage of the Bill rooted primarily in the media generation of a
moral panic. This point is further confirmed by reports of the
Scottish Conference of the Conservative Party (May 1980) where
considerable disquiet was expressed in relation to the proposed
detention powers, four out of five speakers being against the
proposals.[21]

One alternative – in many respects quite attractive in terms of the
likely impact of the legislation – is to link the implementation of the
new police laws contained in the Bill with the economic strategy of
the Thatcher Government. The programme of cuts in welfare
agencies combined with vast increase in youth unemployment
clearly spell new problems of control that could be seen to be
answered by a deliberate policy of increased police powers. In
terms of the genesis of the Bill it is difficult to find such an explanation convincing; it assumes a degree of foresight unusual in the
pragmatism of contemporary British politics.

An approach which would enable us to take a longer retro-
spective view is to relate the 1980 Act to changing patterns of

policing in the post-war period in terms of such developments in the technological and organizational base of police work as have already been described in this book.

Again, however, while recognizing that the powers proposed in the Criminal Justice Bill would undoubtedly facilitate say the gathering of information[22] we are reluctant to assert that any 'conspiracy' took place. There appears after all to have been little if any concerted lobby on the part of the police to obtain these wider powers. The Scottish Police Federation, for example, in their evidence to the Thomson Committee made no such request. Subsequently of course the Federation claimed the powers as necessary common sense, but during the late sixties and early seventies there was little if any pressure from this direction.

Indeed it is, or at least it has been until very recently, a notable feature of policing in Scotland that, unlike their English counterparts, the police have avoided an overtly political stance in Scottish public life.[23] In part at least this can be attributed to the different legal system in Scotland and to the fundamentally different role of the Scottish police in the criminal process. As Paul Gordon has pointed out, the fact that the police 'neither initiate nor conduct prosecutions, and therefore have no direct interest in the prosecution system and the role of public prosecutor, means that the rate of conviction/acquittal is no reflection on their actions or procedures'.[24]

As we shall see, under such circumstances it is less than surprising to find that, initially at least, the pressure for change was to come from the legal profession – albeit a relatively narrow section of that profession.

By the time the issue of police powers of detention and interrogation had first reached the point of legislation, the issue had been politically neutralized. In so far as it had started life as an issue of 'law and order', at the end of the day it had become a technical question of law, in particular of the admissibility of evidence. It was in this light that members of the House of Commons first approached the Bill. The ideological and institutional separation of law and politics, so often commented upon in sociological literature, is nowhere more visible. The Criminal Justice (Scotland) Bill had become 'one for the lawyers'.

There were a number of important contributory factors to the general absence of concern occasioned by the Labour Bill. The lack of a reliable government majority rendered final enactment uncertain. The problems of the 'Winter of Discontent', combined with the protracted debate and referendum on devolution, deflected the political focus from the debate on the Criminal Justice Bill. Yet of themselves these are insufficient grounds to explain (or to excuse) the approach of the Parliamentary Labour Party for, to begin with at least, the new Labour Opposition was again to accept the principle of extended police powers. However, the door was left open for a change of position. Thus Lord McCluskey, leading for the Opposition in the Second Reading debate in the House of Lords, spoke as follows:

> Some of the provisions in this Bill regarding police powers . . . were contained in the Bill . . . introduced by the last Government . . . I want to make it plain that I shall not urge the rejection of any provision which we introduced or might have introduced. But the mere fact that on particular issues the two Front Benches have espoused a particular provision does not of itself make it a good one.[25]

The response of the new Government, however, had been immediately to confirm the line previously established in the earlier debates; thus Lord Mansfield, Conservative leader in the Lords, prefigured the position to be adopted in more exaggerated terms in the House of Commons:

> I want to emphasise that despite the misguided assertions of various vociferous groups and individuals in Scotland, these are provisions limited in nature and in time, and no more than are essential for the police in their function of investigating and preventing crime. (col. 18).

At this stage Labour's opposition remained cautious. Lord McCluskey reiterated the previous Government's position that detention beyond four hours was unjustifiable although in principle acceptable, and maintained opposition to the power to stop and search for offensive weapons. He maintained, however, that interrogations should be tape-recorded, that the power to fingerprint should be expressly withheld, and that the provision allowing re-detention for further periods of six hours was potentially repressive. Perhaps rather surprisingly, he then added that, subject to such limitations, the new police powers should be tried for three years after which they should be reviewed and, if desired, renewed by an affirmative resolution of Parliament.

In Committee Stage in the Lords, the Government was to allow its only important concessions on the matter of police powers, neither of which however were substantial nor went to the principle of detention. First, the proposed power to detain witnesses compulsorily was formally reduced to a power to require identification; and secondly, it was agreed to abandon the clause permitting re-detention. Thereafter, all Opposition attempts in Committee, both in the Lords and the Commons, to secure even the minimal protections of Thomson were blocked. The Lords however agreed the amendments noted above to procedure in judicial examination.

By the time the Bill reached the House of Commons (14 April 1980) the extension of police powers could no longer be described as a 'non-party, cross-political measure' even though in principle the provisions remained unchanged. The whole question of detention powers had been politicized principally as the result of extra-parliamentary campaigning against the Bill.

That extra-parliamentary criticism found its mark is evidenced by the fact that unlike its Labour forerunner, the Bill was introduced by the Secretary of State for Scotland to a full House of Commons. Amongst Mr Younger's very first comments can be found the following statement:

> Many of the arguments so far adduced in criticism of the Bill are very wide of the mark. I cannot help thinking that a very large proportion of those who have violently condemned this Bill have either never read it all or have completely failed to understand it or to compare it with the present practice both north and south of the border.[26]

More significant perhaps was the change of position on the Labour front bench. Although previous prevarication was never finally resolved, a reasoned amendment to the Conservative Bill was moved in the terms:

> This House declines to give a Second Reading to a Bill which will
> damage relationships between the police and public in Scotland
> by giving excessive powers of detention to the police and provid-
> ing them with new powers to stop and search for offensive
> weapons. (col. 830).

At this stage we will not rehearse the rights and wrongs of the
various arguments made outside and subsequently within the
House of Commons. The point is that it was extra-parliamentary
opposition which led to the earlier (quasi-) legal frame of reference
finally being challenged in the Commons although, as it transpired,
the challenge was unsuccessful.

It was argued earlier that the effect of Thomson had been to
'legalize' and thereby to depoliticize the issues as they were encountered by and during the period of the Labour administration,
and that this created a momentum which proved politically
unstoppable. At the end of the day, of course, the Conservative
Government was able to, and did rely upon its 'English' majority to
force through its Bill, yet none the less – and perhaps because the
Conservatives were in a minority in Scotland – a concerted attempt
was made to cling to what now had all the appearance of a fiction,
namely that all that was being engaged in was a tidying-up of the
law. Thus, for example, Mr Michael Ancram, an Edinburgh
advocate and one of the leading Conservative back bench spokes-
men on the Bill who was subsequently to sit on the Standing
Committee, attempted to avoid all the issues raised by arguing
that:

> Since the case of Hartley some 14 months ago, the law of
> Scotland, approved by the appeal court, is that the police can
> detain for uncontrolled periods without creating unfairness in
> regard to any confession that a detained person might make . . .
> We are looking at existing laws and asking whether they should
> be regularised. This is what the Bill tries to do. (col. 859).

Ignoring for the moment the accuracy of Mr Ancram's
interpretation of the law, the approach which his statement

embodied was indicative of one significant aspect of the Conservatives' attempt to legitimate their measures by reference to legal authority: the fact that the police already exercised these powers, *and that it was condoned by the law*, that is, by the judiciary, was adequate and sufficient justification by itself. It was no longer even a question of 'legalization' merely 'regularization'.

With only one exception Conservative representation at Committee stage consisted of members of the Scottish Bar. In this manner Government Ministers attempted to assume the mantle of legal 'neutrality'. The 'political motives' of the Bill's critics were repeatedly impugned. Of 'those who claim to have an interest in civil liberties' the Solicitor-General said in the House of Commons: 'They hide their resentment of the law and those who enforce it behind a pretence of a concern for liberty.' (col. 982).

On frequent occasions Ministers attacked their critics both inside and outside the House of Commons as 'intellectuals of the left' who set out to 'undermine public confidence in our system of justice'.[27] Inevitably perhaps such allegations prompted editorial and readers' comment in the press. But, as one correspondent to the *Scotsman* asked the Solicitor-General: was the Faculty of Advocates – who had published a damning critique of the proposed new powers – therefore to be regarded as a 'hot-bed of Communist activity'?[28]

Little need be said of Committee Stage in the Commons, except that it was marked by a number of features; first, the absolute intransigence of the Government; second, the concern of both sides of the House to quote statements made in relation to the earlier Labour Bill; third, the inconsistency of Members' approaches to the two Bills; and fourth the extent to which the Opposition considered it had won the arguments but lost the vote. Thus, by the seventh sitting of the Committee the Opposition were becoming increasingly worried by the Government's attitude and Mr Ewing was forced to point out that so far *not one* amendment had succeeded. Mr George Foulkes asked for some flexibility and that serious consideration be given to detailed amendments. However the pattern had been set. In the end, on the question of police powers only one minor amendment of any substance was admitted.

The result was never really at issue. The Bill became law and the new powers came into effect in June 1981. By the end of May 1982, 21,435 detentions had been made under Section 2.

## Conclusions

In Scotland in 1978–80 legislation of immense social importance was considered by lawyers without reference to its social or policing context. It instituted powers that may gravely endanger police/public relations, that threaten liberties, that may make policing in Scotland more difficult and that may change our very methods of policing.

The Scottish Act set the scene for the English Royal Commission on Criminal Procedure, which employed similar descriptions of powers as merely 'regularizing' the present position and a similar tendency to treat the debate as an affair solely for lawyers. It is vital to learn from Scottish experience. When legislation of the widest social importance is disguised by reference to 'lawyers' bills', 'legal technicalities', 'tidyings-up', 'regularizing' or 'clarifying', then politicians and the public must not hesitate to lift the legal veil.

## Further Reading

Gordon, P., *Policing Scotland*, Scottish Council for Civil Liberties, Glasgow, 1980.

Renton, R. W. and Brown, H. H., *Criminal Procedure according to the Law of Scotland* (4th ed. by G. H. Gordon), Green, Edinburgh, 1972.

Sheehan, A. V., *Criminal Procedure in Scotland and France*, HMSO, Edinburgh, 1975.

Thomson, Lord, *Criminal Procedure in Scotland*, 2nd Report, Cmnd. 6218, HMSO, Edinburgh, 1975.

# 7

# The Poverty of the Royal Commission

## Background

Whereas in Scotland momentum to change the law on police powers built up within the legal establishment, English and Welsh developments have taken place on a more openly political plane. Throughout the sixties and seventies, dissatisfaction with both the law and practice of policing mounted on several fronts and a public debate had arisen well in advance of the Royal Commission's appointment. As early as 1965 and long before he became Metropolitan Commissioner, Sir Robert Mark had developed in public his later familiar theme that the criminal trial was a 'show jumping contest' full of hurdles at which the prosecution case might fall.[1] As if in response, the Criminal Justice Act of 1967 had provided for majority verdicts in jury trials and pre-trial disclosure of defence alibis.

It was, however, the eleventh report of the Criminal Law Revision Committee (CLRC), published in the year of Mark's appointment to the Commissionership (1972) that was to fuel the fires of debate.[2] Chaired by a High Court Judge and packed with senior lawyers, the CLRC echoed Sir Robert in making unsupported statements about the rules of evidence allowing professional criminals to escape conviction and, by way of solution, proposed to undermine the traditional rights to silence. This was to be done *inter alia* by providing that where an accused failed during police interrogation, to mention a fact subsequently relied on in defence, the court or jury might draw adverse inferences from that silence.

These proposals were met with a barrage of criticism ranging from academic articles to editorials, from letters in *The Times* to speeches by Law Lords.[3] Such widespread reassertion of the presumption of innocence and the traditional view that the onus to prove guilt rested on the prosecution did nothing to please Sir Robert. It was not surprising therefore, that he used his 1973 BBC Dimbleby Memorial Lecture to attack juries for acquitting too many people, to assert once more that the rules of evidence unduly favoured the defence and to threaten that failure to reform the law the way he wanted would increase pressures on the police to 'use more arbitrary methods'. Sir Robert Mark's proposals were taken up by the Police Federation's 'law and order' campaign of 1975–76, which added its expression of police frustration with the rules of criminal procedure.

If there was a police lobby for extended powers, there was, especially in the late seventies, another body of opinion concerned at the extent to which the police were already straying beyond the law. Official confirmation that the police did not follow the rules to the letter came when former High Court judge, Sir Henry Fisher, reported on events leading to trial in the Confait murder case in 1977.[4]

Maxwell Confait was a homosexual prostitute. One night in April 1972 his body was found in his blazing home at 27 Doggett Road, Catford. Three boys aged 14, 15 and 18 were questioned by police, and on the basis of confessions made in separate interviews, were subsequently convicted of a variety of offences ranging from arson to murder. In October 1975 the boys were freed by the Court of Appeal after new scientific evidence had shown that they could not have committed the offences and that the confessions could not have been true.

The Fisher report met with a mixed reception. Some criticized Sir Henry's findings as too supportive of the police. He found, after all, that they had not assaulted the boys, that oral records had not been falsified and that the confessions could not have been made unless at least one of the three had been involved in the killing and arson. Others welcomed Sir Henry's providing authoritative evidence of police methods. He stated that the Judges' Rules and Home Office Directions had been broken in interrogating the boys and that some questioning had been unfair and oppressive. He found, moreover, that some of the Rules and Directions did not seem known to the police or lawyers who gave him evidence; that some Directions were not even published in the standard textbook, 'Archbold', and, most dramatically, he stated of Direction 7 (which provided for a person in custody's having telephone access to solicitor or friends) that this was unknown to both counsel and senior officers who gave evidence to him and that it was 'not observed' in the Metropolitan district.[5] He recommended that such rules be backed with workable sanctions and that any breach of these should constitute grounds on which a judge might exclude evidence from a trial – whether or not such breach sufficed to make a confession 'involuntary'. Since Sir Henry was reluctant to advocate general reform of the law on the basis of a particular case, he suggested that, if such changes were contemplated, then something like a Royal Commission was required.[6]

It was in this climate that Prime Minister James Callaghan announced, in June 1977, the setting up of a Royal Commission on Criminal Procedure (RCCP) to look at the whole of the conviction process from investigation to trial. Official reasons for setting up the Commission were given[7] as a growth of anxiety about rising crime; the confusion of law and practice relating to the investigation and prosecution processes and discontent, on the one hand, with the restraints of criminal procedure and, on the other, with the use made by police of their powers. Further considerations were the failure of governments to mount any similar review in the century beforehand and the fact that the Thomson Report had been sitting unimplemented in Scotland for over two years.

In the wake of Fisher, and, set up by a Labour Government, there was cause to believe that the RCCP was a 'response to demands for greater rights for suspects'.[8] Certainly the police force, for their part, did not universally welcome the new Commission. As has been noted by others[9] Jim Jardine, for the Police Federation, saw the Commission as a stalling device and the Superintendents' Association feared that police powers were about to be reduced by misguided liberals and academics. Sir Robert Mark's successor at the Metropolitan Police, Sir David McNee, was not, however, daunted. He set up a working party to prepare evidence and took the opportunity of his 1977 report to greet the RCCP, to criticize certain restraints of criminal procedure and to warn: 'An excess of liberty which makes ordinary people fear to leave their houses is not freedom under the law as we know it and libertarians should proceed with caution.' Sir David need not have feared, whatever the true intentions of those who set up the RCCP, the last thing that the ensuing report was to do was to increase suspects' rights at the expense of police powers.

A non-lawyer was selected to chair the Commission. Sir Cyril Philips was an ex-professor of Oriental History and head of the School of Oriental and African Studies in London. Of the sixteen Commission members, however, twelve had been involved, or were working in criminal procedure. Notable among these was a former permanent Under-Secretary at the Home Office, a former Chief Constable, a former secretary of the Police Federation, five JPs, a magistrate, a circuit judge, a member of the Law Commission and two solicitors.

Those who had expected a Commission of real independence were to be surprised; the RCCP's secretariat comprised civil servants seconded from the Home Office and was led by Mr Christopher Train from the Home Office Criminal Policy Department. Organizing research was Mrs Mollie Weatheritt from the Home Office and, in a unique position, was Detective Superintendent David Gearon, seconded from the Metropolitan Police, who, in the Commission's words, provided 'insight into the work of the police and helpful liaison with police forces generally'.

The logistic problem for the Commission was to design, farm out and receive back the research it wanted; to do its own collection of information, to hear oral evidence and to write its report – all within three years.

It began by requesting evidence from interested and relevant parties, commissioning research and making visits to see British and other systems of criminal justice in action. Evidence soon poured in, some of which sought to set the tenor of the debate. In August 1978 the views of the Metropolitan Police were leaked in *The Times*, which gave advanced notice of the McNee demands. In what became known as the 'shopping-list' the Commissioner asked the RCCP for greatly extended powers.[10] His general argument betrayed his Scottish roots when he stated that in the past the police had only been able to do their job by taking advantage of a population that was ignorant of its rights. Because the police lacked adequate powers, he said:

> Many police officers have, early in their careers, learned to use methods bordering on trickery or stealth in their investigations . . . One fears that sometimes so-called pious perjury of this nature from junior officers can lead to even more serious perjury on other matters later in their careers.

The answer was not to control officers more rigorously but to give them more powers. In proposals that the TUC was to call 'a substantial move towards the Police State',[11] the Commissioner asked *inter alia*: for powers to hold suspects for questioning for up to seventy-two hours; for reduction of the right to silence along the lines of the 1972 CLRC report; for a general power to stop and search persons and vehicles; for broader powers of search and seizure without warrant; for powers to set up general road block searches and to ease access to private bank accounts, and sanction to fingerprint every person or category of person within a prescribed area. ACPO was to back up Sir David in its evidence to the Commission. The Association thought that no further safeguards for suspects were needed and called for easier majority verdicts in jury trials; it proposed the use of 2 : 1 verdicts (instead of 5 : 1) or else closer control of jury selection to remove people who were 'unresponsible or criminally dishonest'.

As far as the Royal Commission was concerned, the publication of such demands created an environment of police expectation within which to work. Other factors also contributed to a police-oriented approach. The time-scale to which the RCCP had committed itself and its belief in close co-ordination with the police force, led to a strange way of using the mass of information it collected. Sir Cyril Philips has described how visits to police authorities and stations began in the first year of sitting.[12] As research arrived this was, in Sir Cyril's words: 'checked on the ground' and tested with 'people who have to work with the system'. Thus the Commission reversed the normal process in which data is collected on the ground and reflected on in cool detachment. In the case of the RCCP, research was judged in the light of police operations and, no doubt in response to demands made in the heat of investigations. There is evidence, indeed, that on certain issues the RCCP was directly influenced in its recommendations. The *Observer* described how the RCCP had held back from recommending that all police interviews should be taped because of fears that such proposals would be rejected – not by the Government but by the police. A Commission source was quoted:

> We were very conscious that full tape-recording would be too much for them to swallow. It was important that the Police should not come out against the report in its entirety so that our recommendations would at least have a chance of being adopted by the Government.[13]

In other words, instead of proposing a balanced system and letting the Government deal with ensuing political issues, the RCCP tailored its suit according to the political cloth. This general approach, as we shall see, led to a report that placed a high premium on the acceptability of proposals to the police.

The other face to the Commission's pragmatism was in its collective approach to issues. With strong representation of police and prosecuting agencies, together with the presence on the committee of 'liberal democrats' such as Dianne Hayter JP (General Secretary of the Fabian Society), Walter Merricks (former Director of Camden Community Law Centre) and Jack Jones (former General Secretary of the Transport and General Workers' Union) one might have expected some opposition of views on whether or not to increase police powers at the individual's expense. The Commission's response to these issues[14] was not to negotiate on a *quid pro quo* basis, trading some rights for others – it was felt that compromise between two opposing schools would not necessarily produce the right result. Instead, the answer was seen in a 'factual base' on which a framework of first principles could be built. The 'factual base' would be provided by detailed research and 'visits by Commissioners to all police authority areas in England and Wales' (para. 1.34): the general principles would be set down in a process of thinking the issues through from the start.

Those who have spoken of their experience on the RCCP seem unanimous on one point: that the 'two camps' very rapidly disappeared leaving members simply 'to see what would work in practice'. A primary objective was 'getting something that would work'. Those who view the RCCP's proposals cynically may argue either that such an approach was the produce of a liberal collapse, or that the intellectual and pragmatic push of the Home Office/police line proved too strong to resist. The strength of emphasis placed on professional opinion, and the bulk of research that was conducted could have done nothing but shift the balance of power in the Commission away from those members who were non-experts in the field, towards the full time staff and those with prior experience. Commissioner Walter Merricks later wrote 'we were sensibly guided by our Chairman and Secretary into embarking on a research programme enabling us to put a sound basis for the proposals that we were going to try to formulate'.[15] The extent of such 'guidance' we are left to ponder. The fabians on the RCCP would argue, however, that they did not collapse but produced the best and most workable package. One thing, at least, was clear; by 1981 there was very little division in the ranks; there was no minority report and, as we shall see, only on a few points did two members dissent. Those who might have been expected to express reserve were to be seen publicly defending the report in its virtual entirety. Whether they were right to do so will become clearer on looking at the RCCP proposals.

## The RCCP Proposals in Outline

### Arrest

The category of 'arrestable offences' should be widened. Whereas powers of arrest without warrant are now in general limited to offences carrying penalties of five years' gaol or more these powers should apply to all offences punishable with imprisonment. Use of arrest should be limited by the new 'necessity principle' whereby arrested persons should only be detained at a police station if the station officer finds and records one of the following criteria to be satisfied:

a    the person's unwillingness to identify himself so that a summons may be served upon him;

b    the need to prevent the continuation or repetition of the offence;

c    the need to protect the arrested person or other persons or property;

d    the need to secure, to preserve, or to obtain by questioning, evidence relating to the offence;

e    the likelihood of the person failing to appear in court.

There should be a new power to detain persons (witnesses as well as suspects) in the immediate vicinity of a 'grave' incident and to stop vehicles within a reasonable distance of the incident. ('Grave' offences range from serious dishonesty and damage to property to serious offences against the person such as murder.)

## Detention on Arrest

Where criteria for detention at a police station are met a 'custody sheet' should be started to record details of the custody. Instead of the existing position, allowing arrested suspects to be held until brought before a magistrate 'as soon as practicable' (in serious cases) or within twenty-four hours (in others) the position should be standardized. Where detention is justified on the necessity principle it might continue for six hours when the necessity for continued detention should be reviewed by a uniformed inspector unconnected with the case (the reasons for decisions to be recorded and given to the suspect). If detention persists for twenty-four hours without charge or appearance before a magistrate, the suspect must be released except in 'grave' cases where magistrates sitting in private might extend detention for further twenty-four-hour periods.

## Search on Arrest

The common law power to search a person on arrest should be made statutory. A more thorough search should be allowed at the police station where the station officer thinks it necessary. No 'strip search' should be conducted except on suspicion of a grave offence and with the authorization of a subdivisional commander; where necessary it should be carried out by a doctor. Search of premises (and vehicles) following the occupant's arrest should be lawful where there is reasonable suspicion that articles will be found which relate to this or a similar offence, but no warrant would be necessary. As a safeguard the police officer must record his reasons for making the search before the search takes place. Fingerprinting should be allowed either with the written consent of the subject or upon the written and reasoned authority of a subdivisional commander. The same procedure should apply to photographing, and (for grave offences) to any physical examination of a non-intimate nature.

### Questioning and Suspect's Rights

*Right of silence.* The RCCP by a majority recommended there be no change in the suspect's rights to remain silent both in the face of police questioning after caution and in court. The present judicial restrictions on the drawing of inferences from silence should remain.

*At the police station.* Where a suspect is detained at a police station he should be told that he has a general right to have a third party informed of his detention, but the station officer might withhold this right (upon the reasons outlined below) and must record his reason. The suspect should also be told that he has a general right to consult and communicate privately with a solicitor: this right might be withheld for grave offences and upon the authority of a subdivisional commander, if he reasonably believes that the time taken to summon a legal adviser would involve risk of harm to persons or serious damage to property, or that allowing access to a legal adviser might lead to:

*a*  interference with evidence;
*b*  threats or harm to witnesses;
*c*  the alerting of others suspected of the offence; or
*d*  an increase in the difficulty of recovering the proceeds.

Instead of the Judges' Rules and Administrative Directions a 'code of practice' should be drawn up to regulate questioning. It should deal with matters now in Rules and Directions such as cautioning, tape-recording, legal advice and the circumstances of questioning. The nature of questioning would not be covered and the present 'voluntariness' test for the admissibility of confessions would be abandoned in favour of allowing the court to assess the reliability of a confession on the facts presented (including any departure from the code of practice).

The accuracy of recording statements should be improved by the officer's summarizing these orally and recording points in writing and by the use of tape-recorders. Tape-recording to record the whole interview was rejected because of 'operational difficulties'; instead, the RCCP stated that tapes should be used to take down statements or summaries. Video recording on a general basis would be too costly it was said, though selective use should be possible.

*Enforcement.* Compliance with the code of practice and rules on investigation should rely mainly on police disciplinary procedures and civil actions. A rule allowing the exclusion of evidence obtained in breach of the code should only be appropriate in cases where torture, violence or degrading treatment is used. The code of practice's aim is not to discipline the police but to ensure the reliability of evidence. Where a breach occurred, the evidence would be used in court but the judge should warn the jury of the nature of the dangers involved in acting on a statement obtained in breach of the code. Evidence obtained as a result of an unlawful search or by other unlawful means should generally be admissible (unless its reliability is impugned). Exclusion of such evidence is only automatic where it relates to a non-grave offence and was discovered during a search under a specific warrant relating to a different offence.

The present test of the admissibility of statements that they be 'voluntary' should be abandoned as unworkable; instead we should rely, for protection from abuse, on police discipline and training.


## Stop and Search

Various and complex existing powers should be consolidated. Officers should have new general powers to stop and search any person in a public place whom they on reasonable grounds suspect of conveying stolen goods or of being in possession of anything whose possession in a public place is itself a criminal offence (e.g. prohibited drugs, firearms or housebreaking implements). The person stopped must be told the reason for the search, the officer must record the reasons in his notebook, and supervising officers should have the duty to collect and scrutinize figures of searches and their results.

The above new power would authorize some stopping and searching of vehicles. In addition, an Assistant Chief Constable should be empowered to authorize in writing the setting up of road checks for a limited and specified period, principally when it is believed that grave offences may be committed in a particular area at that time.

## Entry to Premises, Search and Seizure

Apart from after arrest, the warrant system should be retained. In the case of prohibited goods (stolen goods, drugs, firearms) warrants should be issued on the basis of reasonable suspicion by magistrates but in urgent cases uniformed police superintendents should now be enabled to authorize this.

A new power should be introduced to allow the search of premises (other than those occupied by the arrested suspect) for evidence relating to 'grave' offences. A circuit judge would be the authority here.

## Prosecution

A Crown prosecution service should be established by statute. Each police area should have a Crown Prosecutor's department, independent of the police but answerable to a joint police and prosecutions authority for the area. It would conduct all cases after the decision to proceed; decide whether to proceed after charge; advise the police on prosecution; provide advocates in the magistrates' courts and brief counsel.

Those who say that the Commission simply gave in to police demands are overstating their case. It did, after all, reject a number of items on the McNee 'shopping-list' such as the seventy-two-hour detention, general powers to detain witnesses, abolition of the right to silence, and general warrants to search for evidence. In many respects, however, the Commission did base its recommendations on a set of assumptions that had been successfully promoted by the Metropolitan Police since the days of Sir Robert Mark. In looking, for example, at some of the reasoning and recommendations, we will see that the language of the Commission reflected a 'police view' that saw suspects as guilty and viewed the primary objective of criminal procedure as the securing of evidence fit to convict. One example makes this point: in speaking of an officer who 'actually sees' someone committing an offence (para 3.86) nothing evidently was thought problematic about leaving out such a word as 'allegedly' and in speaking of 'the offence he has committed'. Such a starting point made relaxing the standards of evidence that bit easier.

Instead of going through the RCCP recommendations one by one, these may be dealt with more succinctly by looking at the hallmarks of the report. The first of these, is the emphasis placed on balancing extensions of police power with protections for the individual (para 2.18–24). The Commission shouts many a liberty from the rooftop but in nearly all cases there is a police discretion that undermines the rhetoric; it speaks of safeguards 'which offer the possibility of . . . immediate challenge and subsequent review' (para 3.4) but the realities of such challenge and review are given little attention. In the case of the freedom from unjustified arrest or detention, protection is offered by the requirement of 'reasonable suspicion' (as in stop and search). How one might challenge lack of reasonable suspicion is not explained – Lord Devlin is even quoted in the Hussien case (para 3.67) as stating that this may 'take into account matters that could not be put into evidence at all'. (Wouldn't this protect a policeman detaining on hunch?) A second protection, however, is provided by 'the necessity principle' which restricts detention following arrest. Unfortunately for suspects this principle is so broad that it justifies detention on the basis of 'the need to secure evidence' or to question. (When, we might ask, would this test be failed?) In similar vein the right to legal advice when in custody is limited by a police discretion to refuse this in 'grave' cases where evidence or witnesses might be interfered with and the right to have intimation of arrest sent to someone could be denied by the police if 'not in the interests of the investigation or the prevention of crime'. As Doreen McBarnet has commented:

> while the safeguards tend to be left at the level of principle, both the police powers that the safeguards limit and the promises that limit the safeguards are etched in fine detail. Why is it that police powers have to be proved workable but safeguards not?[17]

The one-sidedness of a report that places trust in police integrity instead of outlining detailed protections is another feature of the RCCP. In providing for the enforcement of the code of practice that was to replace the Judges' Rules, the Commission could do no more than rely on police discipline and supervision or else the Everest of a civil action.[18] Sir Henry Fisher had already found that (in spite of disciplinary procedures applying to their breach) the Judges' Rules were routinely ignored by the police – why should the RCCP expect the code of practice to be observed to any greater extent?

It is unnecessary to list here all those other points at which protections proposed by the Commission are either made subject to conditions or are reliant on matters within police control such as recording or discipline. The extent to which confidence in systems of internal review allows the Commission both to endorse existing practices and to lead the retreat of law is perhaps best illustrated by one further example. In its proposals on police questioning the Commission rejects the voluntariness test, advocates placing all evidence before the jury, no matter how unfairly obtained (provided torture etc. was not used), urges reliance on the code of practice sanctioned by discipline not law and, apparently as *protection for individuals*, states:

> In addition, police training on interviewing should be developed in ways which will not only improve their interview techniques but also bring home to them the powerful psychological forces that are to play upon the suspect and the dangers that are attendant upon these.[19]

When dealing with a force that can be trusted to this extent, one is tempted to think that there is little need for legal rules to govern police activity.

Whenever there is a balance between extending a power and securing protection the Commission tends to favour the former. In dealing with the need for powers of stop and search (para 3.17) the report states that those who have committed property offences and have articles in their possession 'should not be entirely protected from the possibility of being searched'. If we swallow the image of the suspect as the guilty person seeking shelter behind legal technicalities then it is easy to minimize safeguards. A real point was missed – whether those who have not committed such offences should be protected from interference.

In other assumptions, the RCCP further implies the guilt of the suspect. A feature of the report is the emphasis to be placed on the 'grave' offence.[20] The more serious a crime is then the more imperative it is, in RCCP eyes, to sacrifice the rights of citizens – such rights are seen as impediments to conviction. The opposing argument – that the more serious an offence the more an individual should be protected – is somehow omitted. (The danger that relaxation of standards may increase the risks not only of wrongful conviction but of the genuinely guilty thereby escaping is also forgotten.) The game is given away at paragraph 3.5 of the report where the seriousness of the offence is considered in relation to the exercise of powers that, it is admitted, would normally be unacceptable:

> In assessing whether such powers should be available and the special safeguards to be applied to them if they are, we concluded that account must be taken of the effectiveness of the power in investigating the offence concerned and the importance that society places upon bringing those suspected of it to trial. The seriousness of the offence is, accordingly, a critical consideration.

What might be called the 'argument from exception' is another RCCP hallmark. This principle holds, first, that the police cannot be asked to act illegally. It follows that if examples can be found of circumstances in which *guilty* persons *might* escape justice because police (assuming total non-co-operation) might not have formal powers to act then we must give the police powers to cover such cases. Followers of debates on the Criminal Justice (Scotland) Bill will be familiar with examples of assaults at parties where universal non-co-operation with police is evidenced and of stabbings on trains where witnesses disappear into thin air (see also Report, para 3.91). This argument, however, fails to take into account the *cost* of giving broad powers (e.g. to search for evidence or set up road blocks): it may well be that such powers are unreviewable in courts and cause deep resentment in the community. Occasions on which the police in fact hold back from acting in an emergency are in any case rare, and since the courts will almost invariably support police action on the facts of a particular case, there is little danger that officers 'bending a rule' exceptionally will be either helpless or penalized by the courts.[21]

It is arguable then that the cost of granting extended powers to cover exceptional circumstances should seriously be questioned. This the Commission does not do. A power of compulsory search for evidence in 'grave' offences is proposed (para 3.41–2) to cover 'rare circumstances'. An absolute time limit on detention is rejected with an eye to exceptional cases (para 3.100) and the power of temporary detention (paras 3.91–3) is advocated to cover exceptions in spite of strong arguments that such cases would be the very ones in which public co-operation would provide the basis for the most successful policing. The end products of such reasoning are proposals of a breadth unacceptable to many people, including at least one Chief Constable.[22]

It should also be noted that the argument by exception does not work for safeguards in the way that it does for powers. It is a ground for *refusing* to provide protection if that need arises in remotely exceptional circumstances. Thus a basis for rejecting the rule excluding improperly obtained evidence from court is that it would only help 'the small proportion of cases' that reach trial.[23] The conclusion that it is in those very cases that the necessity for protection is most acute escapes the Commission.

If the RCCP was to be marked out from the other Royal Commissions its claim was to have been the one that 'did its homework'.[24] In its attempts to construct a 'firm factual base' the

Commission expended £1,189,800 and produced a report that, with its twelve research documents, cost potential readers £57.60. Quantity of research was not, however, to guarantee quality of reasoning, the correctness of deductions ensuing, or that an appropriate perspective or depth of analysis was achieved. As has been noted already, the RCCP research was considered against the background of police operational needs, it was organized by Home Office personnel and its data were heavily dependent on police sources. Nor, as has been pointed out by two RCCP researchers, Michael McConville and John Baldwin[25] was the work of uniform quality. The deadlines imposed by the Commission's timetable meant that researchers were asked to produce instant answers on problems defined (narrowly) in advance by the Commission. Key areas of pre-trial procedure were not investigated, much academic work was ignored and even government experiments, such as on Scottish tape-recording, were passed over. How the police actually work on the ground was evidently to be discovered by asking the police themselves rather than seeking any balancing views 'from those with first-hand experience on the receiving end'.[26] Although the RCCP placed great weight on police discipline and internal review, no research was done on the efficiency of these either as means of ensuring compliance with the rules or as remedies in the case of breach. No evidence was produced to show that the recording of reasons for arrest, search, interrogation or refusal of access to a solicitor would act as effective protections in practice. (Indeed, much prior research, including the Fisher Report on Confait indicated that such procedures would be ignored.) The Commission's ideas on extending police powers were set out in detail but as a consequence of its research programme these were matched with only vague notions as to the social costs of extended powers and the effectiveness of safeguards.

What research was done was curiously lacking a critical edge. McConville and Baldwin have commented that:

Almost nothing beyond straightforward description is attempted . . . As a consequence, disturbing findings are often underplayed and inconsistencies not explained. By and large the research is better described as neutered than as neutral.[27]

In moving from research to conclusions the Commission is also suspect; not least so on the two key topics of the voluntariness test (i.e. the rule that to be admissible in court a statement must have been made voluntarily) and the question whether to exclude as evidence material obtained in breach of the code of practice. On voluntariness, as we saw in Chapter 5, the existing law was in a mess. In some cases mere advice ruled out the admissibility of statements, in others quite severe police activity was allowed to pass. The RCCP dealt with this subject largely on the basis of research done by Barrie Irving. In some respects Irving's work confirmed the views of Lord Cooper in Chalmers as to the frightening nature of the police station interview: Irving found that, in the RCCP's words, 'in psychological terms custody in itself and questioning in custody develop forces upon many suspects which . . . so affect their minds that their wills crumble' (para 4.73). There were cases even falling short of conditions that the law would call 'oppressive' in which Irving said voluntariness was ruled out. Irving concluded, therefore, that the legal and psychological concepts of voluntariness did not match.[28]

This was startling; oppression was much more deep rooted than had been thought. The RCCP's deduction however was *not to tighten up* protections for those questioned in custody, it was to abandon the 'voluntariness' test, advocate better police training in interrogation and put all statements before the jury and magistrates for their consideration. (Such logic seems like resuming chain smoking on finding out that one's lungs were more delicate than originally thought.)

More brutally wayward was the reasoning on the use of an exclusionary rule. The RCCP relied on an American study by Dallin Oaks[29] to argue that excluding evidence did not work to deter police from malpractice in dealing with suspects. On reading the Oaks study, however, it is found that he looked not at suspects in custody but at search and seizure. These, as Oaks says, raise very different issues. On *reliability* of evidence, for example, search and seizure produces solid physical evidence (guns, knives, etc.) whereas a confession that results from oppression may be wholly unreliable – the reasons for excluding the latter are clearly stronger. A second difference is in police motivation. Oaks shows that the exclusionary rule will not deter police malpractice in

searches as there are good reasons for this activity that are unrelated to the production of useful courtroom evidence (e.g. searches
to confiscate narcotics, or weapons, or to recover stolen goods or as
summary punishment). Oaks *himself* argues that where activity is
directed towards producing valid evidence (e.g. the interrogation
of suspects) police conduct is 'likely to be responsive' to rules on
admissibility.[30] In short, the Commission used Oaks's work to
prove a point that the research itself contradicted. Those who grant
the RCCP an authority in proportion to the amount of research it
ordered might therefore take heed of McConville and Baldwin's
warning, that the primary role of RCCP research was to 'provide a
cloak of respectability for a series of highly contentious proposals'.

One accomplishment that the RCCP would have been glad to
have seen called one of its hallmarks would have been its clarification of the law. If, however, we look at the difficult areas in
pre-RCCP law we find that little is done by the RCCP to aid
clarification. The slippery concept of 'reasonable suspicion' is not
clarified; instead it is relied upon more heavily in providing the
basis for extended arrest and search powers. The 'voluntariness'
test is not further defined but, as we have seen, replaced by trust in
police training. The RCCP's characteristic way of 'clarifying' the
law is exemplified in its approach to arrests without warrant and
searches: where present powers apply to a complex set of instances
it is easiest to simplify the law by generalizing that power, and
removing what existing rights remain. The RCCP aims at open-
ness, workability, precision and certainty (paras 3.17, 3.56, 4.115)
but what it ends up doing is endorsing much of existing police
practice, relying on systems of internal review that had already
been shown as protective failures and failing to clarify the rules.
The most damning criticism of the RCCP report is, however, that it
does nothing to ensure and offers no evidence to show that all its
proposed new procedures will do anything about the problems of
abuse and of people 'helping the police with their enquiries'.
Nearly all the RCCP procedures are by-passable by the sort of
voluntary 'help' that we saw in the cases of Muir and Swankie. All
the old problems recognized by the Commission are liable to
continue. Nor does the RCCP take the institutional steps that
might help to open out the investigation and so reinforce the
effectiveness of its code of procedure. A prime instance of the

RCCP's failure to look at the organizational context of its proposals was on police complaints. In Chapter 4 the Commission argues that its code of practice should replace the Judges' Rules. As far as enforcing the code is concerned, however, it rejects both the voluntariness test and the exclusionary rule in favour of police discipline. It attaches 'great importance' (para 4.119) to having a police complaints system that is credible with the public and states that such a system is necessary for confidence in police discipline. Having said that, the RCCP is happy to leave it to others to discuss details of reforming complaints and moves on to another subject. It is argued that extended powers of arrest, detention and interrogation should be conditional on creating a strengthened complaints system, but the Commission fails to deal with a central plank on which its fragile edifice of 'protections' for individuals depends. Such neglect is typical of its method.

## The Politics of the Royal Commission

When the RCCP report was published in January 1981, the daily press did not fail to notice the direction of reform advocated by a body that had supposedly set out to respond to the scandals exposed in the Confait case. The front-page stories were headlined 'Sweeping new powers' (*Daily Telegraph*); 'Wider stop and search powers recommended' (*The Times*) and 'Tough proposals on police powers' (*Guardian*). Although Sir Cyril Philips was later to say at Leicester in July 1981 that the RCCP proposals had been given a good reception, the press was not uncritical. A *Times* leader accepted that an impressive report had succeeded in bringing rationality to the laws on police powers but cautioned that 'its recommendations require that society place a level of confidence in police behaviour, and in their commitment to the laws and rules laid down, that cannot be taken for granted'.[31] The *Guardian* leader 'Tilting the scale against innocence!' was critical of allowing continued twenty-four hour periods of detention on the say of a magistrate, and of giving the police a discretion to refuse access to a solicitor to those in custody. 'Even more serious', in *Guardian* eyes, was the RCCP's failure to provide an effective sanction for its code of practice and its extending arrest powers. It regretted that the two commissioners who were most unhappy with the report, Mr Jack Jones and Canon Wilfred Wood had signed the report rather than issue a minority report.[32]

The civil libertarian groups were highly critical of the report. Harriet Harman, in the *New Statesman*, said that in the light of the Fisher revelations of how the police had ignored the Judges' Rules, it was 'incredible' that the RCCP should have suggested leaving the regulation of interrogation to police discipline alone. She attacked the use of prolonged detention, especially in relation to the undefined 'grave' offences allowing twenty-four-hour extensions. It was 'cowardice' on the RCCP's part not to make the code of practice statutory. Police abuse of the rules, she said, would expose them to nothing more than the minimal risk of civil action. The NCCL was shocked that no suggestion was made that increased powers should be conditional on a better complaints system. The 'central absurdity' of the report, Harman said, was its balancing the rights of suspects and those of the community:

> No such conflict exists. If a suspect makes a false confession the individual suffers unfair punishment, and society loses, as in the Confait case, because the true offender goes free . . . No attempt is made to show that greater police freedom to arrest and detain will actually increase the accuracy and efficiency of detention and prosecution.[33]

Such points were not exclusive to radical liberals. Two days later, for instance, Antony Whitaker, legal manager of Times Newspapers, wrote in *The Sunday Times* in terms highly critical of the RCCP proposals to increase powers of arrest and detention without effective sanctions. He warned that the distinction between a policed state and a police state: 'is becoming blurred when the quest for power is motivated more by the sheer appetite for it than by the social need for its exercise'.

Dissent from within the RCCP came very much from the two members already mentioned, Canon Wilfred Wood and Jack Jones. The latter felt that those arguing for extended police powers failed to appreciate the acute social problem of deprived areas.[34] He was 'totally opposed' to removing magisterial oversight of the police in issuing warrants for arrest and in authorizing fingerprinting. It was 'potentially explosive', Mr Jones said, to give a power to arrest for refusal to provide a name and address for committing *any* alleged offence and added that supervision of suspects' rights by senior police officers was insufficient. Jones and Wood thought, in general, that the response to the abuse of power should not be to extend power and 'regularize' the existing position: instead all increases in power had to be justified and scrutinized.

These dissidents signed the report, however, and may be taken generally to favour its implementation. On this point, the NCCL position was to oppose action. It was feared lest the 'law and order' lobby in the Thatcher Government started to select from the RCCP package in the way that had happened in Scotland. It was peculiar that some of the most vigorous defenders of the RCCP package came not from the known political right but from the middle-ground liberals. Walter Merricks, member of the RCCP and former director of Camden Community Law Centre, wrote many articles and letters defending the Commission. He argued that increased powers were matched by better safeguards and that civil libertarians should press the Conservative-run Home Office for implementation. This line was also taken by the *Guardian*'s influential legal correspondent, Professor Michael Zander who noted[35] that the report had been 'comprehensively savaged' by the NCCL, the Legal Action Group, the Law Centres Federation and the Haldane Society. He said, however, that the report was a major step towards better safeguards. He instanced the recommendation that the police record what transpired, for example, on stop searches. This would both aid internal police reviews and influence police behaviour. Tape-recording was also a help, he said, and civil libertarians should welcome the time-limiting of detention. Zander pointed out that if a suspect was told of the right to a solicitor and waived this, that fact would be recorded by signing the custody sheet. As for the exclusionary rule, Zander thought this a weak protection in any case. He concluded by condemning the 'left-wing knee-jerk reaction to the report, virtually dismissing it out of hand'. It was, he thought, 'childish' to expect new safeguards without more police powers and repeatedly advocated implementation.

It was at this time, that the RCCP was dubbed 'The Commission that did its homework'[36] by Malcolm Dean, who, appearing to have temporarily misplaced his critical faculty, argued that the RCCP deserved many more friends than it had got because it had 'vindicated the commission process'. He stressed the amount of work and research done by the RCCP and, as if thinking that this ensured sound proposals, suggested that the RCCP had offered a worthwhile bridge between two opposing standpoints. His viewpoint evidently was not shared by the Labour Party, whose spokesman Robert Kilroy-Silk MP had just announced the creation of a Labour Campaign for Criminal Justice that was, because of the RCCP's neglect of protections, to attempt to stop the proposals becoming law. Tony Gifford, of the Legal Action Group, was also opposed, calling the report 'a cop-out'.[37] He stated that Zander and Dean had failed to understand the realities of police behaviour on the street, of the fear generated even with existing powers, of the hopelessness of obtaining redress from courts and of the tide of ill-feeling running between police and public. In the case of nearly all the new powers – stop and search, detention, to block roads and to take 'body samples' by force – the RCCP resorted only to protections that had been shown not to work. Gifford said that the Chairman of the Bar ('no left-wing knee-jerker') had also refused to accept that the police disciplinary code was an appropriate safeguard for breaches of the rules. He concluded that the RCCP proposals would continue to be opposed across the political spectrum by those who, while concerned about crime, would resist proposals to extend further the control of police over all our lives.

It was in those terms, therefore, that the RCCP was received in the press. As in the days of the 11th Report of the CLRC there were two sides of the debate without much middle ground. The Police Federation's monthly magazine seemed satisfied, stating 'Commission's views come close to Federation evidence'[38], but, in the academic world contributions to the debate in the *Criminal Law Review*[39] and in *Public Law*[40], expressed reservations about the emphasis placed on the police regulating their own investigative methods. Professor Bernard Smythe, in *Public Law*, warned lest the courting of public confidence be neglected in favour of faith in the police: 'Sufficient cynicism can itself destroy any system which is too dependent on trust.' Others said that the RCCP had failed, because of its 'blinkered approach', to clarify the law at all; that

Commissioners' faith in the police was 'touching in its naïvety' and that it lacked 'a coherent theoretical framework'. The progressive element in the police force also found some RCCP proposals too extreme. Although he praised its work in general, John Alderson took the opportunity of the Leicester Conference in July 1981 to argue against powers based on general 'reasonable suspicion' as opposed to suspicion of a particular offence. He pointed out that, in relation to the proposed stop and search powers the new 'stringent' safeguards were already 'current practices in London'. He did not like the power of temporary detention in the vicinity of a 'grave' incident, arguing that use of such powers 'may diminish the persuasive demeanour of the police' and said that it was better to seek voluntary public help than to use such powers. Similarly, Mr Alderson opposed the RCCP proposals to change the age limit for fingerprinting from fourteen to ten. He found the thought of submitting young children to this procedure 'repugnant'.

## Conclusions: A Commission for Poor Law

The RCCP set out to satisfy three standards in arrangements for investigation: 'Are they fair? Are they open? Are they workable?' (Report, para 2.18). It did so acknowledging that previous debates (e.g. on the right to silence) had involved no meeting of minds between opposing groups. Its members succeeded largely in reconciling opposition amongst themselves, and relying on their 'factual base', proposed powers that they emphasized were workable.

Where the RCCP failed, however, was in its perspective. In spite of all its research the Commission failed to come up with a balance of powers and protections that would work in practice. In its one-sidedness the RCCP understood the interests of the force in many respects but, it failed to ask 'What kind of police force do we want?' It failed to absorb and act on the knowledge we have of how social and organizational factors affect police use of their powers. Without considering these matters it would have been well-nigh impossible to have come up with powers and protections that would have reconciled police needs with the requirements of public acceptability. It was especially in respect of the need to build the protection of public confidence into a system of police powers that the Commission failed; this was in spite of its own research having informed it of the enormous extent to which both uncovering and solving crimes depended on public support and co-operation.[41] That the RCCP has made proposals on police powers without discussing, for instance, the implications for different styles of policing, or the use of criminal intelligence or complaints and disciplinary systems, demonstrates a belief similar to that found in Thomson[42] – that it is possible in some way to divorce legal powers and controls from their social and organizational context.

To some extent criticism of the RCCP proposals from the libertarian lawyer's perspective adopted above involves a narrowness that reflects the report. What this chapter has not discussed is the wider context, whether, for instance, the extent of police powers is a far less important question than the nature of the policing employed in Britain (a topic that will be returned to below). It may therefore be unwise to become as involved in the minutiae of balancing powers against protections that we lose sight of the need to broaden the debate itself. McConville and Baldwin again:

> The primary objection [to the RCCP proposals] is not that police decisions would be unreviewed or unregulated (though in practical terms they would be both) but that the powers are of their nature unreviewable and uncontrollable.[43]

It is by its narrowness of view that the RCCP has a tendency to lead the reader astray: with its broad powers of arrest, search and detention and its vague protections ('reasonable suspicion'; 'interests of the investigation'; 'necessity principle') we are driven to a stage where the role of law is diminished and all faith is placed in police integrity. The move away from law, however, involves obligations that are unfulfilled by the RCCP. If we really are to rely less on legal controls then we have to ask not merely what will be the role of police in society but what are the other kinds of rule or control that will replace legal norms. If we are to look to such matters as internal accountability, organizational pressure, social review or external accountability then these matters have to be investigated, researched and understood. The RCCP did not engage in such work because its terms of reference, as interpreted, were too narrow. It is in moving away from legal regulation and in

failing to substitute other kinds that the poverty of the RCCP lies.
Proponents of the Commission philosophy will undoubtedly claim that legislation as proposed would in practice tighten up controls on the police. What they fail to recognize, however, is that to adopt such a strategy is only to confirm the drift away from policing by consent. The fact that the Commission did not consider recent developments in 'fire-brigade' and pre-emptive policing not only demonstrates the inadequacy of its research but further emphasizes its fundamentally legalistic attitude, one in which the essentially collective nature of police work is neglected and problems of accountability are left unresolved.

Since the Commission reported Britain has experienced the street disturbances of 1981. Such events have redefined the parameters of the debate and demand that policing is placed squarely in its social and political context. The costs of ignoring public co-operation and consent and their centrality for policing have been only too clearly and painfully demonstrated.

## Further Reading

Fisher, Sir H., *Report of an Inquiry into the Circumstances leading to the Trial of Three Persons on Charges arising out of the Death of Maxwell Confait*, HMSO, London, 1977.

Oaks, D., 'Studying the Exclusionary Rule in Search and Seizure', *University of Chicago Law Review*, 37:4, 1970, p.665.

Price, C. and Caplan, J., *The Confait Confessions*, Marion Boyars, London, 1977.

Royal Commission on Criminal Procedure: Report (Chairman: Sir Cyril Phillips), Cmnd. 8092, HMSO, London, 1981.

Royal Commission on Criminal Procedure: *The Investigation and Prosecution of Offences in England and Wales: the Law and Procedure*, Cmnd. 8092–1, HMSO, London, 1981.

Royal Commission on Criminal Procedure Research Series:

No. 1: Barrie Irving and Linden Hilgendorf, *Police Interrogation: The Psychological Approach*, HMSO, London.

No. 2: Barrie Irving with the assistance of Linden Hilgendorf, *Police Interrogation: A Case Study of Current Practice*, HMSO, London.

No. 3: Pauline Morris, *Police Interrogation*, HMSO, London.

No. 4: Paul Softley, with the assistance of David Brown, Bob Forde, George Mair and David Moxon, *Police Interrogation: An Observational Study in Four Police Stations*, HMSO, London.

No. 5: John Baldwin and Michael McConville, *Confessions in Crown Court Trials*, HMSO, London.

No. 6: Julie Vennard and Keith Williams, *Contested Trials in Magistrates' Courts: The Case for the Prosecution*, HMSO, London.

No. 7: David Steer, *Uncovering Crime: The Police Role*, HMSO, London.

No. 8: J. A. Barnes and N. Webster, *Police Interrogation: Tape Recording*, HMSO, London.

No. 9: P. Gemmill and R. F. M. Morgan-Giles, *Arrest, Charge and Summons: Current Practice and Resource Implications*, HMSO, London.

No. 10: K. W. Lidstone, Russell Hogg and Frank Sutcliffe in collaboration with A. F. Bottoms and Monica A. Walker, *Prosecutions by Private Individuals and Non-Police Agencies*, HMSO, London.

No. 11: Mollie Weatheritt in collaboration with Joan MacNaughton, *The Prosecution System: Survey of Prosecuting Solicitors' Departments*, HMSO, London.

No. 12: David R. Kaye with the assistance of R. L. Redman and G. J. Brennard, *The Prosecution System: Organisational Implications of Change*, HMSO, London.

# Community Policing and Scarman on the Riots

The kind of policing philosophy adopted by a force may be a far more important factor in the style of policing seen on the street than the extent of any formal powers possessed. This is because, although it is important to limit formal powers, these *alone* cannot dictate the sort of policing we have. Treating the law as a variable independent of policing strategies was a major error of the Royal Commission: whatever the limitations imposed on them, powers will always be considerable and open to a wide range of uses. If we first look at the main options in police style we may then consider in more detail what many people think is the modern answer to the old problems of control – community policing.

## Styles of Policing

We have examined two identifiable styles of policing: the 'fire-brigade' or reactive method (Chapter 2) and the pre-emptive strategy with its emphasis on local intelligence (Chapter 3). These may be grouped together as the developed forms of non-consensual policing. Reactive policing puts a premium on the tactical and rapid response and sees 'response time' as the yardstick of efficiency. It has relied upon developments in technology and communications within the force rather than on information and co-operation supplied by the public. This has tended to encourage a belief in police autonomy and professionalism.

The increasing resort to intelligence-gathering that typifies preemptive policing (see Chapter 3) can be seen as a response to the lack of public contact engendered by reactive policing. The two styles have a mutually reinforcing effect. As the police are distanced from the public they are led increasingly to make two assumptions: that past offenders will commit further crimes and that the police must inform themselves of those who, though having committed no offence as yet, are thought likely to do so.

The drift away from policing by consent is to be seen in the prevalence of these policing strategies. The ensuing spiral of confrontation, to which we referred in Chapter 1, has been diagramatically presented by John Lea and Jock Young with the inner city in mind:

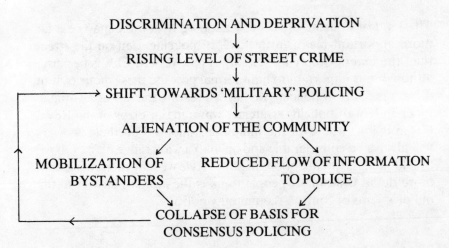

Taken from Lea and Young, 1982.

The inner-city riots of 1981 gave prominence to the problems of non-consensual policing. The easy answer, it seems, is simply 'to put the bobbies back on the beat', the ready assumption is that more police is the answer to our problems. An old response is updated by calling these 'community' officers. As we shall see, however, the philosophy of community policing is complex and involves far more than increasing manpower on the streets.

At this point, care should be taken not to confuse 'community involvement' or 'liaison' with the more comprehensive strategies of community policing. Community involvement and liaison both exist as adjuncts of reactive policing. They attempt to increase contact with the public but typically involve no readjustment of the dominant reactive and pre-emptive policies within a force. They are based on the post-war movement towards rationalization and specialization in police work as described above, they involve low levels of manpower and are organized around specific tasks. Community policing, on the other hand, actively attempts to move away from specialization towards a general re-evaluation of both policing aims and the wider role of the constable working the streets. It puts stress upon the 'pro-active' function of the police in strengthening social discipline and the 'self-policing' of a community. Further, there is stress on moving away from enforcement and the 'capture-culture' towards more informal methods of social control.

## Community Involvement and Prevention

Most police would argue that close involvement with the community is a traditional element of policing. Although juvenile liaison schemes have been operated in England since 1949, when a specialist service was set up in Liverpool, it was in Scotland in 1957 that the police first took steps towards the introduction of specialist community involvement departments. This lead in part reflected the responsiveness of a national force considerably smaller than that in England, in part it also reflected the appalling conditions of unemployment and housing that prevailed in Scotland at the time and which struck police officers as obviously 'crimogenic'.

In 1957 the Chief Constable of Greenock, David Gray, took action in the Gibshill area to set up a youth liaison scheme. He wrote to the Town Clerk stating that boys were engaged in vandalism 'not because of inherent badness' but because they were merely conforming to a communal disrespect for property, law and order. He advocated selecting an area and concentrating on it a broad range of services from police and local authority to church and teachers. Gray proposed to police the district with chosen officers who would liaise closely with all services, with children and with parents.

Specialist youth liaison in Gibshill was to broaden in character over the years but real progress had to wait until 1972 when a newly active Tenants' Association was set up. This change coincided with the instalment of a Labour council and resulted in action to redevelop the area, improve landscaping and housing and organize youth activities. In response, the police agreed to reduce the resented 'panda' patrols and to devote further staff to beat policing. This was specialist community involvement with volunteer officers aiming to cultivate good relations not merely with youths but with all the locality. Whether one believes that the prime movers behind changes in Gibshill were the police[1] or the organized members of the local community[2] there was evidence of success in the mid-1970s. A police report of September 1976 showed that crimes by Gibshill youngsters had been *halved* over the preceding year.[3]

The police, as might have been expected, experienced difficulties that flowed directly from the use of a specialist team of individuals: notably an antipathy between officers engaged in more conventional policing and those on the community project.[4] In spite of these problems however, the project demonstrated to many people the value of community involvement. In the end, its success, as far as the police were concerned, was found to depend on a factor that we should bear in mind in looking at more recent work in Devon and Cornwall – leadership by senior officers. A Strathclyde Police Working Party concluded from its researches that 'the community involvement posture adopted by senior officers is contagious and generally reflected in the attitudes of subordinates'. A recent commentator has emphasized 'without this wholehearted support from the top, any efforts at street level will fail'.[5]

Following the Greenock example, community involvement projects were set up in other areas in Scotland, e.g. at Linwood in Renfrewshire. New support for rethinking relationships between the police and especially young offenders came in the 1960s with progressive legislation. Following the report of the Kilbrandon Commission in 1964 with its new proposals for young offenders, and after a White Paper on 'Social Work and the Community' in

1966 the Social Work (Scotland) Act was passed in July 1968. For the police this was significant in integrating all social services into one department in the local authority and, transitional hitches apart, in facilitating co-ordination.

A major change came in 1971 when Part III of the Act was implemented so as to remove child offenders from the criminal justice system and replace juvenile courts with children's panels. Space here does not allow description of the panels; it suffices to state that the prime factor in their decisions was the welfare of the child rather than any notions of punishment or retribution. For the police, the panel system involved a process of adjustment. An inter-departmental working party reviewed police procedures in relation to children and advocated, among other things, closer co-ordination between police and other social services and a new way of handling child offenders to reflect the philosophy of welfare, not punishment. The Scottish Home and Health Department responded in 1971 by issuing a circular to Chief Constables calling for more progress in and rationalization of community-related policing. It recommended the creation of 'community involvement branches' comprising 2 per cent of each force who were, among other things, to liaise with social work departments (not merely in relation to juveniles but also on all social welfare matters); to organize crime prevention, foster community involvement by area constables and to arrange communications with youth associations, clubs and schools.

Since the 1971 circular, all Scottish forces have responded by creating departments under such titles as 'Liaison Department' or 'Community Involvement Branch'. These moves, however, have been treated merely as adjustments in the development of unit beat policing.[6] Research by the Scottish Office in 1980[7] shows that there have been no radical changes in policing methods; nor have changes been across the board. The 1980 report stated of newly created community departments that 'the existence of such separate branches inevitably encouraged many officers to evade or neglect their own responsibilities in this respect, and to regard the development of relationships in the community as a matter for the specialists'. Far from modifying the 'capture-culture' it seems then that specialist community involvement reinforced it.

The Scottish Office found that most Chief Constables saw

community work as peripheral to mainstream policing and a look at the resources devoted to the task reveals a muted enthusiasm. In only one force out of eight was the recommended 2 per cent figure met. Those therefore who think that Scotland's capital has been or is 'community policed' might be shocked to read the Scottish Office figures: Lothian and Borders police out of a total strength in 1980 of 2,342, employed twenty-eight community involvement officers (1.21 per cent) on a special budget of £600 per annum[8] with no separate community involvement officers in the four Edinburgh divisions of the force.[9] Even after the 1981 riots and, in anticipation of the Scarman Report, Lothian and Borders only proposed to increase their number of community involvement officers to forty-seven (or 1.99 per cent of the force).[10]

Not only has the complement devoted to such work been small and specialist, but a narrow conception of community involvement has prevailed. The Scottish Office discovered that in all Scottish forces physical crime prevention accounted for much 'community work', the 1980 report said that 'in the eyes of policemen and outside agencies, the credibility of community involvement . . . is enhanced by virtue of its association with the tangible matter of locks, bolts, bars and alarms'.[11]

In England progress has been even slower. As early as 1962 the Royal Commission on the Police looked in detail at community relations and stressed that the police 'cannot successfully carry out their task of maintaining law and order without the support and confidence of the people' (para. 326). Suggestions were made on how relations could be furthered (e.g. by putting enough men on beat duties and by residence within the working area) but positive action was not taken. England, furthermore, has yet to match the Social Work (Scotland) Act of 1968. In 1965 the Ingleby Committee was followed by a White Paper on 'The Child, the Family and the Young Offender' but no change was made from the judicial to the welfare model of dealing with young offenders. The Children and Young Persons Act (1969) still retained the juvenile courts system. As for the police they were largely left out of English deliberations on young offenders and did not receive the community impetus that had been supplied in Scotland by the 1971 circular. Apart from sporadic attempts to set up juvenile liaison schemes, such as the Metropolitan Police Juvenile Bureau of 1968, and occasional experiments with extra beat officers as in South Yorkshire and Sussex, English forces had to wait until 1976 until positive proposals for bringing the police closer to the community emerged. When they did, however, they aimed not at 'community involvement' but at comprehensive 'community policing'.

## Community Policing in Devon and Cornwall

John Alderson has long been a progressive thinker in a police hierarchy comprised, especially at the highest levels, of conservative men. A former barrister and Commandant of the Police Staff College at Bramshill he was an Assistant Commissioner at New Scotland Yard in the early 1970s when he made a mark as a theorist of community policing. The style of policing he espoused, however, seems not to have endeared him to the then Commissioner – Alderson recently described how he came to move west:

I rather suspected that Robert Mark thought it wouldn't be a good thing to have too many reformers at the Yard. It's a very tight-knit little community, and the Commissioner likes a degree of harmony . . . So he kindly suggested one day that I apply for Devon and Cornwall – which I wasn't particularly interested in . . . I was thinking very much of continuing in the Met. But eventually I applied and was appointed.[12]

The new exile's philosophy was soon made clear. Alderson feared that the police, as they were going about things, could not control crime. They did not have the resources, and even if they did, he said that reactive policing was not the effective method of control. He emphasized that the level of crime depended not so much on the effectiveness of the Home Office or police but on the agencies controlling such matters as housing, employment, planning and education.

His new policing depended on activating the good in society by police initiative:

Unlike reactive policing and to some extent preventive policing, pro-active policing envisages a more pervasive effect. It seeks to reinforce social discipline and mutual trust in communities, whilst having due regard for legal discipline. Although it makes heavy demands on police leadership, it strives to activate all possible resources in support of the common good.[13]

Why police leadership? Alderson believed that 'with their unrivalled knowledge of crime and social awareness'[14] they were ideally placed to lead. As for the common good, this was assumed to be in some way identifiable; the model thus was not of policing a society of plural, conflicting interests but one in which there was a consensus. He said of democratic community policing:

It would exist in its purest form where all the elements in a community, both official and unofficial, would conceive of the common good and combine to produce a social climate and an environment conducive to good order and the happiness of all those living within it.[15]

Before looking at how the Alderson philosophy was put into action it is important at this stage to see how his new policing style was supposed to differ from previous experiments. Alderson himself considered this point in a letter to *New Society*.[16] He replied to allegations that his policing was 'nothing new' by distinguishing his own 'community policing' from 'community involvement' schemes as seen elsewhere. There were, he said, critical differences: 'community involvement' by one or two per cent of the force, as found in Scotland, meant that community constables were alienated from the mainstream, or other 98 per cent, of officers. Such a small allocation of manpower to community activity did nothing to change cultural biases favouring traditional policing. Community policing in Devon and Cornwall, he said, constituted the mainstream police activity, it was run by a major department (preventive policing) and was commanded by a senior assistant chief constable. It was not, therefore, cut off from 'operational policing' but was its backbone. His community policing style was said to have six characteristics: it emphasized prevention; it involved localities in a dialogue on the nature of policing; it analysed crime patterns in public meetings, it put a significant proportion (25 per cent) of PCs on the beat as community constables; it maintained a major public and educational programme on community policing and it aimed to reduce fear and tension by encouraging co-operation between residents, social agencies and the police. Central to this philosophy was the rejection of specialist community relations or public relations departments within forces: the cultivation of good community relations was, in Alderson's view, a task, not for some but for every police officer.

The first practical step taken in Exeter was to set up a Crime Prevention Support Unit (CPSU) in 1976 with a remit to identify crime and community problems, to gain public support and to work out ways in which crime prevention initiatives could be taken by the police. A staff of four, headed by Chief Superintendent Colin Moore, worked out of a prefabricated hut at Exeter police headquarters. On the streets, the first move was to change from centralized policing to a devolved beat system. Exeter was divided into five sections in which, apart from the more concentrated city centre, a sergeant and twelve constables were made responsible for policing each area. Each section contained a number of resident (or community) constables who were free to choose their own hours of work.[17]

At headquarters CPSU analysed information about crime. Spot maps were compiled so that, by overlaying perspex charts, comparisons could be seen between, for example, sources of crime and facilities for recreation. More importantly, this allowed the display of such information at public meetings where communities would be 'confronted' with their crime problems. A first activity the CPSU engaged in was football; they put on track-suits and organized games in the summer holidays. A gratifying decrease in juvenile crime followed the experiment. Others were tried: CPSU did a publicity campaign, ran competitions and explored initiatives on recreation in particular. The Exeter Youth and Community Officer was approached and arranged a meeting involving the police, other agencies and councillors. An Action Committee was formed. While this went on, surveys were conducted of social attitudes and public meetings were set up by CPSU to discuss with residents what went on in their areas. At these meetings CPSU staff described the criminal activity of the area in question and remedies were discussed.

A feature of CPSU activity has been the leadership shown by the police. Alderson distinguishes the passive form of preventive policing (burglar alarms, locks etc.) from pro-active policing which 'reaches out to penetrate the community in a number of ways'.[18] In accordance with this philosophy's emphasis on police leadership it was the CPSU who took it upon themselves to organize and run public meetings. These met with good public responses but with some suspicion from other agencies. To allow better understanding CPSU arranged for officers to meet with personnel from the probation and after care and social services. As more information was collected by CPSU, the value to other agencies of close police contacts became more apparent and the youth and community services began to make use of such data.[19]

Reactions to the CPSU were mixed at first: other officers saw the work as gimmicky and as too demanding of manpower; social workers feared the police bulldozing into their patches; politicians and the public, however, seemed to welcome the new approach. The CPSU saw a need to take a further step towards better co-ordination. A list was drawn up of all persons and agencies thought potentially to influence crime, from the manager of the Job Centre, to county councillors, social service staff, magistrates and journalists. All were invited to a meeting to establish an advisory panel. After explanatory talks, a Policing Consultative Group was proposed and a steering group was set up under the head of the CPSU and comprising representatives of youth, housing, probation, education, social services, leisure, voluntary services and health. This steering group, amidst co-ordinating difficulties set out to bring different field workers together in order to increase mutual understanding. There were understandable problems arising from the demands and ambitious aims of the group but field workers did begin to meet each other regularly. Increasingly the steering group became involved in local government and the city planning officer, for instance, sought advice on housing plans.[20] Police input has not been trivial: in recent years the proposal to build a 500-home council estate was abandoned after police criticism of its lack of amenities and, in another case, small units of houses were preferred to a large Plymouth scheme. On the general running of the area, members of the consultative group began to think about how best to influence local politicians.

Moore and Brown note that after a year members of the consultative group viewed their role very differently: the police saw it as fostering 'the Anglo-Saxon concept of policing' (i.e. the responsibility of all citizens for policing); the probation service saw it as a forum for discussion; the youth and community service saw a source of shared resources and the planners had found a new advisory body. Two groups were still suspicious; the social services feared a police invasion of their territory and were reluctant to work with them; the councillors had reservations about the strength of police representation on the group and the challenge to their democratic status.

In spite of these difficulties the group has survived since shedding the steering committee. Meetings are held every three months at which officers identify problems of crime or delinquency and a working party is usually set up to recommend action. Helped by the group, relationships between the police and the social services have grown closer. Constables, for example, have been attached on a regular basis to probation officers in districts near their working area. After some initial reluctance, the social services department began to take on groups of four constables to observe work at institutions such as old people's homes, advice surgeries and mental hospitals. In return reciprocal placements were made. On such experiences Moore and Brown concluded:

> In general, all workers who had the experience of a placement became ambassadors for the host agency. Their experiences were told and retold in the canteen, on training courses and in others' work situations. This helped to change the deep-rooted prejudices which were held by the many members of their own peer work groups, and released many of the sources of frustrations with other agencies.[21]

Politically, the Devon and Cornwall police have become involved as observers, if not actors, in nearly all levels of local and county life. The community meetings organized by CPSU have served both to give the police feedback on local opinions and to bring home to residents the policing choices that have to be faced in their areas. Police officers attend council meetings and are able both to listen to points made there and to report back to the CPSU and the Chief Constable.

As to the use of CPSU research, it is freely acknowledged[22] that this has encountered mixed reaction, with some people fearing its effect to stigmatize certain areas of the city. Such information-gathering has, however, led to greater agency co-operation in Devon and Cornwall and has given the police a method of putting their views to such individuals as town planners and councillors. As for the future and more general plans, John Alderson has argued (for example to Lord Scarman in 1981) that at local government level the Police Authorities should be responsible for setting up district community police councils and neighbourhood community police councils in urban areas (in rural areas parish councils would fulfil these functions). These bodies would represent the public interest in policing and would be empowered both to make representations to the Police Authority and to observe Police Authority meetings. (In London similar arrangements would operate at the borough level.) They would, furthermore, have a say in the appointment of their local police commanders.

At a national level, Alderson's view of community policing demands that the police force is not left merely to pick up the pieces after social and economic policies have been formulated; he wants to see a forum created in which the police may advise various government departments on the policing implications of different policies. (Here again one might ask: 'Whose definition of the "common good" will be involved in describing these implications?') He proposes that the four main ministries, Home Office, Environment, Employment and Health and Social Security should set up a Standing Advisory Body on Preventive Policing to co-ordinate community policies. A similar commission is suggested at the local government level. Alderson argues: 'It must be driven home to Government that public order and crime have to be approached on a broad inter-ministerial basis, not just through the Home Office.'[23]

This outline of Alderson's community policing is hopefully enough to show that if it has a claim to originality this lies in its emphasis on a comprehensive general approach throughout the force rather than as an after-thought or public relations exercise. In political terms, its striking feature is the prominence of the police part in directing social action and in setting down what is acceptable behaviour in society. If Sir Robert Mark saw the police leading 'a perplexed society' to salvation, then, similarly, there seems no doubt to whom John Alderson is referring when he says:

> Where communities exist they will be strengthened by mutual concern; where they don't exist they will be created by it. The key is leadership which is like gold. (*Communal Policing*, p. 35)

## Selling Community Policing

Although it was the present Metropolitan Commissioner, Sir David McNee, who introduced community involvement to the Strathclyde force in the mid-1970s, he, like the vast majority of the Association of Chief Police Officers (ACPO) has consistently rejected the Alderson notion of comprehensive community policing. Instead ACPO leaders have emphasized specialist liaison and, in effect, adjustments to the non-consensual forms of policing that were described in Chapters 2 and 3. This point emerged clearly from replies to Alderson's evidence at the Scarman Inquiry. In September 1981 ACPO outgoing president, George Terry, Chief Constable of Sussex said:

> Mr Alderson polices a pleasant part of England . . . the philosophy in that environment is quite different from inner city areas . . . the British Police can deal with any situation where there is a challenge.[24]

Nor are the two competing philosophies always compatible; Moore and Brown[25] describe how the Police Federation's orchestration of the hard-line 'law and order' campaign of 1976 affected Exeter community policity. Senior officers, they say, were encouraged to criticize 'do-gooders' and 'namby-pamby social workers' with the result that prejudices were confirmed and both social workers and police were hindered in their jobs. The propaganda of capture, it seems, was not conducive to consensual policing.

Such has been the resistance of senior officers to the community

style that one of its notable proponents was induced to throw in the
towel. In early October 1981, Superintendent David Webb, who
had spent four and a half years transforming the Handsworth
division in the West Midlands into a prime example of community
policing, annouced that he was to retire from the force twelve years
prematurely. He argued that, although polite interest was shown
by senior officers in his ideas, they in turn rejected and scorned
them:

> The way to the top is not by doing what I'm doing . . . They say
> what a good job we're doing, but when they go back they don't
> want to get involved in that scene themselves. You have to be
> available on the phone 24 hours a day and give up some of your
> weekends. (*Observer*, 18 October 1981)

Where the top man is the radical then success is more likely.
Soon after Alderson first went to Exeter, a Police Federation
deputation came to him to complain that he was misdirecting
resources to community work that should be applied to real
policing on the streets. Within eighteen months, however, another
deputation from rank-and-file constables came to him to offer full
support for his policies. Alderson has recounted: 'If I had any
problems, they said, it was with the senior men. The constables
split off to identify with me . . . so there was more identification
with my ideas from top to bottom than there was through the staff
chain of command.' The problem of selling community policing to
officers is a matter we will return to below; as for convincing the
Government, the Chief Constables and the public, a real
opportunity to do this followed the 1981 street troubles with
publication of the Scarman Report.

## Disturbances and Lord Scarman

What could not be doubted in 1981 was the extent of disquiet; a
year after one hundred persons were arrested and forty-nine police
injured at St Paul's, Bristol, following a raid on an illegal drinking
club, there came riots in Brixton in the period 9–13 April 1981 that
resulted in injuries to 279 police officers and uncounted civilians.

July was worse; on the 3rd a confrontation between white skin-heads and young Asians at Southall turned into a battle between Asians and the police that ended in 105 police and thirty civilians being injured with twenty-three arrests being made. Further north in Toxteth, Liverpool, the arrest of a youth on a motorcycle turned latent hostility between a community and the police into a massive riot that produced 250 police injuries and over 200 arrests; in other deprived and decaying areas, such as Moss Side, Manchester and Wood Green, London, simultaneous and similar events pushed injury and arrest figures even higher and were repeated in West Midland areas like Handsworth, Wolverhampton and Smethwick.

The taking to the streets of hundreds of mostly young people, jolted the authorities into action. Mrs Thatcher revised a party political broadcast on 8 July to omit references to unemployment and to call on parents to dissuade their children from breaking the law. Apparently failing to see any connection between the subject of her original speech and the troubles, she said: 'I had expected tonight to talk wholly about unemployment but events in Liverpool have changed that.'[26]

The Government considered a mass of proposals to quell the riots: laws to make parents responsible for their children; summary riot courts; army camps for temporary detention centres; limitations on the right to trial by jury; new Riot Acts; Ulster-type water cannon, and 'snatch-squads'; CS gas; armoured vehicles and plastic bullets. A leader in the *Guardian* of 15 July expressed dismay at Mrs Thatcher's unwillingness to look to root causes and said of the Home Secretary:

> Mr Whitelaw's comments seem alarming for two reasons: it means the Government is not prepared to tackle this problem at source, and it means that it is contemplating changing the fundamental nature of British policing. At present, we are policed by consent; a switch to aggressive policing could do untold damage to our society.

Amidst reports that Kenneth Oxford's Merseyside police had fired CS gas bullets into crowds with Ferret guns that were designed to pierce doors and toughened glass, a divide in the police ranks was emerging. This was made public in evidence to Lord Scarman, who had in April been asked by Mr Whitelaw to enquire into the Brixton riots, but who was considering later events also. John Alderson criticized governmental and police overreaction to the riots, he said to Scarman:

> Some seem hell-bent on sacrificing a police style which is the envy of the world just becaue of a few hours madness on the streets.[27]

He urged the need to preserve the tradition of policing *with* rather than *against* the people and, calling plastic bullets, CS gas and new detention camps 'de-humanizing', he warned that

> Once we start tooling up to declare war on the public, the policemen become the unwilling victims of violence.[28]

Other policemen took a very different line, Kenneth Oxford defended his use of CS gas in Toxteth and Mr Jim Jardine of the Police Federation accused Alderson of being irresponsible and out of touch. Sussex Chief Constable, George Terry, the ACPO chairman emphasized that Alderson did not speak on behalf of the association, but, two days later, chief officers at ACPO's annual conference said that they did favour using PCs on the beat rather than solely reactive policing methods. New ACPO vice-president, Kenneth Oxford, claimed that shortage of manpower had forced Merseyside into 'fire-brigade' policing and predictably George Terry warned that a doubling of manpower would be necessary if we were to return to the policing standards of years gone by.[29]

When Lord Scarman reported in November 1981, he dealt in some detail with conditions existing in the Brixton area and the events of 10–12 April. The people, he said, suffered from decaying housing, they felt rejected and insecure both politically and economically. The accumulation of these frustrations was no excuse for disorder, he stressed, but the riots could not be understood unless seen in the context of political, social and economic factors. There had been in Brixton, he concluded: 'a set of social conditions which create a predisposition towards violent protest'.[30]

Scarman found that, like the other disturbances, Brixton's had been triggered by minor events. On the warm Friday evening of 10 April 1981, uniformed officers had stopped a cab in an attempt to assist an injured youth. Soon, thirty to fifty people, mainly black youths, gathered and shouted to the officers to leave the youth alone. Police assistance was called for, the young man was taken to hospital but bricks and bottles had started to be thrown at the police. More police arrived to find their colleagues being stoned by a group of youths in Railton Road ('The Front Line'). Three people were arrested and six policemen injured. There was a lull before police vehicles arriving on the scene were stoned. After a period of missile throwing, the incident ended at 7.30 p.m., with a total of six arrests, six police injuries and damage to four police vehicles.

That evening twenty officers were left to patrol the area and a number of what Scarman called 'crucial police decisions' were taken. Additional officers were called into reserve in Brixton and mobile patrols were reduced. Foot patrols, however, were increased to twenty-eight officers patrolling in pairs. Most importantly the Chief Superintendents discussed whether 'Operation Swamp', an exercise aimed at street crime and involving extensive use of stop and search powers, should continue on Friday evening and Saturday. It was decided that it should.

At this time the police called in community leaders because they were worried about the circulation of rumours of brutality both to the injured youth and in dealing with crowds. The community representatives were asked to help dispel the rumours and in return expressed concern about police tactics and the number of police in their area. No mention was made by the police of 'Operation Swamp'.

On Friday's events, Lord Scarman commented that the reaction of the crowd was not planned but probably came as no surprise to the officers concerned, he said:

Distrust of police action on the streets was too common a phenomenon of life in Brixton . . . It was a spontaneous act of defiant aggression by young men who felt themselves hunted by a hostile police force.[31]

As for the decision to go ahead with 'Swamp '81' this was in Lord Scarman's view 'unwise' in the circumstances: given public feeling, it should have been discontinued.

Saturday the 11th began in fine weather and almost normally, except that instead of the usual eight officers on foot patrols in Brixton there were an extra twenty-eight officers in the area of Railton Road. The previous night had, in addition, left a residue of tension and rumour. In the early afternoon the forty-eight 'Swamp' officers assigned to Brixton started duties. Later on two young officers from the 'Swamp' squad (aged twenty and twenty-four) saw a man putting pieces of paper into his sock while sitting in a car outside the S & M Car Hire Office. Suspecting him of a drugs offence, they questioned him but he told them that, as a mini-cab driver, he usually put his money in his socks for safety. While he was being searched and bank notes were being found, a group of thirty or so mainly black youths gathered. As the hostile crowd watched and the driver objected, the officers searched the car. The crowd shouted abuse and accusations of harassment. There was a scuffle and the officers arrested a young black man who put up a struggle. By this time assistance had been requested and the crowd had grown to 150 or so.

Several police vans and a dog van arrived, missiles were thrown and a van window smashed. It was nearly 5 p.m. when senior officers arrived on the scene and they soon faced a large angry crowd who complained about police harassment and alleged that some officers had been seen wearing National Front badges.

A young black man warned the Chief Superintendent present that unless officers left the area a riot would ensue – by this time fifty or sixty officers had come to the locality in response to the calls for assistance and the crowd numbered some 200.

Before a decision could be taken, a barrage of missiles hit the police vehicles. A police car and van were set on fire. Chief Superintendent Bayling called for urgent assistance from all over the Metropolitan district and ordered a truncheon charge on the crowd. By this means, Atlantic Road was cleared but windows were now being broken in Brixton Road and looting had begun. Another crowd of about 150 formed in Leeson Road and showered oncoming officers (who at the time possessed no shields) with bricks and bottles. A vehicle was set on fire, petrol bombs were for the first time thrown at the police and assistance was called for again.

At this point a local white woman came from the crowd to warn the police that their presence was provocative and she proposed to mediate with the crowd. The Chief Superintendent in charge refused this offer and shortly afterwards both a supply of shields and a dozen SPG officers arrived. There were more cars set alight and missiles were causing heavy police casualties. In the next hour there was an almost continuous series of battles in the area, a bus was taken over by the crowd and more petrol bombs were being used. Both sides began to organize their battle formation and receive reinforcements.

At about 7 p.m. a four-man mediation team again suggested that the police leave the vicinity so as to allow the crowd to disperse but the police refused to run the risk of disturbances spreading. The crowd told the mediators their conditions for dispersal, these were: police withdrawal, an end to police harassment and the release of those arrested. Deadlock was reached and, as the crowd's attack on the police cordon continued, some officers began to fling missiles back at the mob.

At this time disorder had spread all over central Brixton with substantial looting taking place. Fire engines and ambulances coming to the scene were attacked, with resulting injuries to personnel. Devastating onslaughts were now made on premises in Railton Road with buildings set on fire and two pubs laid waste. Where fires burned in Railton Road crowd hostility was preventing the fire-brigade taking action and a cordon of sixty to seventy officers attempted to clear the way. Behind shields, they met 300 to 400 people in Railton Road and were stoned; ferocious battles continued and more police arrived continually.

By about 8.30 to 9 p.m. the police were beginning to collect together enough officers to disperse the crowd, but the route to the fires in Railton Road was not cleared without heavy casualties. Finally, as the police's pincer movement came into effect, the crowds dispersed down side streets and by 10.00–10.15 p.m. the main disorders had ended. In all, eighty-two people had been arrested, 279 police officers injured, forty-five members of the public (probably more) were injured, sixty-one private and fifty-six police vehicles damaged or destroyed and 145 premises damaged (twenty-eight by fire).

All, however, was not yet over; Sunday continued the disorders on a less intense but more widespread scale. On Sunday afternoon the police met community leaders, groups of youngsters were throwing missiles at the police and looting. Again further incidents followed police attempts at 5 p.m. to arrest a youth for obstruction and a familiar pattern of activity followed with both sides calling for reinforcements, more sporadic missile attacks and looting. As a kind of finale, the weekend came to a close with a crowd gathering outside the Brixton police station, which was protected by seventy or so officers. As Sunday ended the incidences of looting and disturbance grew less and Brixton was quiet again.

## The Scarman Findings

On the causes of the disturbances Lord Scarman ruled out conspiracy or prior organization, though once started, he said, elements of leadership did emerge.[32] He concluded that genuine riots had occurred, but:

> The evidence I have heard indicates that the disorders originated as a spontaneous crowd reaction to police action which, rightly or wrongly, the crowd believed to be harassment of black people.[33]

The disorders, Scarman said, arose from a 'complex political, social and economic situation' that was not special to Brixton; there was a strong racial element involved but these were not 'race riots'; they were triggered by police action that was common on Brixton streets but in essence the riots were 'an outburst of anger and resentment by young black people against the police'. (para. 3.110)

Turning to the police's relations with the community Lord Scarman found that a major cause of hostility by young blacks was loss of confidence in the police by significant sections of the Brixton public. The reasons for this loss of confidence included the collapse of the police liaison committee in 1979; the 'hard' policing methods adopted in Brixton (particularly the use of the SPG on the streets, use of the 'sus' law and exercise of stop and search powers); lack of consultation about police operations; distrust of the procedure for investigating complaints against the police and unlawful and, in particular, racially prejudiced conduct by some officers.

Before dealing with the principal criticisms of the police that were put to him, Lord Scarman set out two guiding principles that he said were necessary for policing a free society. The principle of 'consent and balance', derived from the philosophy of Peel, held that preservation of tranquillity and a stable state of society came before simple law enforcement:

> Inevitably there will be situations in which public interest requires the officer to test the effect of law enforcement by its likely effect upon public order. Law enforcement, involving as it must, the possibility that force may have to be used, can cause acute friction and division in a community . . . it can lead a policeman into tactics disruptive of the very fabric of society. (para. 4.51)

The second principle of 'independence and accountability' emphasized in Lord Scarman's words:

> the independence of the police, coupled with the need to ensure that the police operate not only within the law but with the support of the community as a whole. (para. 4.60)

The criticisms themselves he dealt with under six headings, an arrangement that we will follow. He came to the following conclusions:

## 1 Racial Prejudice

The direction and policies of the Metropolitan Police were not racist but such accusations were given some plausibility because of 'the ill-considered, immature and racially prejudiced actions of some officers in their dealings on the streets with young black people' (para. 4.63). Placing responsibility squarely on the *individual* rather than the organization (see Chapter 1), Scarman said that senior officers were not prejudiced but 'a few' junior officers manifested prejudice in public.

## 2 Harassment

He said (again with individual aberrations in mind):

> I do not doubt that harassment does occur. Stop and search operations in particular require courteous and carefully controlled behaviour by the police to those stopped, which I am certain was sometimes lacking. And in Brixton even one isolated instance of misconduct can foster a whole legion of rumours which rapidly become beliefs firmly held within the community. Whether justified or not, many in Brixton believe that the police routinely abuse their powers and mistreat alleged offenders. The belief here is as important as the fact. (para. 4.67)

The police could point to the complaints procedure as a remedy, said Scarman, but many people had no faith in its impartiality and efficiency and 'a significant number of people' had such little faith in it that they did not bother to make formal complaints.

## 3 Unimaginative and Inflexible Policing

The Metropolitan Police were aware of the need for good community relations but in Lambeth they had failed to gain the degree of approval and respect necessary for effectively fulfilling their functions and duties: the police had not adjusted to the problems of policing a multi-racial community. Two main factors in the breakdown of relations were the police's failure to consult the public on police operations and their 'hard policing' approach. The Lambeth commanders had not consulted community leaders (or informed their own home beat officers) before 'Swamp '81' because they saw consultation as an intrusion on their independence of judgment. This, said Scarman, was 'an error of judgment'. As for 'hard policing', involving extensive use on the streets of stop and search powers and 'saturation' exercises, this was often necessary to act, for example against 'mugging', but where a community became resentful and restless, police methods had to be reviewed: 'Operation Swamp was a serious mistake, given the tension which existed between the police and the local community' (para. 4.76). It was remarkable that the home beat officers had not been consulted on

'Operation Swamp', he said, and it seemed that the police had misconceived the place of community relations in policing. Such relations, Scarman emphasized again, 'are central, not peripheral to the police function' (para. 4.80).

## 4 Over-reaction to the Disorders

Lord Scarman again treated mistakes as exceptional: the police, he said, had not in general over-reacted although there was misconduct by some officers. The force in his view had been correct in not withdrawing on the Saturday.

## 5 Delay and Lack of Vigour in Handling the Disorders

There had been some weakness in the police's preparedness and capacity to respond firmly to street violence. The police equipment and, in particular their shields and helmets, had proved inadequate.

## 6 Failure to Act against Looting

Police delay in preventing looting had been due to their lack of resources and their inability to combat the disorders and the looting simultaneously. They were right to give priority to the former said Lord Scarman.

## The Scarman Proposals on Policing

It was clear from Scarman's 'two principles' of policing and his emphasis on both consent and the preservation of order as priorities over law enforcement that he thought changes were necessary in police methods. First steps, he proposed, would be to consider ways of increasing the number of black entrants into the police; a way to do this, he suggested, might be to provide additional training for black applicants. Efforts should be made to stop racially prejudiced people entering the police and the Home Office was to work on ways to do this. On entry to the police, he said that the length of initial training should be increased to a minimum of six months and attention given to direction in the prevention as well as

the handling of disorder. Training should also cater for an understanding of ethnically diverse sections of society and probationary
officers should be instructed in street work with ethnic minorities.
Probationers should not, however, go out alone in inner city or
racially sensitive areas. Above all, a central theme in training
should be the need for officers to secure the consent of the public.

As far as supervision of young officers was concerned Scarman
argued that, as well as being removed from sensitive areas,
attention should be given to training inspectors and sergeants in
supervising junior officers: close supervision was particularly
important in stop and search type of operations. He endorsed a
Commission for Racial Equality (CRE) suggestion that racially
prejudiced or discriminatory behaviour should be a specific offence
in the Police Discipline Code.

On methods of policing, Scarman had clearly been won over by
the community philosophy; he visited David Webb in Handsworth
three times during his inquiry[34] and had been impressed. His 'two
principles' of policing owed much to the evidence of the Chief
Constable of Avon and Somerset and clearly reflected Alderson's
words on balancing enforcement and keeping the peace:

> if in order to enforce the laws, methods are used which in
> themselves result in widespread disorder then the Queen's Peace
> has been disproportionately broken. Thus, in striving to enforce
> laws, police have to do so in a manner which would not be
> disproportionate in social damage caused by police law enforce-
> ment activity. In practice this can mean achieving enforcement
> objectives by prevention and pro-activity rather than solely by
> reaction.[35]

Policing, said Scarman, had to operate by consent in all aspects
of police work, and concern with the public's good opinion was not
something to be pushed aside into a box called 'community relations'. It was surprising that Lord Scarman continued to hold that:

> There will in my view continue to be circumstances in which it is
> appropriate – even essential – for police commanders to utilise
> stop and search operations or to deploy special units such as the
> SPG.[36]

This is the more surprising when put next to his comment:

> the evidence (para. 4.21, supra) is not clear that a street satu-
> ration operation does diminish street crime: it may well only
> drive it elsewhere. And, after the operation is ended, street
> crime returns. If, therefore, such an operation is, in the short
> term, the only direct action possible against street crime, its
> efficacy is doubtful. But in the long term the development of a
> style of policing which is designed to secure public approval and
> respect is likely to be more effective. (para 4.78)

(Why, if 'Swamp'-type of operations were so ineffective yet
offensive, did not Lord Scarman go the whole way and condemn
their use?)

In order to establish policing by consent on the streets Lord
Scarman advocated a review of the Home Beat Officer's role.
These officers he said were regarded by others as 'outside the
mainstream of operational policing', they had not been informed of
'Swamp '81' nor involved in quelling the disorders and their nick-
name 'hobby bobbies' summed up their status in their colleagues'
eyes. Scarman argued that Home Beat Officers should not be at the
bottom of the police pecking order, but at its apex. As for their
presence on the street, the public, he said, did not object to patrols
by individuals known in the community but to a sudden influx of
unknown officers.

Just as Scarman did not rule out further stop and search operations, he rejected the view that the SPG should be abolished:
there was, he thought, a need for a small mobile reserve. He
stressed, however, that a regular turn-over of officers was essential
to prevent too inward looking and self-conscious an *esprit de corps*
developing. When the SPG was used, he added, that this should be
done with discretion and after proper consultation with the
community.

On the role of community leaders, Lord Scarman had high
standards. The history of police/public relations in Brixton in
recent years had been 'a tale of failure' but the police were not
solely to blame. Local leaders, he said, had been wrong to abandon
the liaison committee in spite of past police assertions that they
alone would decide what policing should go on in the area; in spite

of aggressive SPG operations being kept secret from the committee; in spite of the arrest and questioning of committee members on a suspicion that derived solely from their possession of sheepskin coats; in spite of police refusal to give evidence to the Lambeth Council's Working Party on police/public relations and in spite of the Working Party's conclusion that the police in Lambeth acted like an army of occupation. Lord Scarman's view was that a body committed to improving relations in the community should have continued to liaise even given its deep-seated suspicion of the police. He proposed that changes be made. Most forces had community relations branches but a number of these served only as public relations exercises. The whole police force, he argued, should co-operate with the public and community involvement in the policy and operations of policing was 'perfectly feasible without undermining the independence of the police or destroying the secrecy of those operations against crime which have to be left secret'. (para. 5.56)

The way forward was via consultation and accountability and this had to be provided for in new legislation. Scarman explained:

> Under the existing law consultation is largely but not entirely an administrative matter: accountability has to be statutory. Accountability is, I have no doubt, the key to successful consultation and socially responsive policing. Exclusive reliance on 'voluntary' consultative machinery will not do, as the Brixton story illustrates. It must be backed by law. (para. 5.57)

The solution was not to change the powers of the existing Police Authorities, but to get them to set up local consultative arrangements. He said that a statutory duty should be imposed on Police Authorities and Chief Officers to set up such consultative bodies and that, within London, a statutory framework should provide for consultative groups at the borough or police district level. In terms of legal accountability he rejected proposals for a new Riot Act but argued that the complaints system ought to be reformed to restore public confidence and bring an independent element into the investigative process. In a new proposal he suggested that there be a statutory system of random checks by independent people (perhaps police committee members) of the interrogation and detention of suspects in police stations.

## Scarman in Perspective

The Scarman Report is a model of clear exposition and is written with a reserve that borders on understatement. In terms of the arguments made in this book, however, it is severely limited in scope. The report makes a number of criticisms of the police and offers recommendations for the future but there is a fundamental omission in the analysis offered. Lord Scarman fails to connect either the riots or the police failings that he lists to the *organization and styles of policing* in force in Brixton in 1981. If we read his report we find no account of the sort of policing that was practised in the area. We are not told whether it was a 'fire-brigade' service or pre-emptive or even whether a computerized command and control system was in existence. We have seen how important intelligence-gathering techniques are to police/community relations in Chapter 3 but Scarman in looking at Swamp '81 does not, for instance, examine how such operations related to police perceptions of intelligence-gathering.

Because Scarman fails to analyse police methods, he is forced to deal with policing issues in the abstract, severed from their organizational contexts. Thus he both criticizes 'hard-line' policing as alienating and he recommends closer community involvement by the police, but he does not make it clear whether he is advocating replacing 'fire-brigade' policing as the prevailing style with something else, nor does he explain how community involvement can be made compatible with the (undescribed) type of policing dominant in Brixton.

Failing to put the general strategy of the force under the spotlight, Lord Scarman leaves out notions of collective responsibility and, like the Royal Commission on Criminal Procedure, places emphasis on individuals' shortcomings. (Again this relieves any pressure to relate organizational issues to general policing philosophies and these in turn to particular events.) We see, therefore, that in Brixton racial prejudice and harassment did not flow from the police style adopted but from the lack of maturity or inexperience of a few young officers. The 'Swamp '81' operation is explained not as the product of reactive or pre-emptive policing methods but as a 'one-off' mistake and over-reaction came not from the force but from 'some officers'. Perhaps it is understatement that leads Lord Scarman astray for when he talks of policing by consent he again fails to hold the policy-makers to account. He states (p. 66) that 'the basic policy of the Metropolitan Police is to police with the consent and approval of the people' but Brixton is explained as exceptional, as a particular instance of 'a certain lack of flexibility'. Scarman does not ask whether Brixton merely exemplified the failings of certain styles of policing, by confrontation that are widespread in the Metropolitan area.

The Report is nowhere less clear than in its endorsement and simultaneous condemnation of 'hard-line' operations like 'Swamp '81'. Having failed to relate such manoeuvres to pre-emptive styles of policing, Scarman seems unable to decide whether this kind of operation serves a useful purpose or not. He might have explained the conditions that could conceivably justify such exercises, he could have recommended that they be abandoned as counter-productive but, instead, he sidestepped and stated of the decision to use 'saturation' policing methods: 'It is a situation calling for the exercise of a professional judgement.' (para. 4.75)

Perhaps if Brixton showed anything it was that professional judgment may within certain organizational structures and policing philosophies, lead to most undesirable results. It seems from Lord Scarman's 'two principles' of consensual policing that he would disagree with the Powis line of argument – that to create 'hot spots' by frequent stops and searches is a good way to police so as to reduce crime (see page 261) – but he fails to follow through by advocating a change of policy rejecting this form of policing, nor does he examine how in practice one might reform the organization and policies of Brixton policing in order to replace 'hard-line' attitudes with something else.

When reforms are considered, collective issues again disappear and the individual is highlighted. The way forward is to improve the training, supervision and monitoring of officers and to use individuals of greater maturity on the beat. When it comes to overall policy changes in policing the issues once more are left unresolved. On the one hand, Scarman seems to favour an Alderson/Webb form of community policing in so far as he advocates an (unexplored) system of local consultation and says that beat officers should be moved from the bottom of the 'police pecking-order' (by unspecified means). On the other hand, he speaks the language of community involvement by treating community work as subsidiary to a reactive policing that retains the option of SPG 'hard-line' operations and by omitting to make recommendations that would shift police culture away from reaction, pre-emption and capture (e.g. by specifying a percentage of officers to work in the community). Such vagueness is the product of a failure to get to grips with police organization and method. The major point Scarman misses is that a degree of community involvement cannot simply be 'tagged-on' to a predominantly reactive, pre-emptive and non-consensual form of policing – the whole of policing strategy and organization has to be reformed or else all his proposals amount to little.

Whether or not Lord Scarman's generalized recommendations amount to community involvement or community policing, what they did provide was a political thrust in the general direction of consensual policing. How far in that direction it is possible to go depends on the feasibility of replacing reactive or 'fire-brigade' policing with alternatives. Since liaison or community involvement involves no such radical change, it is necessary to ask whether community policing can be put into practice in an acceptable form. So far the reader of this book may have been given a somewhat utopian view of Alderson-style policing: at this point it may, therefore, be best to use the Alderson model as a means of looking more critically at one form of community policing.

In doing so, it may be helpful to summarize aspects of the types of community and reactive policing we have been concerned with above. It should of course be stressed that there is in practice no such simple division of police styles, there is a great diversity even among 'community' schemes ranging from the use of area constables, the co-ordination of police and agencies, 'team' or 'zone' policing to 'situational' policing and variations of these and others.[37] What follows, then, is based on two *models* subject in practice to variation and fusion.

| *Community Policing* | *Reactive/Pre-emptive ('hard')* *Policing* |
|---|---|
| 1. A large percentage of officers on the beat in community police work. (High status in the force) | 1. A small number of community involvement and liaison officers. (Low status within the force) |
| 2. A community perspective for the whole force. | 2. A specialist community relations branch. |
| 3. Emphasis on prevention. | 3. Reaction and 'response-time' stressed. Emphasis on criminal intelligence collection. |
| 4. Consultation and accountability at many levels. | 4. Emphasis on independence, professionalism and being left to 'do the job'. |
| 5. Political involvement and acknowledgement of political decision-making. | 5. Claim to non-political stance i.e. of merely 'applying the law'. |
| 6. Policing by consent and co-operation. | 6. Equipping properly to 'fight crime'; notions of 'professional criminals'. |
| 7. Self-policing by encouraging 'the good'. | 7. Deterrence via effective application of criminal sanctions. |
| 8. Circumscribed powers and their use limited to publicly acceptable ends. Protecting individuals with defined civil rights. | 8. Advocacy of extended police powers; wide discretions, based on trust. |

## A Critical View

Criticisms of community policing can mostly be arranged under three headings: it will not work in the cities; it is difficult to fit within police organizations; and it threatens liberties.

### i  It Won't Work in the Cities?

Representatives of ACPO and the Police Federation portrayed the Alderson evidence to Scarman as idealistic dreams that 'village' policing could be transferred from rural areas into the inner cities. Urban areas, they retort, involve higher levels of crime, ethnic mix and turnover of population, together with lower social cohesion and less opportunity for the police to exert social leadership. Michael Banton also has argued: 'In the anonymity of the city street, the factory, and the market place, the opportunities for crime are multiplied – social and geographic mobility have created relationships that cannot be governed by informal controls.'[38] The Alderson reply to this is that in cities things will be more difficult, that the police will have to work harder but that the 'village in the city' can be created just as it has been created in Exeter and Plymouth. More difficulty would be encountered in the commercial than the residential areas, it would be admitted, but, by resort to local institutions and media, the sense of social identity can be maximized. The 'most potent jolt' in this direction can come, says Alderson[39] from police crime surveys and their discussion at public meetings. (The police's 'unrivalled view of crime' means, furthermore, that it is highly important for city administrations to have access to such police information.) Surveys would identify existing communities and their remnants where sprawl has led to disintegration. They would also help to establish new communities and, through meetings, would reinforce or create a sense of identity. Alderson favours the creation of community police consultative groups via small steering committees, so as to form the start of the community. He then says: 'Having embarked on this course of social action . . . the potential for its growth and purpose is only limited by the scope of imagination.'[40]

Critics will again point to the difficulties of police leadership by fostering the common good where different communities may have different notions of what 'the good' is. What Alderson and Webb, may, however, point to is the apparent failure of 'hard-line' or 'arm's-length' policing in such areas as Toxteth and Brixton. They are able to argue that even if the 'village' is only established in limited form in the city it will lead to more effective policing than operates at present. Even forgetting prevention and assuming that the conviction process does operate as a major deterrent, they would say that it will do so more efficiently where a degree of co-operation is fostered: Alderson warns:

> if the policemen are disliked, mistrusted or even hated, people will not go to court as witnesses for police prosecutions . . . people on juries will not believe their evidence, they will not line up on identification parades, the lay magistrates will not believe the police and the whole system of criminal justice is diminished.[41]

Given that the police only come to know about a tenth of crime,[42] given the evidence that *public* response time is a primary determinant of an incident's outcome,[43] and knowing the heavy reliance that must be placed on public co-operation in detection and conviction,[44] there is some substance in this argument. Recent studies of community experiments at Highfields in Leicestershire and in Gainsborough[45] further indicate that, in the police's view, greater community involvement does lead to an increase in the flow of useful information from public to the force.

If we refer back to the above differences between the two models of policing, it is arguable that Lord Scarman, in looking specifically at difficult inner city areas of ethnic mixture, has favoured a community policing style in so far as he advocates more beat officers, better integration of these in the mainstream of operational policing, limiting new powers (e.g. as contained in new Riot Acts) and greater community consultation and accountability. It is ironic that it is in such areas as Toxteth, St Pauls and Brixton that there are fewest problems in creating a village or community identity. Some would say that it has already been shown in Toxteth and Brixton that police action is most capable of stimulating social cohesiveness: it is unfortunate, however, that this stimulus has flowed from an adverse rather than sympathetic reaction to the police. Whether limited forms of community policing will improve matters in all circumstances will be an issue to which we will return shortly.

## ii   *Community Policing Faces Organizational Hurdles?*

A first problem for nearly all community constables is the reaction of other officers. The Scottish Office study of 1980 called this a 'principal difficulty' saying:

> Over the years there has been evidence of apathy, scepticism and outright hostility, and it is clear that such attitudes will exist; on the whole . . . the position has improved . . . but the incidence of indifference, legpulling or misunderstanding is still fairly widespread.[46]

The Scottish study pointed to a number of suggested reasons for resistance to the community idea. Some officers resented it as a new 'gimmick' or, being a separate unit, as an attack on their work (did they not have concerns for the community?) and some saw it as a soft option in relation to 'real police work'[47] – 'R' Division referred to 'the family planning department' and Scarman notes the term 'hobby bobbies' in Brixton use. A comparison between community involvement work, as found in Scotland and community policing in Devon and Cornwall indicates different methods and rates of integration into the force. In Exeter the Alderson style was at first opposed by the Police Federation officers, but within a short time gained their wholehearted support. Community policing enjoyed a stronger position there for three main reasons apart from social conditions: officers were placed full-time on this form of work in numbers sufficient to influence the opinions of others; community policing was deemed to be a part of all officers' work – not a specialist activity – and it was the Chief Constable's pet concern.

This last point is important not merely in terms of the community constable's morale but also in relation to other factors. It is often stated that beat work is difficult to put into operation or to staff properly because it is boring, it is of low status and it is (as Inspector David Webb said) no way to gain the promotion that comes the way of those doing the 'real police work' of 'feeling collars'. Alderson claims that he has 'made inroads' into this problem. He argues that community policemen are not bored:

They are highly regarded in the community, they have status
these boys and they love it . . . they wouldn't give you tuppence
for going into the CID these people.[48]

On the issue of status Alderson has attempted to counter the
process of de-skilling (described in Chapter 3) by emphasizing the
expertise required for community policing:

Now the CID have had their nose put out of joint in this force
because they were originally the élite . . . and these guys know
that I don't regard them as an élite at all; the people that I have
always championed . . . are the constables on the ground. How
we have done it is because I personally have made it possible for
them to survive in the organization: they have direct access to
me.[49]

Such is this access that, especially in the early days in Exeter,
Alderson stated that there was more identification of ideas from
the top of the force directly to the constables than through the
chain of command. It is again consistent with his philosophy for
Alderson often to have communicated with his constables via the
media rather than through formal organizational structures.

The position of the beat constables in Exeter then is very different from their counterparts' in many forces in Scotland. Whereas
the former are locked into a comprehensive community approach
and have the Chief Constable as a patron, the latter are more the
relics of a declining beat system who do not fit into modern reactive
policing and who feel that they occupy a forgotten backwater.
Alderson makes clear the amount of work that a Chief Constable
must put into community policing to keep in touch with the PCs on
the ground. It has to be questioned, therefore, whether such a
system could be made to work on a sufficiently large scale to
operate in cities where personalized supervision would be more
difficult (more so under command and control systems) and
whether, operated without Alderson's drive and determination,
the community constables can be sustained and motivated. The
latter is no mean task. Community constables are so much left to
their own devices (even choosing their own work hours in the
Exeter force) that they are very difficult to control in ways other

than firing them with commitment to an ideal. Charismatic leadership may therefore work but, if this is lacking, it is hard to see how senior officers, dealing with hundreds of responses daily, can easily keep a check on their PCs on the ground by resorting to the usual chain of command or bureaucratic methods. If uncommitted, community officers may do little good in the community or even little work at all. Related to this commitment is the kind of status attributed to such officers. Unless this is high, it will prove difficult to retain officers of sufficient quality on the street. The role of a personally interested Chief Constable is again important here for there are considerable organizational pressures in police forces to seduce good PCs away from the work of the beat, leaving it in John Brown's phrase to 'green lads and old sweats'. Little can be expected from beats policed by very young officers lacking the maturity of judgment necessary for this kind of work.[50]

In looking at police organizations, the issue of resources is an all-important factor. Many Chief Constables in urban areas would argue that Alderson's model would demand enormous increases in manpower. They point to panda cars as the only way of satisfying public demands for a responsive police *service* with the resources available. Community policing, they say, would simply be too expensive.

What is clear is that a failed or half-hearted community system of policing is not only objectionable in libertarian terms (see below), it also necessarily involves the distancing of community constables from the mainstream operational officers. Such a divorce would isolate, undermine and demoralize the PCs on the beat: real community policing would be impossible and a harder form of policing would take over.

### iii   *Community Policing is Dangerous to Liberties?*

In all relationships there is a point at which closeness becomes oppressive. Critics of community-styles of policing start to worry when John Alderson talks of 'pervasive' policing that 'penetrates' society. This seems, they say, to be extending the tentacles of control too deep into the social fabric. Still more concern is expressed at the paternalistic elements in such policing. The orthodox conception is of the police neutrally applying 'the law';

they do not legislate, act politically or assume the right to direct society – that is a job for democratic institutions. Be that a trite model or not, it certainly involves moving in a different direction for Alderson to say: 'The police have a role to facilitate the progress of society . . . they always have in a sense.'[51]

In the new community policing there is a frankness that acknowledges that the police do have to make political choices. It will be pointed out that emphasizing different aspects of crime, or prosecution activity has always involved the police in politics to some extent. What demands close scrutiny, however, is the idea that the police should not so much apply the law in exerting social control but should seek to promote some 'good'.

We have seen, above, that Alderson repeatedly emphasizes self-policing by communities who are encouraged and even led by the police to further the good. He says: 'The common good is a kind of consensus . . . it is the common needs.'[52] Some would argue that this involves 'the return to some arcadian existence'[53] but Alderson is not a trite theorizer. He recognizes that:

> The concept of the common good is elusive in a society where individualism and permissiveness are established, as in Great Britain. The cultural diversity of some neighbourhoods makes the concept of the common good difficult to envisage, let alone achieve.[54]

In spite of this, however, he sees it to be a police function to define this good; not only that, but the police force is the best suited of all social organizations to provide this kind of leadership.[55] Just as other very different policemen have taken the police to represent 'common sense' or to 'discharge the communal will',[56] so Alderson also accepts this need to promote a social ideal. Many, of course, would argue vigorously that in a plural society there is a mass of conflicting interests and no 'common' good at all; what, they say, the police in fact are assuming is the right to promulgate not the law or any commonly agreed view but some personal ideas of the 'right' direction in which society should progress. They point to the dangers of unmandated police 'crusades'.

If this argument is put to Alderson he is liable to reply that a pragmatic approach has to be taken by Chief Constables, that defining the social good is unavoidable but that it is done in a context in which Chief Constables and officers are subject to democratic consultations and accountability. The way his system works in practice was, however, seen in a different way by journalist Jean Stead:

> The police exert a benevolently autocratic rule in the whole of the region . . . there are parents in areas like Truro who feel that their teenage unemployed children are being too heavily supervised by the police force.[57]

Where the public meetings system is relied upon to act as a check on police paternalism, there is another snag: the police have acted as leaders in the public hearings also. In her study of the first year of the Exeter Community Policing Consultative Group, Ann Blaber states that it was 'generally agreed' among agencies that the police should take the lead in creating consultative groups. Although there was talk of policemen merely acting as 'catalysts', their falling back into a secondary role has been slow, largely due to perceptions of them as being in the useful position of political neutrality.[58] Such neutrality may exist in a party political sense but, as Moore and Brown point out,[59] it does not mean that the force avoids heavy involvement in local politics. The critics will again question both the extent to which such involvement can really be called neutral and the effect of such activity in tainting the police's reputation as impartial enforcers of the law.

Paternalism is a tag that police forces can perhaps live with. There is, however, another view of community policing that sees it as a more dangerous method of social control. This view emphasizes the ease with which this form of policing can be used as a method of surveillance and as the ultimate in pre-emptive control. It is argued, first, that the research used to identify persons at risk and locate them socially and geographically is open to abuse and, second, that constables who are involved in all kinds of social activity will place too dazzling a legal searchlight on people's behaviour.

Let us take the first point. Research showing 'crime areas' or city districts in which juveniles are 'at risk' may be seen as both questionable yet also attractive. This was shown in Exeter when the new CPSU revealed their research to other agencies – planners, social services, educationalists etc. Moore and Brown say:

> Some were suspicious of police motives and questioned us closely as to what use we were going to put it. They were afraid it would be used to create further stigmatisation of certain areas in the city. Some were concerned that it would expose weakness in agencies' use of resources. Others expressed the opinion that the information should be kept confidential. Some saw it as raising questions about certain decisions by local politicians. *Gradually, however, more and more took an increasing interest in the data.*[60]

Amidst all the range of sentiments from altruistic liberalism to professional defensiveness, all social agencies seemed irresistibly attracted to such data. Two concerns arise here, first, that political use may be made of this information (as it was in relation to an Exeter housing estate)[61] and, second, that, where agencies such as the police and social services are exchanging information, there are liable to be breaches of confidentiality that might prejudice particular individuals. Blaber argues[62] that community research involves no information concerning individuals and suggests that public fears can be allayed by the production of guidelines on information collection, but the problem is more complicated than she makes out. The full community policing model involves not mere co-ordination but exchanges of staff between police and many agencies including social workers. Apart from questions whether officers on secondment will see information of police interest when working in the social services, there must in such a situation be a public fear that individuals or bureaucratic organizations in this position will inevitably – as a matter of organizational fact – indulge in informal bargaining and exchange information. No matter how high-principled individuals and agencies are, it would seem very difficult to convince the public that this danger does not exist. The implications are severe: are, for example, people to be expected to talk freely to social workers about family, marital or social problems when the fear that information concerning illegitimate activity may find its way back to the police?

This takes us on to the other major difficulty: that community policing involves too close a scrutiny for comfort. The rules of law are so extensive now that strict enforcement would make 'criminals of us all'. This being so, constant attention to individuals, like the Truro unemployed already mentioned, is liable to make them feel uncomfortable and even vulnerable whether they are law-abiding or not. Such anxieties will perhaps not be allayed on, for example, a group of youths seeing that the police have both mapped out their area of town as a 'crime area' and even tagged them 'juveniles at risk'. Such research has its productive side, it should be emphasized, but there is a danger, nevertheless, that unless used with restraint and acted upon with discretion, such research may alienate individuals who feel that they are being 'picked-upon' or have been 'convicted' in advance of committing any offence. In so far as police activity is seen as extending into other agencies' work, feelings of insecurity stand to be magnified.

Such points do not indicate that community forms of policing cannot be made to work, nor is it contended here that the results achieved may not vastly exceed those of more reactive styles; what is argued is that this is a high-risk strategy. Notable achievements can be made but this takes a lot of effort and to fail may lead to disastrous results.

To explain, let us look at the likelihood and costs of failure. Like others, we have said of Devon and Cornwall that much depends on strong leadership from the top and a police organization that caters for committed community constables. In such a system PCs on the beat might be expected to serve the community in the sense of *watching over* rather than *watching* its citizens. As we have also noted, such is the freedom given to community constables, that it is difficult to impose a style or approach upon them other than by instilling a personal commitment. Given this difficulty little can be done where the various preconditions of acceptable community policing are lacking; let us take some examples:

## i No Leadership from the Top

Unless the officers on the beat are given a lead they may both despair in terms of promotion prospects and may lose interest in doing any kind of work at all. They may revert to a conviction – oriented style of policing or keep a low profile and 'take the pay'.

## ii   Insufficient Resources are Allocated

If community officers constitute a minority then their position within the force and community will be prejudiced. If limited to a public relations role this would be detrimental to their own work and also to the relations between the other operational officers and the public. General police/public relations would be made worse by the imposition of a barrier to wider communications. Thus, for example in Brixton in 1981 the home beat officers seemed to be driven into a negative 'buffer' role that both operated cosmetically and obstructed good relations between the operational officers and the public. (Scarman 4.37)

## iii   Insufficient Economic Support

Where community policing is attempted in areas of great deprivation a difficult choice faces Chief Constables. They have to provide a reactive motorized capability, perhaps combined with a small community force, or else they have to devote a large amount of resources to offer a community force of sufficient size to reduce needs for specialist reactive officers. In a time of economic recession, the latter is difficult. There are many areas of the country where inner city conditions would demand a tripling or quadrupling of police numbers in order to establish proper home beat policing. If the compromise position is adopted there is a grave danger that the few PCs on the ground will operate within a general police culture that stresses not community prevention but pre-emption and a deterrence based on efficient reaction and conviction. Officers in such positions may be driven to act not so much as community constables but as agents of covert surveillance.[63] Instead of being known for protective patrolling and for encouraging legitimate activity in the community there is a danger of their being seen as 'collectors of dirt' ready to pounce on suspected offenders on the basis of evidence of a dubious nature. They would be seen not as friends of the neighbourhood but as 'spies'.

What makes an individual beat constable into a community worker as opposed to a person engaged in surveillance is a delicate balance; leadership, manpower and resources are factors mentioned, another is the socio-economic condition of the area. Thus, a particular form of policing may work in a district of low-quality mixed housing that would not work in the worse conditions of some housing schemes in, say, Liverpool and Glasgow. To repeat an earlier statement; there is in practice no crude distinction between community and reactive/pre-emptive policing. The two may fuse and, depending on the conditions, certain forms of community technique may work either on a preventive or on a reactive/pre-emptive basis.

Here we have explored some of the difficulties of community policing where resources are not so limited as to result in 'crisis' policing. If there are two conclusions to be emphasized in this chapter they are these: first, the amended community style is not suited to 'crisis' policing where extreme deprivation is met with inadequate resources. If in such conditions, a combination of community and reactive strategies is adopted then beat officers will be driven to act in an insidious reactive manner. The only real course in those circumstances is for all agencies, including the police, to stress to politicians that humane policing cannot be accomplished without substantial improvements in the social and economic conditions that prevail.

The second and final conclusion is this: community policing, though it can work commendably, is a difficult machine to operate and control, and the risks of both failure and abuse are great. When we think of the RCCP and systems of protection, we should remember that the kinds of diffused responsibility and individual autonomy that prevail in some systems of community policing might not readily be susceptible of either legal or organizational control (with increased democratic review there is perhaps more reason for optimism). The Exeter experiment is impressive but the imaginative test is to think of Alderson's 'benevolently autocratic' system being operated by one or two of our more celebrated 'hard-line' Chief Constables. Community policing is all very well when administered by a charismatic liberal but it might very easily turn into a fearsome machine for surveillance if placed in the wrong hands.

## Further Reading

Alderson, J. C., *Policing Freedom*, Macdonald & Evans, Plymouth, 1979.

Banton, M., *The Police and the Community*, Tavistock, London, 1964.

Belson, W. A., *The Public and the Police*, Harper & Row, New York, 1975.

Blaber, A., *The Exeter Community Consultative Group*, National Association for Care and Rehabilitation of Offenders, 1979.

Demuth, C., *Sus: A Report on Section 4 of the Vagrancy Act 1824*, Runnymede Trust, London, 1978.

Humphry, D., *Police Power and Black People*, Granada, London, 1972.

Institute of Race Relations, *Police Against Black People*, Institute of Race Relations, London, 1979.

Lambeth Borough, *Working Party on Community/Police Relations in Lambeth, Report*, Lambeth, 1981.

Lea, J. and Young, J., 'Urban Violence and Political Marginalisation: The Riots in Britain; Summer 1981', in *Critical Social Policy* vol. I, no. 3 Spring 1982, pp. 59–69.

Moore, C. and Brown, J., *Community versus Crime*, National Council for Voluntary Organizations, London, 1981.

National Council for Civil Liberties, *Civil Disorder and Civil Liberties*, National Council for Civil Liberties, London, 1981.

Police Federation, *The Police in Society*, Police Federation, London, 1971.

Scarman, Lord, *The Brixton Disorders, 10–12 April 1981: Report of an Inquiry*, Cmnd. 8427, HMSO, London, 1981.

Schaffer, E. B., *Community Policing*, Croom Helm, London, 1980.

# Alternatives and Conclusions

A constructive approach to police reform must give attention to the social, political and organizational considerations that have too often been neglected in the past. We will, therefore, start but not conclude with specific proposals on the legal regulation of police powers. To end with, we must look to more fundamental questions concerning the kind of police styles and organizations that are socially and politically acceptable in Britain.

## Police Powers at Law

Although the Royal Commission on Criminal Procedure may be criticized for its legalism, it is worth repeating that the law does have a role to play in the field of police activity and in its control. Formal limits must be imposed if powers are to exist as other than broad discretions. In this section we will, therefore, look at the major police powers, consider proposals for law reform, and discuss both criticisms and alternatives.

### *a* Stop and Search

As noted in Chapter 5, there are at present a limited number of statutes that give to the police powers of stop and search for specified articles (drugs, birds' eggs, firearms, etc.) and local legislation in major cities gives such powers in relation to stolen goods. There is, however, no general police power to stop and search. The Commission recommended that, for the sake of 'greater clarity and certainty', there should be a general power to stop and search in a public place without arrest but based on reasonable suspicion of carrying stolen goods or carrying anything whose possession in a public place is itself an offence.[1] This power would be available not merely to uniformed but to *all* officers. The Commission puts 'great weight' however, on certain safeguards. These are that there should be 'reasonable suspicion', that persons be notified of the reasons for a search, that these be recorded by officers and that supervising officers should monitor these records.

It is in relation to this power that the Commision said that those possessing illegal goods 'should not be entirely protected from the possibility of being searched'. This phrase speaks volumes of the Commission's approach: it utterly fails to consider the position of the innocent person who may not want to be searched and whose resentment may affect subsequent relations with the police. It assumes that the police somehow 'know who is guilty', but are inhibited by the law from acting. The existing evidence shows otherwise: of searches under the Misuse of Drugs Act 1971 figures given to the Commission by the Metropolitan Police indicate that of over 10,000 'stops' on reasonable suspicion carried out in 1978 outside London only 22.4 per cent disclosed possession.[2] A minority of the Advisory Committee on Drug Dependence (1970) argued that once search on suspicion without arrest was allowed, it tended to result in 'some kind of random search'[3] and two of the Commission's own researchers have stated that 'random searches are not obviously authorised by the Royal Commission, but they would be the inevitable consequence of its recommendations'.[4]

Were such powers given then we would enter a difficult area since it cannot be assumed that all police officers use a concept of preventive policing that significantly differs from harassing a community. Those who doubt that such harassment can occur and be endorsed as a policy matter by senior officers are referred to the unofficial training manual written by David Powis, Assistant Deputy Commissioner of Scotland Yard. 'The Signs of Crime' warns young officers never to be disappointed if stopping an innocent person in the street results in no arrest:

> Who is to say that an apparently unsuccessful stop is not a crime prevented? Real effort will give your police area a reputation that it is a hot place . . . activity by uniformed officers in speaking to loiterers and suspicious persons is what is required to reduce the incidence of serious crime.[5]

Whether such activity affects levels of crime at all – or simply moves criminal activity from one patch to another – it is clear from experience in Brixton with 'hard policing' and intensive operations such as 'Swamp '81' that policing philosophies designed to create 'hot places' can deeply alienate the residents of those areas.

As far as the law is concerned, legal limits on the use of potentially blanket stop-and-search operations are difficult to enforce. The Commission's protections are also weak: 'reasonable suspicion' is a notoriously loose concept, and this the Commission admitted[6] in turning its attention to its proposed recording procedures. One must be sceptical of these as added protections: first, because the duty falls on officers, who are to use their own notebooks for records; second, because such recording is already standard practice in most forces (including the Metropolitan Police), yet serves as little protection and third, because monitoring by supervising officers is not reliable as a control mechanism in the light of evidence that lower ranks of officers consistently 'protect' their superiors from unwanted or embarrassing information.[7]

For our own part we would oppose the creation of a general power of stop and search as being too broad and incapable of effective review. We do so in spite of Lord Scarman's acceptance of the necessity of intensive stop-and-search operations in certain circumstances[8] and question whether such operations are other than exceptionally of policing value. Although the present law is confused, it is better to give powers that do relate to particular items or types of goods (e.g. drugs or offensive weapons). A preference for particularized powers as opposed to general areas has been expressed by Chief Constable John Alderson[9] and seems the one effective method of rendering the concept of 'reasonable suspicion' more precise – at least an arresting officer then has to be prepared to say whether and why he or she suspects a person of carrying birds' eggs or offensive weapons. If suspicion does not allow the making of this kind of distinction then it does not seem 'reasonable', and, if acted on, seems likely to cause public offence out of proportion to any potential value to the police.

Where particularized powers of stop and search are not justified there seems no good reason for having a power of stop and search on grounds less rigorous than those that would suffice for arrest: if the test for both is the same (i.e. reasonable suspicion) then to create a power of stop and search that is separate from arrest may, as the Haldane Society argues, only give legitimacy to random stops and searches.[10] This is of particular significance in the context of intelligence collection.

Recording procedures should not be relied upon as an effective counterbalance to powers of the broadest kind but they may be of some limited value. We suggest that persons stopped and searched against their will should be given written notice of the reasons for so doing; this is an improvement on mere recording in the officer's notebook as required by the Commission. Notice should be delivered on the spot, in non-urgent cases and not as the Commission says 'within a reasonable period on request'.[11] Recording by the constable should, of course, be retained so that, as the Commission states, such records may be of evidential value in any allegations of unlawful search or in officers defending themselves against such allegations.

## b  Arrest and Detention

We saw that the Commission's proposal was to extend the power to arrest without warrant – at present limited to offences punishable by five years' imprisonment – to cover all imprisonable offences. Although, as we have seen, there is at present no legal power to detain for questioning, the Commission envisaged such a power in its proposals to 'limit' detention upon arrest according to 'the necessity principle' (para. 3.83). These suggestions are seen to be seriously flawed on examining the grounds on which the necessity principle justifies detention. The first is 'unwillingness to identify himself' – but it is clear that it is the police who will judge whether identification is satisfactory. Another ground is the need to secure evidence or 'to obtain such evidence from the suspect by questioning him'. This provision endorses a notion of policing alien to the Scottish idea of detection outlined in the Chalmers case: Lord Cooper would not countenance procedures that used questioning to make a person 'condemn himself out of his own mouth'. Why not? Because the dangers of oppression and unreliable confession were too great. The Royal Commission clearly has lower standards, since, in spite of being told by its own research that mere entry to a police station may suffice to remove the voluntary element from a subsequent statement,[12] it recommends a power to detain for questioning on reasonable suspicion.

To enact such proposals would be to give the police another wide and almost uncontrollable discretion. Uncontrollable, because it is based on considerations of such a subjective nature that judges, in the unlikely event of challenge to the exercise of such powers, would find it difficult to do anything other than give way to the picture of operational needs put forward by police officers in particular cases. The judiciary, moreover, would find it almost impossible to develop any standards via case law that would have application beyond the case in hand.[13]

Implementation of such proposals would give the police significantly extended powers. 'Reasonable suspicion' would be required as a ground of action but the standards for this would be so low as to afford little protection – low standards are envisaged in any case by the Commission endorsing the notion that detention may be used not to verify evidence or organize it but actually to produce and collect it. The locus of trial takes another step away from the court into the police station.[14] Although the Commission asserts the right to silence repeatedly, its proposals undermine this; it advocates detention to question in spite of actually quoting the Irving finding that:

To remain silent in a police interview room in the face of determined questioning by an officer with legitimate authority to carry on this activity requires an abnormal exercise of will. So uncommon is it for a person to remain silent while being questioned that, when it does occur, any observer would be forgiven for making the fallacious assumption that the abnormal behaviour is associated with some significant cause (in this context guilt as opposed to innocence).[15]

We oppose the power to detain merely for questioning on the grounds of its breadth and because of the difficulties of review. It is important to see the difference between the present law which connives at custody for questioning and the proposed law which endorses it wholeheartedly. As far as the public is concerned there is a great deal of difference between a constable who can often 'get away with' questioning suspects on 'holding charges' and one who may arrest them for questioning with virtual impunity. Officers should as far as possible seek to gain the public's co-operation and to endorse compulsory questioning is to run the risk of sacrificing too much public goodwill. Why this risk should be run is a key issue. Harriet Harman of the NCCL emphasized this point in saying of the Commission Report:

> No attempt is made to show that greater police freedom to arrest and detain will actually increase the accuracy and efficiency of detention and prosecution.[16]

It has been claimed that most, perhaps 80 per cent, of crimes are solved by confessions.[17] If it were the case that to regulate police questioning more effectively would allow 80 per cent of guilty persons to go free then the cost of protecting liberties would be great. The evidence is, however, that the value of admissions has been greatly exaggerated. In their recent study McConville and Baldwin conclude that confessions frequently make little difference in a case since they are usually made where other evidence is sufficient to convict. In only 20 per cent of cases, they conclude, would the prosecution case be vitally affected by excluding all admissions.[18] That interrogation plays a relatively minor role in conviction is also indicated by Softley's study for the Royal Commission[19] which found that in only 8 per cent of cases would the police have dropped proceedings had the suspect refused to answer questions.

In spite of these findings it is clear from the Irving study for the Commission[20] that police officers see interrogation as important in investigation. McConville and Baldwin argue that the premium attached by the police to questioning derives from the value they set on it for purposes collateral to conviction (e.g. information-collecting concerning other persons and offences). Their study, like others, reveals that these collateral benefits are exaggerated since the police role in detection (as opposed to merely assembling the prosecution case by collecting information from civilians) was comparatively small and the overwhelming majority of suspects that are convicted are caught in the act, identified by witnesses, found in possession or seen with suspects.[21] McConville and Baldwin conclude:

> The combined effect of all the studies on reported as well as detected offences, whether based on police files, case papers, or observational exercises, is that, in relation to indictable crime, the police are in essence a reactive organisation and that interrogation is in fact a relatively unimportant part of the total law enforcement picture.

To organize policing around the collection of evidence via admission is thus to make a double error. It is to give way to a distorted view of the police's own role in detection and conviction and it is to pursue ends that are defined in terms of the police organization (e.g. 'good convictions') to the detriment of ends desired by society in general (i.e. more efficient prevention and detection of crime). The product of this misconception is to place more emphasis on arrest, questioning and the overruling of rights in custody than on the seeking of public co-operation. It is to move towards an inefficient system of policing by confrontation.[22]

Until there is clear evidence that by giving up their most valuable commodity, public goodwill, the police will improve detection to such an extent that overall crime solving will be improved, it is unwise to expand powers of arrest. As for powers to arrest and detain for questioning, it is arguable that unless there exists evidence sufficient to charge a person with an offence then there should be no power to arrest at all – this was the Scottish position at least in the 1950s and the evidential test to be satisfied for both arrest and charge is still the same in Scotland. To allow arrest on evidence that is too weak to justify a charge and to endorse questioning for the purposes of 'topping-up' existing evidence is a dangerous practice as has been seen in a number of recent cases where persons are led to admit to crimes they have not committed (as in the Confait case) or to confess to crimes that did not happen at all – as with Erroll Madden.[23] If there are arguments for compulsory detention to question in certain narrowly prescribed circumstances – perhaps those of extreme urgency where a suspect is about to flee the country – then these should be argued for in relation to particular circumstances and not imposed in blanket form.

## c   Searches of Persons and Premises

Apart from powers to stop and search persons there were Commission proposals to change the law on a number of search powers:

### i   Powers to Search Premises before Arrest

The warrant system exists as the safeguard of what Lord Scarman has called a 'fundamental right of privacy'.[24] It involves independent judicial intervention in the investigation process but, like other ways of regulating police action, is often short-circuited: research for the Royal Commission showed that most searches are done without warrant but under 'consent' of householder or suspect.[25] The Commission argued that magistrates should in general issue warrants and proposed a new recording procedure in which applications for search warrants would be lodged in writing in court and would specify the objects of search. Such proposals are to be welcomed but the Commission's response to the problem of 'fishing' may meet with mixed reaction. In recent years statute and case law has allowed the police to use warrants to cover not just the items specified but the taking (and use in court as evidence) of goods believed to be stolen and even evidence of crimes unrelated to the subject matter of the warrant.[26] The Commission answer is to state that the police should be allowed to seize not only the goods specified in a warrant but also any prohibited goods or any evidence of a 'grave' offence found in the course of a search which is carried out in a manner appropriate to the items listed in the warrant. Somewhat exceptionally in view of its rejection of the exclusionary rule elsewhere (e.g. in relation to breaches of the Code of Practice and evidence derived from unlawful stop and searches) the Commission says that evidence obtained where a warrant is used, and which does not fall within its scope as newly defined, should not be admitted in court. This proposal might be welcomed by some people as a clarification of the law and a boost to the exclusionary rule in this area; others might argue that the question of exclusion will hardly ever arise because it will be almost impossible to prove that, where 'fishing' produces results, the form of search used was inappropriate to the items specified on the warrant. Those legislating on the Commission proposals will, if they aim for an effective exclusionary rule and an end to 'fishing', have to make further attempts to distinguish between those cases of genuinely 'stumbling over' evidence and cases where warrants have been used deliberately to search for any prejudicial evidence.

As far as the use of magistrates is concerned, the Commission acknowledges, in relation to stop and searches, that they can do 'little other than endorse a police request'.[27] It is vital, therefore, that any future legislation imposes in the new warrants system a duty on magistrates to review the reasons justifying any warrant powers positively and with some vigour.

As with arrest, the status of searches by 'consent' should, we think, be clarified by recording that consent. The Commission recommends that such recording should be undertaken by police officers for their own protection (para. 3.50) but a written record should also be given to householders for the same reasons.

## ii  Powers to Search for Evidence

Although the Commission advocates no new power of entry without warrant, it does suggest a new procedure under which police officers might search premises other than those of an arrested person to look for evidence (paras 3.40–3.52). This would apply to 'grave' offences before charge and a warrant from a circuit judge would be required. The judge would have to be satisfied of a number of conditions, for example, that other methods of investigation had failed and that an item could be specified precisely. 'Fishing expeditions' would be guarded against by describing the subjects of search in the deposition lodged in court which, under

Commission proposals is necessary to obtain all warrants. Evidence could be used in court where it accords with the warrant or where evidence of a grave offence is found in a lawful search that is appropriate to specified items but, again, the Commission would exclude evidence that does not conform to such terms.

In view of these protections this suggested power appears to be useful and to establish a reasonable balance of powers versus protections – assuming, that is, that judges will follow the spirit of these proposals and enforce the rule that items be specified with some precision. Such an assumption is not, however, to be made unthinkingly and it is therefore vital that the conditions to be satisfied before such warrants are granted be set out fully by statute and an instruction given that reasons for deeming these conditions to be met should be recorded by the circuit judge.

### iii   *Search of Persons and Premises after Arrest*

There is at present no general police power to search individuals or their houses and premises after arrest: only when there are reasonable grounds to suspect the possession of weapons may persons and their surroundings be searched – and only after actual arrest (the existence of grounds for arrest is insufficient). The Commission, however, recommended more police powers. In the case of persons taken to the police station under arrest it was acknowledged that they are in practice, and for administrative reasons, searched in spite of there being no statutory authority to do this (para. 3.116). Though accepting that people may find such searches 'humiliating and disturbing', the Commission recommended the creation of a statutory power to allow police to carry them out whenever detention is felt justified by the officer in charge of a case. (If a 'grave' offence is alleged then 'strip' and body searches would be allowed.) As for safeguards, the Commission declined to lay down any guidelines and stated:

> Station officers will have to be left to use their discretion sensibly, but if that is so they should not be blamed or be liable to an action if something goes wrong. (para. 3.117)

A similar approach is adopted in relation to an arrested person's premises. The present common law power allows search only of the arrestee's 'immediate surroundings' but the Commission thinks that there is a need for a power to search premises and vehicles on arrest since such searches 'can and do contribute to the investigation and detection of offences' (para. 3.120). What the Commission does not ask is whether this contribution justifies the offence caused by the use of such powers. (Unless it is accepted that a point is reached where such a trade-off is unjustified we may as well grant to the police unrestricted powers to search for evidence.)

It is, however, on the issue of who is to grant warrants for search of premises on arrest that the Commission is least convincing. It argues that the police should write out their own warrants (para. 3.121) because the need to obtain a warrant elsewhere might delay a suspect's release from custody; it might place undue pressure on suspects to consent to searches and because, in operational matters, magistrates were seen by the Commission as merely rubber-stamping police decisions (para. 3.33). These proposals, however, would make an arrested person's rights less fundamental than those of a free individual in spite of both being innocent at law until proven guilty. One commentator has said that the suggestions are: 'astoundingly naïve and tantamount to making an arrested person's premises "open water" for fishing expeditions'. He concluded:

> There is a risk that requiring a warrant in such cases will delay the suspect's release from custody but the answer is surely to improve the administrative procedures to avoid any delay rather than to strip the suspect of a right because its exercise may cause him inconvenience.[28]

We agree; having said that general supervision of searches under warrant should fall to magistrates[29] it is difficult to see why magisterial ineffectiveness should be a reason for allowing the police to supervise themselves when arrest has occurred. If the rationale for abandoning magisterial oversight is based on considerations of operational urgency then the case is not argued through by the Commission. The effect of instituting police warrants is not merely to prejudice arrested suspects but it is to place undue pressures on officers to use arrest as a device to facilitate searches.

## *d*  Questioning in Custody and 'Helping with Enquiries'

After arrest, suspects are taken to the police station where they are
either set free, released pending further investigation, charged
with an offence and bailed to attend at a magistrates' court or
charged and kept in custody to be brought before a magistrate as
soon as possible. Where formal arrest does not occur, persons may
still attend at a police station to 'help with enquiries' and, in
practice, may be treated similarly. In the light of increasing
orientation of the police towards the collection of evidence by
admission, and given such cases as Confait and Madden, it is
understandable that there has been some concern in recent years
over the rules governing the treatment of suspects in custody.[30]
The Fisher Report on Confait, we should remember, was a major
reason why the Royal Commission was set up – it was embarrassing
that the Metropolitan Police were not observing some Judges'
Rules and did not even know of the existence of others.

The Commission would allow detention for questioning subject
to broad conditions. As was the case with arrest, however, extended powers supposedly went along with protections: to limit
detention it was proposed that after six hours without charge an
officer unconnected with the investigation would review the need
for continued detention and, if the need for this was found, he was
to record relevant reasons in writing. Release from detention or
appearance in court was to follow within twenty-four hours – not of
arrest but of arrival at the police station. In relation to allegations
of 'grave' offences, however, further periods of detention for
twenty-four-hour periods might be authorized by magistrates sitting in private.

It follows from our comments above that we see little justification for the imposition of such periods of detention and their use to
collect evidence: this would be another step from trial by jury to
police inquisition.[31] As for the time-limits system, this is of little
comfort to any suspect involved. Six hours (e.g. 11 p.m. to 5 a.m.)
is a considerable period of time – long enough in three quarters of
cases for suspects to be dealt with[32] and equivalent to the longest
period of detention allowed under the heavily resisted Criminal
Justice (Scotland) Act 1980. Review after six hours is conducted

not by an independent official but by another police officer and repeated periods of detention (allowed, sceptics will say by 'tame' magistrates) were likened by both major parties in Scottish debates (including Ministers in the Conservative Government) to South Africa's detention laws.

As far as the treatment of suspects in custody is concerned, the present system depends, in the main, on the Judges' Rules, the rule that to be admissible in court statements must have been made voluntarily and the judicial discretion to exclude from trial any evidence that is obtained by irregular or unfair means. The Commission, it will be remembered, proposes to replace the Judges' Rules with a Code of Practice but to make the enforcement of the latter depend on internal police discipline and supervision.[33] As we also saw in Chapter 7, the voluntariness and exclusionary rules were both rejected on the basis of weak reasoning and a distortion of research findings.

Like many of the Commission's critics, we would retain both the test of voluntariness and the exclusionary rule. For all its vagueness and difficulty the voluntariness test does at least give judges a discretion to intervene in extreme cases. As for exclusion, some have argued that evidence derived from any breach of the Judges' Rules or Code of Practice should *automatically* be excluded from use in court. They say that only strict exclusion will deter officers from 'chancing their arm'[34] so as to gain evidence by dubious means and that only this rule would offer any guarantee of suspects' rights. This is a hard proposal to sell since it is too easy to think of trivial breaches of rules and to ridicule the exclusion of important evidence on such a basis. Such difficulties can be overcome, however, by dividing rights in custody into two groups, the first of which would involve rights whose breach would be an issue of discipline but not always of exclusion, and the second group would comprise rights fundamental to lawful treatment and breach of which would result in automatic exclusion of any consequent evidence. Any judicial discretion to allow the production of evidence derived in the breach of fundamental rights should be framed in the narrowest terms (e.g. that errors resulted from factors beyond police control and could not reasonably be said to have prejudiced the accused in any way). Where a breach of non-fundamental rights in custody occurs, then Sir Henry Fisher's suggestion in the Confait

Report should be implemented: that no person should be convicted on the basis of evidence derived in breach of the Code or Rules (here the first group) unless there is corroborative evidence obtained legitimately. This would offer some protection to the wronged suspect, which is something that cannot be said for the Commission's own proposal – that all evidence be put before a jury whose members are to be warned of its possible unreliability and are to be directed to 'look for independent support'. We think that it is no use thrusting the forbidden fruit before juries and then warning them about their waistlines.

The brief criticism of the Commission's proposals for treatment in custody is therefore that they offer no workable protections and, as legal rules, fail to improve on existing provisions. There is, however, another absolutely fundamental point: all of these proposals do very little to change the practice, so much criticized, of 'helping with police enquiries'. Since the notion of arrest is so vague it would still be possible to by-pass the Commission's custody procedures, the 'reasonable suspicion' test and the 'necessity principle' by deeming a person not to have been arrested or to be in detention but to be 'helping' the police voluntarily. Unless the role of this fiction is excluded any regulatory regime governing arrest is liable to be short-circuited.

The Commission's recording proposals might be improved to contribute usefully at this point: they involve opening a 'custody sheet' when an arrested person comes to a police station or as soon as a person who has come to the station voluntarily is put under arrest. The latter suggestion is of value in the Inwood[35] kind of case where attempts to leave the station are 'discouraged', but contention can best be eradicated by requiring that on entry to a police station a record be made not only of arrests but also of those volunteering help. We propose, therefore, that volunteers be invited on entering a station to sign a form offering help for a limited period (e.g. two hours). Coupled with provision for the admissibility of 'custody sheets' and such 'voluntary attendance forms' as evidence in cases of unlawful detention, such a system would go some way to remove doubts as to the status of persons at the police station.[36] To those who argue that too much time-wasting paperwork would be involved in such a process and that officers cannot be expected in practice to observe such a system (see Chapter 2) it should be conceded readily that officers will routinely avoid the use of such forms. They will not formalize most 'friendly five-minute chats' and short interviews. What can be expected, is that where an extended or rigorous interview is intended, or where there is any possibility of contention, the form system will be used. It is this small minority of cases that gives rise to trouble and here that the aims of this recording system will be achieved. Other critics will say that persons will be pressured into signing 'voluntary attendance forms' but one cannot legislate against such dangers: once such a level of distrust of the police is reached, we may as well abandon proposals for legal control in this area.

There is a further suggestion made, not by the Commission but by Lord Scarman, which would be useful in counteracting public distrust of what goes on in police stations. Scarman advocated a statutory system of independent inspection together with the supervision of interrogation procedures and detention in police stations:

> I suggest that, if it were known that members of police com-
> mittees (outside London) and of the statutory liaison (or con-
> sultative) committees, whose establishment I recommend both
> in London and outside, had the right to visit police stations at
> any time and the duty to report upon what they observed, the
> effect would be salutary.[37]

Together with provision for elected consultative police councils this proposal would be a major step in keeping questioning practices to acceptable limits. It would mean that any officer holding a person for questioning against their will and without grounds for arrest would always run the risk of inspection and consequent disciplinary action. (If there is reasonable suspicion and a 'custody sheet' or else a 'voluntary attendance form' then there would be no issue to be answered.) Libertarians cannot aim for more extensive control of police activity without running the risk that evasive action will be taken. If officers see themselves as compelled to interview suspects in police cars in back streets then all efforts to control questioning at the police station amount to very little.

Another way, of course, to regulate what goes on in interrogations is to tape-record them. Recording was, as we saw in Chapter 6, a precondition of the Thomson proposals on Scottish powers of detention and was seen by many as an important method of judging whether questioning was too harsh; of ensuring that statements were in fact made (rather than 'verballed') and of guaranteeing the accuracy of statements.[38] It has been clear for some time that a significant problem has existed in the accounts that are given of statements made in police custody and allegations of 'verballing' have been too frequent.[39] The Royal Commission's response to this has been weak in the extreme: it rejected the recording of whole interviews as 'not yet practicable' and, instead, envisaged that recording be used only to take down an officer's summary of points made in the interview. McConville and Baldwin comment of the Commission: 'The problem as it sees it, is not that verbals might be false but that the recording of them might not be wholly accurate.'[40]

Suspects would, under the Commission system, be asked to comment on their treatment and upon the officer's summary[41] but the latter would be admissible in evidence whether a comment is made or not and even if there is a failure to invite comment. These proposals on taping amount to poor protection for suspects yet a significant inconvenience for the police.

*Conclusions on Questioning.* There should be no police power to detain simply for questioning (or a power that has this effect): instead, questioning should depend on public co-operation and detention should rest on there being sufficient evidence to justify arrest except in narrowly defined cases of urgency. At the police station, a two-form system should be applied to remove doubts as to whether attendance is voluntary or not. So as to make the suspect's right to legal representation effective he or she should be asked to sign a section of either the 'custody sheet' or 'voluntary attendance' form stating that the presence of a solicitor has been offered and has been accepted or refused. The right to a solicitor should not be subject to a general police power to deny this but if, as the Commission suggests, there has to be a power to refuse advice where there are good reasons for fearing interference with witnesses or evidence in a particular case then this power should only be exercisable by a senior officer (say divisional commander; the Commission suggests a subdivisional commander or above.)

This system would involve solicitors attending at police stations more often than at present but this is a price (about £30m per year) that should be paid.[42] Given our proposed right to have solicitors present during an interview, it is necessary, if the right is to count for anything, to make inadmissible in court those statements obtained where legal representation has been wrongly denied (here again, we differ from the Commission).[43] Unless a waiver is recorded, therefore, all questioning should be conducted in the presence of a solicitor if it is to be admissible in court except in two circumstances in which statements would be usable: where a senior officer overrules the right to a solicitor, on grounds that are recorded on the custody sheet or where a suspect makes a statement in the absence of a solicitor when such absence is not due to factors within police control (e.g. he or she volunteers a statement in the period before a solicitor arrives at the station).

Proposals for tape-recording are more difficult to make a judgment on since the findings of relevant experiments are not yet public. In principle we would advocate their use but should research and experience indicate that such factors as time, expense and operational difficulty lead to interviews being conducted outside the police station (where, for example, no council visitors may appear) then, even from the civil libertarian point of view, this would be undesirable.

The Code of Practice governing treatment of suspects in custody should, we think, be of legal significance rather than a matter of administrative practice backed up by threat of disciplinary action. The voluntariness rule should be kept, automatic exclusion should apply where certain rights in custody are breached and, in the case of the breach of others, there should be a discretion to exclude or (if not exercised) a requirement of corroboration. Protection of certain rights would, accordingly, be absolute but in the case of 'lesser' rights in custody the exercise of a discretion to exclude might be based not merely on the need to discipline officers or to ensure the reliability of evidence, but on the 'protective principle' outlined by Dr Andrew Ashworth, who said:

If a legal system declares certain standards for the conduct of a criminal investigation . . . then it can be argued that citizens have corresponding rights to be accorded certain facilities and not to be treated in certain ways. If the legal system is to protect those rights then it is arguable that a suspect whose rights have been infringed should not thereby be placed at any disadvantage: by 'disadvantage' is meant . . . that evidence obtained by the investigators as a result of the infringement should not be used against the subject.[44]

### e  Prosecutions

Most prosecutions in England and Wales are brought by the police, a position that differs from Scottish practice in which the Lord Advocate, a political appointee and Law Officer of the Crown, brings almost all prosecutions with the assistance either of his civil-service-staffed procurator-fiscal service or, in more serious cases, his Advocates-Depute (who are appointed from the ranks of advocates).

South of the border there are two ways to prosecute: by arrest and charge or by information and summons. Where arrest is used the charging officer takes his report to the station officer (usually a sergeant or Inspector), who decides initially whether to dispose of a case with a caution, whether to prosecute at all or whether to prosecute by accepting a charge. (In more serious cases more senior officers from the prosecution department or from general command are consulted.) Following a charge, a person must be brought before a magistrate within twenty-four hours if practicable or released on bail or brought before a magistrate 'as soon as practicable'.

Where summons procedure is used, an information is first laid before a magistrate by the police. This describes the alleged offence and requests the issue of a summons which is served on the accused, sets out the offences charged and gives a date for appearance in court. In terms of reviewing the evidence against a person, the summons procedure gives an opportunity to seek legal advice before proceedings are started. The problem with arrest and charge is that the charge sergeant must decide whether or not to accept a charge at so early a stage in proceedings (e.g. before witnesses have given statements) that the police have committed themselves before there is time either to take legal advice or to appraise the evidence fully.[45]

When legal advice is obtained, this comes from the force's prosecuting solicitor or *ad hoc* from a private or local authority solicitor. There is, among forces, a wide range of prosecution departments and procedures that are subject to no single legislative foundation but the general functions of the solicitors are similar:[46] to advise the police on prosecutions, to conduct prosecutions in magistrates' courts and to brief counsel in trials on indictment. The solicitors are not responsible for investigations and the final decision on whether to prosecute or not lies with the police. The police do not have to seek advice at all and, since they are the clients of the solicitors, they are not obliged to act on any advice they receive. The result is that the police control the prosecution process to such an extent that prosecution solicitors are sometimes given cases that they would not have proceeded on and few cases involve abandoning prosecution before committal on the basis of legal advice. The formal position again contrasts with Scotland where the final say on whether to prosecute or not rests with the procurator-fiscal.

Chief Constables thus have the final authority in England and Wales on whether prosecutions should be undertaken but their discretions are limited in so far as the Director of Public Prosecutions (DPP) has powers to take over the conduct of any prosecution at any stage. He or she may even discontinue a case and it is the DPP who both supervises private prosecutions and has the power to 'call in' certain classes of case. It is possible, therefore, for the DPP to impose some overall policy control over at least major prosecutions. Further oversight is imposed by the rule that in certain classes of case a prosecution requires the consent of the DPP or the Attorney-General.

The issue in recent years has been whether prosecutions should be taken away from the police and given to an independent body on the basis that investigation should be separated from prosecution and that the present system allows too many prosecutions to be brought where there is insufficient evidence. Research indicates that in a significant number of cases charges are pressed in the absence of supporting evidence and where convictions are unlikely. In 1972, McCabe and Purves found that in a number of cases 'policy prosecutions' took place in which charges were pursued with ends other than conviction in view.[47] In 1977 Sir Henry Fisher in the

Confait Report argued that committal proceedings (where the prosecutor first asks the court to commit for trial) could be used to test the prosecution's case but said that this would not happen 'unless there is a careful and dispassionate survey and review of the evidence by the counsel, solicitor or police officer responsible for presenting the case'. He argued for a review of evidence both for and against the accused but, as presently organized, committal proceedings are not used to test the prosecution's case since police control means that once a charge is laid it has sufficient momentum to carry it to the Crown Court.[48]

Recent work by McConville and Baldwin has shown the extent to which the present prosecution system fails to weed out cases which are based on evidence that is insufficient to justify a prosecution.[49] Over 800 contested cases from Crown Courts in Birmingham and London were studied. The statements and depositions in the committal papers were examined by two experienced assessors, a retired Chief Constable and a retired Justices' Clerk, who judged whether there was a proper case to answer. They found that between 6.2 and 8.3 per cent of the cases pursued in trial were hopelessly weak. Leaving out eight cases where insufficient information was available for the assessors, it was found that at trial all the defendants in the weak cases were acquitted either on judicial direction or order or by the jury – thus reinforcing the accuracy of the assessor's judgments. Even in cases where defendants pleaded guilty the assessors found that 2.2 per cent of cases did not justify prosecution.

We return to the question: how can we best screen out these cases so that individuals are not put through the considerable anxiety of being prosecuted unnecessarily? One reform would be to reduce the growing role in the adversary system of the police who not only prosecute and not only investigate but, as we have seen in earlier chapters, are increasingly directing their policing styles towards obtaining evidence via admissions and confessions.[50] Lord Devlin has said:

> What happens now is that the inquisitorial procedure is conducted but by the police, and the collection of facts is done by the police     we rely upon the police to do the job that the procurator fiscal or the juge d'instruction does abroad. And, to that

extent, we have made the police inquisitors.[51]

Commenting on the additional finding that only one in twenty defendants actually end up opting for trial by jury, McConville and Baldwin add,

> The police assemble the evidence, control its content, select, authenticate and validate it. They interrogate the suspect on their own territory and on their own terms and their record of the encounter is virtually unchallengeable and for the most part unchallenged.[52]

When the Royal Commission looked at the problem, it accepted that in about a fifth of ordered and directed acquittals there was doubt as to whether the evidence was sufficient to justify the decision to prosecute at the time when the decision was made. The Commission went on:

> it is said to be unsatisfactory that the person responsible for the decision to prosecute should be the person who has carried out or been concerned in the investigation. A police officer who carries out an investigation, inevitably and properly forms a view as to the guilt of the suspect. Having done so, without any kind of improper motive, he may be inclined to put his mind to other evidence telling against the guilt of the suspect or to over-estimate the strength of the evidence he has assembled.[53]

Such arguments clearly favour the separation of investigative from prosecution functions but the Commission warned that the provision of legal advice might not necesssarily improve fairness: it was in any case difficult to separate out investigation from prosecution and the police would tend to make the effective decisions. Looking north – where at committal the police give the procurator-fiscal a summary information and the fiscal has the task of deciding whether to proceed – the Commission said:

> Our impression from our visit to a number of fiscal's offices in Scotland was that this is a formal and routine task of endorsing a police decision to proceed, an impression which is, we under-

stand, confirmed by research recently done by the Scottish
Home and Health Department . . . In effect . . . the police
decision to report to the fiscal is the critical one in the bringing of
proceedings in the majority of cases.[54]

It was for these reasons that the Commission rejected both the idea
of removing the decision to prosecute entirely from the police so as
to place it with an independent legally qualified prosecutor and also
the Scottish and American systems in which the lawyer is involved
after investigation is complete but before the court is approached.
It favoured leaving the decision to initiate proceedings and to
charge with the police but establishing a Crown prosecution service
for each force that would take responsibility after the summons or
charge stage. A national body was rejected in favour of a local
service accountable to a local supervisory authority based on the
existing police authority areas, but national co-ordination was to be
imposed by making the Attorney-General or the Home Secretary
responsible for the prosecution and by having the DPP promulgate
national guidelines on prosecution matters.

For our part we would argue in favour of greater responsibilities
being given to the Crown Prosecutor so that, as in Scotland, the
prosecutor not the police would have responsibility for the initial
approach to the court. Though no complete answer this would
encourage a more objective evaluation of evidence. The Royal
Commission stated that Scottish Home and Health Department
research confirmed its 'rubber stamp' view of fiscals but offered no
explanation of why it did so. The research referred to did indicate
for instance, that 92 per cent of cases reported by the police were
proceeded with by fiscals[55] and it did show that fiscals have relatively little time or opportunity to conduct an effective review of
the evidence summarized in a police report. What was not
explained by the Commission was whether the independence of the
fiscal service does or does not act to deter the *reporting* of weak
cases by the police – in so far as it does the statistics, paradoxically
will indicate the ineffectiveness of the fiscal service as a filter of
weak cases since the reports they receive will be of a higher quality
than otherwise, and less in need of weeding out.

This dispute is, however, marginal: the Commission was right to
point out that the police do take the important steps in so far as they

control the collection of evidence. Our preference for the Scottish system does not assume that the fiscal's position differs greatly from that of the prosecuting solicitor: for all their independence the fiscals do depend heavily on police decision-making. More important than independence is access to information and the stage at which the prosecutor takes control from the police. We do argue, however, that where time does allow and where fiscals are involved in investigations (as in serious cases such as murders) there is value in independence.

There are other ways to discourage weak prosecutions apart from attempting to structure relations between prosecution and the police: these involve judicial discouragement. One method would involve a change of attitude at committal proceedings. Were judges to encourage prosecutors to take a more objective view at this stage, and were they more critical of prosecutors when directing or ordering acquittals at trial then this would do much to reduce unwarranted prosecutions. A second idea is to extend the judicial discretion to award costs against the prosecution where persons have been acquitted by the judge's order or direction (where the prosecution's evidence does not reach the level at which it would be safe to put the issue before a jury) or where it can be shown that the decision to proceed was unreasonable in the circumstances. When assessing such costs judges might be encouraged to take into account not merely legal fees but such factors as loss of earnings. This would be a more radical solution than proposals for independent prosecutors and might do something about the remarkable fact disclosed in recent Lord Chancellor's 'Judicial Statistics' that over four in ten acquittals are by order or direction of the judge rather than the jury.[56]

## Styles and Organizations

As important as resisting the temptation to give the police unrestricted powers is the need to encourage consensual styles of policing. The failings of non-consensual methods are manifest not merely in their alienating effect but in their inefficiency. There is, however, no simple blueprint for success. We should bear in mind a number of general points before offering any models of policing.

First, it is impossible to separate policing problems from social and economic ones. There are, therefore, limits to what policing can achieve. To be too ambitious in attempting to reduce crime is to risk over-policing and alienation. No lesser person than Sir Robert Mark has said recently:

> A great deal of crime is simply not preventable . . . Any suggestion that the police and the courts can by numbers, or severity, reverse or suppress widespread social non-conformity is simplistic.[57]

A second point to remember is that the same model of policing may not simply be applied throughout the country. Different problems arise in city, borough and country districts, in vast housing estates and in suburbia. Not only that but different demands are made of policing in different areas: the affluent may want first and foremost a rapid response for the protection of their property, whereas the residents of a hard-pressed council estate may resent 'fire-brigade' methods and respond more readily to a more community-based style.

With these qualifications in mind, we advocate a general policy of policing by consent. This does not, however, rule out a reactive capability – there will always be the urgent telephone call that demands immediate assistance. The gain of consensual policing is in fostering public trust of the police and so in increasing the speed with which the members of a community report crime. Many people are at present reluctant to call the police when they see something suspicious because they 'don't want to get involved': they may distrust the police, they may think that nothing will happen or they may fear inclusion in the criminal process as, say, a witness. Such reluctance arises from a lack of contact with the police and an ignorance of police needs and capabilities. With the consensual approach the aim is, therefore, not merely to provide a preventive presence on the streets but also to increase reactive capability (whether on foot or by car) by decreasing the time taken to report crime – a factor which has almost always greatly exceeded the police's own response time.[58]

The ability of the police to inform the public of their capabilities is an important factor in making policing more efficient. When people are told what the police can do they may attune the demands they make of the force to realities rather than fictions. This would lead to less time-wasting on trivial demands and more efficient responses to genuinely urgent cases. This is one important function of the consultative councils and reformed Police Authorities as advocated in Chapter 4.

We argue then, for community-based policing rather than 'community involvement'. This demands considerable changes in policing since it requires that consensual methods rather than reactive or pre-emptive ones be made the dominant styles of policing within a force. It recognizes that since the police only find out about around a tenth of all crimes and only deal with a tiny percentage of these without public help, what they can accomplish is critically affected by public attitudes. The courting of public assent is, as John Alderson stresses, a concern of all police officers, not merely of a specialist group.

Part of the process of building trust in consensual policing is the police force's ability to respond to public initiatives or demands: to watch, *on behalf of*, rather than to watch the community. This is a critical point in community policing and one where we differ from John Alderson. We reject his emphasis upon the central role of the police in leading and initiating community action. Equally we reject any notion that the police have some special status as definers of the social good. The police have to apply the law but they have to do so in an openly political context. Were they to assume to define the social good, the political process would be circumvented. Not only that, but assumed political superiority would undermine the force's main justification of its neutrality: 'we apply the law, not politics'. All law is clearly the outcome of political decision-making and to a limited extent the application of law necessarily involves political choice. In a democratic society, however, the choices must be kept within the legitimate political arena rather than delegated to a privileged group of experts.

On the role of the police in the political process we advocated in Chapter 4 the implementation of a two-tier system of local accountability in all areas including the Metropolis, with strengthened police committees of local authorities and the introduction of statutory consultative councils at divisional and subdivisional levels.

At the level of national politics we reject the Alderson proposals for a multi-departmental committee to oversee policing policies. Though of dubious practicality this is also undesirable in principle. To increase the power of central government would conflate the sensitive areas of education, welfare and policing as well as undermine the locally established Community Police Councils and Police Authorities. More can be accomplished by rendering the Home Secretary and the Home Office properly accountable for the undoubted influence they exert over every force in the country. This would best be achieved by setting up a Select Committee of the House of Commons to monitor the police and the co-ordination of national policy. In local terms, the relationship between the Home Office and individual police forces would be more open to review were full provision made to Police Authorities for access to and review of all material relevant to the relationship between central government and particular forces. (This would include, for example, circulars, policy guidance, budgetary and planning advice issued by the Home Departments.)

Reform of police styles and philosophies is valueless without attention to organization. Policing by consent requires, in the first instance, a reduction of the size of police bureaucracies. Realistically, this means a substantial devolution of power within the system so as to promote autonomy and responsibility at divisional and subdivisional level. Commanders at these levels should be given the authority to negotiate with and implement policies agreed at local level through the consultative process we have outlined. In this manner a local station would have responsibility for precise formulation of initiatives and strategies within its area.

Reorganization within the force, in order to implement the form of community policing we advocate, must also restore and revalue beat work. This is not a matter of simply putting more men back on the beat but demands the countering of those bureaucratic tendencies (especially towards increased specialization) that make impossible any acceptable form of local policing.

The evaluation of police work must no longer rest upon simple law enforcement and the number of captures made or the amount of intelligence collected. The adequacy of policing, and the test of a constable's performance, must instead be based on a community's response to its force. The issue should be acknowledged as one of qualitative judgment rather than numerical analysis. In such a method of evaluation the role of the Community Police Council would clearly be of significance.

To secure the status of beat officers each force should devote a sufficient proportion of personnel to the beat to make community policing the dominant culture rather than one based on captures. In terms of training, greater emphasis should be placed on street supervision by experienced beat constables. This would be supplemented by a more sensitive and extended police training course.

Small-scale policing reduces the value of much computerized work. There will clearly be a role to be played by police computers in future – we would not do away with the officer's ability to check out, say, a suspicious car nor deny the value of the crime information computer in highly complex investigations such as that undertaken in the case of the Yorkshire Ripper – what diminishes under-devolved policing is the need for computerized local intelligence. Officers on the beat are in the position not only to accumulate but also to evaluate the information they acquire. In consequence there is less point in recording via the collator every small scrap of information and gossip. To reduce reliance on local computers is also to relieve the temptation for officers to gain intelligence non-consensually – by spying, surveillance, 'swamp' operations or interrogation under pressure. This move is unlikely to eliminate all such practices but it is an essential step in the right direction.

## Conclusion

We have argued the case for a more acceptable and effective system of policing. It could be said in reply, however, that there is no point in debating consensual forms of policing if economic and social conditions preclude their realization. Instead, it could be said that emphasis should be given to the economic structure of Britain, to poverty, unemployment and bad housing: that creating jobs would do more to reduce all forms of crime than could ever be done through policing.

We agree. The particular reforms we propose will come to nothing unless pursued within a broader programme of economic and social reform. Policies that result in lowering the standard of living of the least well-off, that exacerbate the problems of large-scale unemployment and that generate fears of discrimination do not permit policing by consent. The non-consensual policing that results in this way only compounds the very problems to which it is meant to respond.

The need for change is immediate. The question: 'What kind of policing is acceptable in society?' is by its very nature a question of politics that demands a decision on the kind of society wanted. Those who advocate hard-line policing must be prepared for a society based on confrontation.

## Further Reading

Devlin, Lord, *The Judge*, Oxford University Press, Oxford, 1979.

Hewitt, P., *The Abuse of Power*, Martin Robertson, Oxford, 1982.

Holdaway, S. (ed.), *The British Police*, Edward Arnold, London, 1979.

McConville, M. and Baldwin, J., *Courts, Prosecution and Conviction*, Oxford University Press, Oxford, 1981.

Morris, P. and Heal, K., *Crime Control and the Police*, Home Office Research Unit, Study 67, HMSO, London, 1981.

Taylor, I., *Law and Order: Arguments for Socialism*, Macmillan, London, 1981.

Wilcox, A. F., *The Decision to Prosecute*, Butterworths, London, 1972.

# Appendix: Job Specification for Area Constable (Research Force 1982)

The duties specified are within the overall obligation of the police to preserve peace, protect life and property and prevent and detect crime.

*Job Title*            – Area Constable
*Immediate Superior*   – Operational Sergeant

*Duties and Responsibilities*
1. Is responsible to the duty Operational Sergeant for effectively patrolling the area allotted to him and for efficiently dealing with matters arising therein.
2. Will normally work in uniform, but may wear plain clothes when circumstances warrant and with the concurrence of the Area Inspector.
3. Each officer will be equipped with a personal radio and will patrol his/her area on foot.
4. His/her role will be to maintain personal contact with members of the public and although his/her primary role will be concerned with crime and criminals he/she must also attend to the various other duties in the normal manner. *HE/SHE*

*MUST NOT BECOME OFFICE BOUND* and *MUST* spend as little time as possible away from his/her area.

5. Areas in the vicinity of shopping centres and busy road junctions etc., will be given special attention and any information obtained by the Area Constable will be passed to the divisional intelligence officer.

6. He/she should:

   a Secure the services of at least one observer in every street, not a paid professional informant, but someone who knows the inhabitants and is inquisitive enough to find out what is going on and who is willing to pass on such information gained;

   b get to know the habits of and all other information about criminals in his/her area;

   c cultivate shopkeepers, tradesmen and garage proprietors who are a good source of information;

   d keep observations in parks, playing fields, schools and other places where children congregate.

7. He/she will ensure that complaints from members of the public are followed up. This not only applies to reports of crime and other serious matters but to minor complaints and the subsequent action taken by the Police in respect of them. Many complaints of lack of attention are unfounded and unjustified. These have arisen, in many cases, where the complainers have not been made aware of the action taken, or the problems with which the police are faced. 'Follow-ups' by the Area Constable will lead to a better understanding between the police and the public.

8. His/her effectiveness to some degree will be judged by the amount of information he/she feeds to the records of local crime intelligence, together with the general crime situation in his/her area.

9. The area constable must be fully aware of all youth clubs and other such organizations meeting in his/her area and he/she should be on speaking terms with the leaders of such organizations.

10. On commencing duty, the area constable will examine the Log Book at his/her Station and bring himself/herself up-to-date with all incidents, complaints etc., which have occurred

in the area during his/her absence.

11. Is responsible for the service of Copy Complaints and Witness Citations in the allotted area.
12. Rest Days will be taken on Saturday and Sunday, and Sunday and Monday on alternating weeks.
13. Will submit for approval on Form No. 43–3 to his/her supervisory sergeant fourteen days before the commencement of each week, details of the shifts he/she will be working during that week.
14. As it is desirable that a record be kept of the enquiries and duties carried out by the area constable, he/she will submit a report on a fortnightly basis giving the following information:

    *a* brief details of enquiries and other work carried out during the previous fortnight;

    *b* how contacts or other possible sources of information have been cultivated;

    *c* nature of any advice sought by the public; and

    *d* any other relevant information.

# Notes

## Chapter 1. Slogans or Policies?

1. Sir Robert Mark, *Policing a Perplexed Society*, Allen & Unwin, London, 1977, p. 20.
2. S. Cohen, *Folk Devils and Moral Panics*, Penguin, Harmondsworth, 1973; J. Clarke *et al.*, *Policing the Crisis*, Macmillan, London, 1978. See also R. V. G. Clarke and J. M. Hough (eds.), *The Effectiveness of Policing*, Gower, Aldershot, Hants, 1980.
3. P. Colquhoun, *Treatise on the Police of the Metropolis*, 1795, p. 2.
4. Quoted in Clarke *et al.*, op. cit., p. 4.
5. Bill Walker MP, House of Commons, 14 April 1982.
6. 'Programme Analysis and Review 1972: Police Manpower', Home Office and Scottish Home and Health Dept., 1973, unpublished.
7. Ibid., para. 2.3.
8. Ibid., para. 6.7.
9. Ibid., para. 6.7.
10. *Committee of Inquiry on the Police*, Reports I & II (Chairman, Lord Edmund-Davies), Cmnd. 7283 and 7633, HMSO, 1979.
11. *The Times*, 24 Dec. 1908.
12. T. A. Critchley, *A History of the Police in England and Wales*, Constable, London, 1967, p. 10.
13. Ibid., p. 50.
14. *The British Magazine*, Oct., 1763, p. 542.
15. *General Instructions to the Metropolitan Police*, 1829.
16. Sir Leon Radzinowicz, *A History of the English Criminal Law*, vol. 4, Stevens, London, 1968, p. 164.
17. C. Reith, *British Police and the Democratic Ideal*, OUP, Oxford, 1943, pp. 153–9.

18. *The Times*, 2 Dec., 1845.
19. T. Bunyan, *The Political Police in Britain*, Quartet, London, 1977, ch. 2.
20. Sir Ronald Howe, *The Story of Scotland Yard*, Barker, London, 1965, p. 171.
21. Royal Commission on the Police 1962, Minutes of Evidence: Evidence of ACPO, HMSO, London, 1962, p. 256.
22. Ibid.
23. Ibid.
24. Royal Commission on the Police, Interim Report, Cmnd. 1222, HMSO, London, 1960, p. 12.
25. Ibid.
26. J. McClure, *Spike Island*, Macmillan, London, 1980, p. 29.
27. Sir Robert Mark, *In the Office of Constable*, Collins, London, 1978, pp. 55–6.
28. Chief Constable Ian Oliver, quoted in the *Sunday Times*, 7 June 1981.
29. Sir David McNee, 'Policing Modern Britain', in J. Stott and N. Miller (eds.), *Crime and the Responsible Community*, Hodder & Stoughton, London, 1979, p. 76.
30. R. F. Sparks, H. G. Genn and D. J. Dodd, *Surveying Victims*, Wiley, New York, 1977, ch. 6.
31. Sir Robert Mark, *Sunday Telegraph*, 7 March 1971, quoted in T. Bunyan, op cit., p. 89.
32. 'Minority Verdict', the Dimbleby Lecture 1973, BBC TV, reprinted in Mark, 1977, op. cit., pp. 55–73.
33. Ibid., p. 65.
34. McNee, loc. cit., p. 85.
35. Ibid., p. 78.
36. Ibid.
37. Colquhoun, op. cit., p. 85.
38. Mark, 1977, op. cit., p. 20.
39. Mark, 1978, op. cit., p. 161.
40. Ibid., p. 281.
41. Royal Commission on the Police, 1962: Minutes of Evidence of Superintendents' Association, HMSO, London, 1962.
42. Mark, 1977, op. cit., pp. 19–20.

*Chapter 2. The Organization of Police Work I: 'Fire-brigade' Policing*

1. Lord Scarman, *The Brixton Disorders*, 10–12 April 1981, Cmnd. 8427, HMSO, 1981, p. 63.
2. 'Programme Analysis and Review, 1972: Police Manpower', Home Office and Scottish Home and Health Dept., 1973, unpublished.
3. Ibid., para. 5.17.
4. *Police Manpower, Equipment and Efficiency* (Taverne Report), HMSO, 1967.
5. 'Programme Analysis and Review, 1972', p. 18.

6.   Ibid.
7.   M. Chatterton, 'Practical Coppers, Oarsmen and Administrators: Front-line Supervisory Styles in Police Organizations', ISA Conference, Oxford, 1981.
8.   To provide 24-hour cover the police work three eight-hour shifts per day – the cycle starting at 6 a.m. There are four shifts – necessary to cover days off through the month. Each shift works a monthly pattern starting with seven consecutive nights; the turn on nights (10 p.m. – 6 a.m.) is followed by two days off, two days on the back shift (2 p.m. – 10 p.m.), three days on early shift (6 a.m. – 2 p.m.), and then two further days on the back shift. (This is the 'relief week', the broken pattern covering the days off of the other three shifts.) After two further days off, the shift works three days back shift followed by four days early shift.
9.   M. Chatterton, 'Police in Social Control', in J. F. S. King (ed.), *Control Without Custody*, Institute of Criminology, Cambridge, 1976, pp. 104–22.
10.  Ian Lund, Home Office/Electrical Engineering Association Symposium and Exhibition, London, 21–3 Nov. 1977, unpublished.
11.  Ronald Broome, Assistant Chief Constable, West Midlands Police, in Home Office Symposium, 21–3 Nov. 1977.
12.  Arthur Burrows, Director of the Police Scientific Development Board, in Home Office Symposium, 21–3 Nov. 1977.
13.  G. A. Fraser, 'The Applications of Police Computing', in D. W. Pope and N. L. Weiner, *Modern Policing*, Croom Helm, London, 1981, p. 215.
14.  Research in Kansas City indicates average citizen-reporting times of sixty minutes for assaults and twenty-three minutes for burglaries, compared to police-response times of three and three and a half minutes respectively: see P. Manning, *Police Work*, MIT Press, 1977, p. 215.
15.  *State Research*, vol. 3, no. 19, 1980.
16.  R. Reiner, *The Blue-Coated Worker*, CUP, Cambridge, 1978, p. 188.

*Chapter 3. The Organization of Police Work II: Local Intelligence*

1.   G. A. Fraser, 'The Application of Police Computing', in D. W. Pope and N. L. Weiner, *Modern Policing*, Croom Helm, London, 1981.
2.   In the research force there were no female Divisional Information Officers.
3.   See Appendix.
4.   See D. Campbell, 'Society under Surveillance', in P. Hain (ed.), *Policing the Police*, vol. 2, John Calder, London, 1980.
5.   Report of the Committee on Data Protection (Chairman: Sir Norman Lindop), Cmnd. 7341, HMSO, London, 1978, para. 3.15.
6.   BBC, Panorama, March 1981.
7.   See articles by Duncan Campbell in the *New Statesman*, 23 and 30 October 1981. Allegations concerning the misuse of the Thames Valley Police Computer were investigated by the Thames Valley Police in accordance with the Police Act 1964 in a report dated January 1982 and found to be wholly unsubstantiated. This report is not publicly available.
8.   See P. Hewitt, *The Abuse of Power*, Martin Robertson, Oxford, 1982, p. 50.
9.   M. Chatterton, 'Police in Social Control', in J. F. S. King (ed.), *Control*

*without Custody*, CUP, Cambridge, 1976.

10. T. Bunyan,*The Political Police in Britain*, Quartet, London, 1977, ch. 2.

## Chapter 4. The Politics of Local Accountability

1. James Anderton, Chief Constable of Greater Manchester, *The Guardian*, 17 March 1982.
2. G. Marshall, 'The Government of the Police since 1964', in J. C. Alderson and J. Stead (eds.), *The Police We Deserve*, Wolfe, London, 1973, p.57.
3. G. Marshall, *Police and Government*, Methuen, London, 1965, pp.9–14.
4. Royal Commission on the Police, 1962: Report, Cmnd. 1728, HMSO, London, 1962, paras. 89–90.
5. P. Hewitt, *The Abuse of Power*, Martin Robertson, Oxford, 1982, p. 60.
6. Marshall, loc. cit., p. 59.
7. See *Newsletter*, Labour Campaign for Criminal Justice, Winter, 1981.
8. See Hewitt, op. cit., p. 62, n. 16.
9. *Police Review*, Nov. 1981, p. 24.
10. But for proposals on non-statutory district police committees see Marshall, loc. cit., p. 61.
11. J. C. Alderson, 'The Case for Community Policing: Submission to Scarman', 1981.
12. See Hewitt, 1982, op. cit., p. 68, n. 25.
13. Alderson, op. cit.
14. Lord Scarman, The Brixton Disorders, 10–12 April 1981, Cmnd. 8427, HMSO, 1981, para. 4.37 (Scarman Report).
15. *The Times*, 15 Dec. 1981.
16. See press reports of 8 Dec. 1981. Postscript: in June 1982 the Home Office sent a circular to all police authorities and chief officers instructing the creation and offering guidelines on the running of police–community consultative committees. The committees as such will not have Lord Scarman's proposed statutory basis. (*The Times*, 17 June 1982).
17. Quoted in R. S. Bunyard, *Police Organization and Command*, Macdonald & Evans, Plymouth, 1978, p. 44.
18. See *Laker Airways v. Department of Trade*, [1977] 2 WLR 237 and article by G. R. Baldwin in *Public Law*, 1978, p. 57.
19. For details of the 1976 Act and the politics behind it, see D. Humphry 'The Complaints System', in P. Hain (ed.), *Policing the Police*, vol. 1, John Calder, London, 1979.
20. See Home Office Circular 63/77.
21. D. Humphry, loc. cit., p. 49.
22. Triennial Review Report, 1980, Police Complaints Board, Cmnd. 1966, 1980, para. 34.
23. Annual Report, 1977, Police Complaints Board.
24. *The Sunday Times*, 23 April 1978.
25. Scarman Report, para. 5.43.

26. See Hewitt, op. cit., p. 72.
27. Triennial Review Report, 1980, Police Complaints Board, paras. 60–2.
28. Hewitt, op. cit., p. 73.
29. See Home Office Circular, 32/80.
30. Triennial Review Report, 1980, Police Complaints Board, para. 97.
31. Ibid., para. 100.
32. Ibid.
33. *The Establishment of an Independent Element in the Investigation of Complaints against the Police,* Cmnd. 8194, HMSO, 1981; see also 'Police Fend off Reform of Complaints Procedure', *Rights* May/June, 1981.
34. *The Times,* 31 July 1981.
35. *Police,* Nov. 1981.
36. *Observer,* 15 Nov. 1981.
37. Scarman Report, para. 7.23.
38. See statement by William Whitelaw to the House of Commons, 10 Dec. 1981. Postscript: the House of Commons Select Committee on Home Affairs reported in June 1982. It favoured the appointment of assessors to oversee the investigation of serious complaints (suggesting the PCB might do this) but the majority rejected a system of investigating complaints by independent body. (*The Times* 2 June 1982).
39. Humphry, loc. cit., p. 63
40. M. Chatterton, 'Police in Social Control', in J. F. S. King (ed.), *Control without Custody,* CUP, Cambridge, 1976.
41. J. Mervyn Jones, *Organisational Aspects of Police Behaviour,* Gower, 1981, p. 100.
42. Ibid., p. 91.
43. M. Chatterton, 'Practical Coppers, Oarsmen and Administrators: Front-line Supervisory Styles in Police Organisations', ISA Conference, Oxford, 1981.
44. R. Reiner, *The Blue-Coated Worker,* CUP, Cambridge, 1978, p. 188.

## Chapter 5. The Police and the Law

1. On the police inquisition and judicial connivance see P. Devlin, *The Judge,* OUP, Oxford, 1981, and D. J. McBarnet, *Conviction: Law, the State and the Construction of Justice,* Macmillan, London, 1981.
2. For a detailed exposition see the Royal Commission on Criminal Procedure, *The Investigation and Prosecution of Criminal Offences in England and Wales: The Law and Procedure,* Cmnd. 8092–1, HMSO, London, 1979 (*Law and Procedure*).
3. Royal Commission on Police Powers and Procedure, Cmnd. 3297, HMSO, London, 1929, para. 15.
4. See also Lord Cooper in *Lawrie v. Muir* 1950 JC 19 on common law residual powers.
5. Lord Denning in *R v. Metropolitan Police Commissioner ex parte* Blackburn (no. 1), [1968] 2QB 118 at p. 136.
6. The Ombudsman's jurisdiction does not cover the police (Parliamentary

Commissioner Act 1967, s. 5(3) and schedule 3). The Police Authority is not responsible in law for a constable's acts since officers are servants of the state and not the authority. See *Fisher v. Oldham Corporation*, [1930] 3 KB 364.

7. Criminal Law Act 1967, s. 2(2) and (3).
8. See Royal Commission Research Study, no. 10 by K. W. Lidstone, R. Hogg and F. Sutcliffe, HMSO, London, 1980.
9. *Halsbury's Laws*, 4th edn., vol. 11, para 99. See also *Spicer v. Holt*, [1976] ALL ER 71, 78 and David Telling, 'Arrest and Detention – the Conceptual Maze', *Criminal Law Review*, 1978, p. 320.
10. *Christie v. Leachinsky*, [1947] AC 573.
11. *Spicer v. Holt*, [1976] 3 ALL ER 71.
12. (1976), 64 Cr App R 231; [1977] RTR 160.
13. See [1977] RTR 164–5.
14. See Telling, loc. cit.
15. [1977] RTR, at p. 166. See also those cases in which courts have arrest has taken place where a person reasonably infers from an officer's action (e.g. detention for questioning) that he is under arrest, e.g. *Campbell v. Tormey*, [1969] 1 ALL ER 961, or where arrest is said to occur on a person's accompanying a police officer voluntarily but only because he feels constrained to do so, eg. *R v. Jones, ex parte Moore*, [1965] Crim LR, p. 23.
16. *Swankie v. Milne* 1973 SLT (Notes) 28.
17. *Muir v. Magistrates of Hamilton* 1910 1 SLT 164.
18. See Lord Scarman in *Morris v. Beardmore*, [1980] 3 WLR 283.
19. Criminal Law Act 1967, s. 2.
20. 'Reasonable cause' must exist for such arrest (though a workable definition of 'reasonable cause' is hard to find). There is no Scottish general power equivalent to section 2. Extensive common law powers of arrest exist but there is no distinction between either felonies and misdemeanours or between arrestable and non-arrestable offences. It will 'always be a question whether the circumstances justify the apprehension' (*Peggie v. Clark* (1808) 7 M 89).
21. See *Law and Procedure*, Appendix 9 for details.
22. Ibid., Appendix 9.3.
23. For Scotland, see Criminal Procedure (Scotland) Act 1975, ss. 321 and 12.
24. *Christie v. Leachinsky*, [1947] AC 573, pp. 587–8. For the position in Scotland see *Chalmers v. HM Advocate* 1954 JC 66.
25. Criminal Law Act 1967, s. 3(1).
26. See Criminal Law Revision Committee, 7th Report, *Felonies and Misdemeanours*, Cmnd. 2659, HMSO, London, 1972.
27. See also *DPP v. Carey*, [1969] 3 ALL ER 1662, p. 1680.
28. *Rice v. Connolly*, [1966] 2 QB 414. For the similar Scottish rule see *Chalmers v. HM Advocate* 1954 JC 66.
29. *Kenlin v. Gardiner*, [1967] 2 QB 510; see also *R v. Lemsatef*, [1977] 2 ALL ER 835.
30. [1970] 1 ALL ER 987.
31. [1966] 2 QB 414, 419; see also *Ricketts v. Cox*, [1982] Crim LR 182.

32. See Lanham, 'Arrest, Detention and Compulsion', *Criminal Law Review* 1974, pp. 288, 290.
33. *R v. Inwood,* [1973] 1 WLR 647.
34. See Lord Devlin in *Hussien v. Chong Fook Kam,* [1970] AC 942, 947 (PC).
35. See *Chalmers v. HM Advocate* 1954 JC 66, especially Lord Cooper.
36. *Shaaban bin Hussien v. Chong Fook Kam,* [1969] 3 ALL ER 1626.
37. *Law and Procedure,* para 3. 66.
38. *Wiltshire v. Barrett,* [1966] 1 QB 312, and subsection 28(4) of the Children and Young Persons Act 1969.
39. *Law and Procedure,* para 64.
40. Magistrates' Courts Act 1980, s. 43.
41. Ibid., s. 43(4). In Scotland the common law position is similar: R. W. Renton and H. H. Brown, *Criminal Procedure according to the Law of Scotland,* 4th edn., by G. H. Gordon, Green, Edinburgh, 1972, pp. 34, 60. The Police (Scotland) Act 1967, s. 17(1) prohibits unnecessary or unreasonable detention. See also Criminal Procedure (Scotland) Act 1975, ss. 101, 321(3).
42. *R v. Voisin* (1918), 13 Cr App R 89; *R v. Praeger,* [1972] 1 WLR 260.
43. *R v. Lemsatef,* [1977] 2 ALL ER 835.
44. [1966] 2 QB 414.
45. *R v. Sang,* [1979] 2 ALL ER 1222, 1230.
46. *R v. Thompson,* [1893] 2 QB 12; Sir Rupert Cross, *Evidence,* 5th edn., Butterworths, London, 1979; *R v. Cleary* (1963) 48 Cr App R 166; *DPP v. Ping Lin,* [1975] 3 ALL ER 175; [1976] AC 574 and *R v. Rennie,* [1982] 1 ALL ER 386.
47. (1966) 50 Cr App R 183.
48. [1972] 1 WLR 260; but see for oppression the case of *Hudson* (1981) 72 Cr App R 163.
49. [1975] 1 ALL ER 77. See also *R v. Houghton and Franciosy* (1978) Cr App R 197 in which statements following detention incommunicado for five days were admitted.
50. Report, para. 4. 123.
51. *R v. Praeger,* [1972] 1 ALL ER 144.
52. *Chalmers v. HM Advocate* 1954 JC 66.
53. Ibid., pp. 98–9.
54. See *Thomson v. HM Advocate* 1968 JC 61; *Jones v. Milne* 1975 SLT 2; *Murphy v. HM Advocate* 1975 SLT (Notes) 17; Balloch 1977 SLT (Notes) 29; *Hartley v. HM Advocate* 1979 SLT 26.
55. See *HM Advocate v. McFadden* (unreported) 12 August 1980 (Perth High Court).
56. L. J. Lawton in *R v. Chandler,* [1976] 1 WLR 575. For Scotland see *Robertson v. Maxwell* 1951 JC 11, p. 14.
57. See *R v. Christie,* [1914] AC 548.
58. *Law and Procedure,* para 80.
59. See Cross, op. cit., p. 548, n. 7.
60. *R v. Gilbert* (1977) 66 Cr App R 237.
61. Cross, op. cit., pp. 548–9.

62. See the list in *Law and Procedure*, Appendix 1.
63. *Dillon v. O'Brien and Davis* (1897), 16 Cox CC 245 (IR); *R v. O'Donnell* (1835), 7 C & P 138; *Yakimishyn v. Bileski* (1946) 86 CCC; 179 and cases listed therein; *Adair v. McGarry* 1933 JC 72.
64. *Barnett and Grant v. Campbell*, [1902] 2 NZLR 484.
65. *Entick v. Carrington* (1765), 19 State Tr 1029.
66. See *Law and Procedure*, Appendix 4.
67. Ibid., para. 29. *Dillon v. O'Brien and Davis* (1897), 16 Cox CC 245 (Ir).
68. *Law and Procedure*, Appendix 5.
69. See *Law and Procedure*, Appendix 5.2.
70. *Launock v. Brown*, (1819), 2 B and Ald 592.
71. *Thomas v. Sawkins*, [1935] 2 KB 249.
72. Archbold, *Pleading, Evidence and Practice in Criminal Cases*, 40th edn. by S. Mitchell, London, 1979, para. 1410.
73. [1968] 2 QB 299.
74. [1970] 1 QB 693.
75. *Police Powers in England and Wales*, Butterworths, London, 1975, p. 31.
76. See D. J. McBarnet, *Conviction: Law, the State and the Construction of Justice*, Macmillan, London, 1981, esp. ch. 3.
77. [1977] RTR 160.
78. [1970] AC 942.
79. See for example *Miln v. Cullen* 1967 JC 21.
80. *Callis v. Gunn*, [1964] 1 QB 490; *Jeffrey v. Black*, [1978] QB 49
81. [1979] 2 ALL ER 1222, at p. 1230.
82. See *Law and Procedure*, p. 48.
83. *Miln v. Cullen* 1967 JC 21.
84. For example, *Hartley v. HM Advocate* 1979 SLT 26; *Thomson v. HM Advocate* 1968 JC 61. In England, see *R v. Houghton and Franciosy* (1978) Cr App R 197 (suspect detained for five days) compare *Dodd* (1982) 74 Cr App R 50 and *Hudson* (1981) 72 Cr App R 163.
85. See *HM Advocate v. McGuigan* 1936 JC 16.
86. [1973] 2 ALL ER 645.
87. *R v. Bass*, [1953] 1 QB 680; *Dunne v. Clinton*, [1930] IR 366; *Hussien v. Chong Fook Kam*, [1970] AC 942, p. 847.
88. *Criminal Procedure in Scotland, Second Report* (Thomson Committee), Cmnd. 6218, HMSO, 1975.
89. HC (1977/8) 90. The inquiry followed the mistaken conviction of three youths following the death of Maxwell Confait in April 1972 (see ch. 7).
90. Ibid., para. 2. 17.
91. Ibid., para. 2. 17(d).
92. Royal Commission on Criminal Procedure, Report, Cmnd. 8092, HMSO, 1981, para. 3. 15.
93. Submission of the National Council for Civil Liberties to the Royal Commission on Criminal Procedure: Pt. 2 (Arrest), 1979.
94. See D. J. McBarnet, *Conviction: Law, the State and the Construction of Justice*, Macmillan, London, 1981, ch. 3.

95.   Royal Commission Research Study, no. 7 by David Steer, HMSO, London, 1980, p. 122.

## Chapter 6. *Reforming the Law or Legalizing Abuse?*

1.   *Second Programme of Law Reform,* Scottish Law Commission, no. 8, 1968.
2.   *Fourth Annual Report,* Scottish Law Commission, no. 13, 1969, emphasis added.
3.   *Chalmers v. HM Advocate* 1954 JC 66, 78.
4.   See *Brown v. HM Advocate* 1966 SLT 105, *Miln v. Cullen* 1967 JC 21, *Thompson v. HM Advocate* 1968 JC 61.
5.   *Journal of the Law Society,* 14 (1969), p. 309.
6.   Law Commissions Act 1965, s. 3(1).
7.   *Criminal Procedure in Scotland, Second Report* (Thomson Committee), Cmnd. 6218, HMSO, 1975, para. 3.11. (emphasis added).
8.   G. H. Gordon, 'The Admissibility of Answers to Police Questioning in Scotland', in P. Glazebrook (ed.), *Reshaping the Criminal Law,* Stevens & Sons, London, 1978.
9.   HC Deb., Scottish Grand Committee – Criminal Justice (Scotland) Bill, 1st sitting, cols. 2–3 (12 Dec. 1978).
10.  HC Deb., Scottish Grand Committee – Criminal Justice (Scotland) Bill, 2nd sitting, cols. 109–10 (14 Dec. 1978).
11.  *Hartley v. HM Advocate* 1979 SLT 26.
12.  Thomson Committee, para. 3.19.
13.  HC Deb., Scottish Grand Committee – Criminal Justice (Scotland) Bill, 1st sitting, col. 35 (12 Dec. 1978).
14.  Following the General Election in Scotland, the Conservative Party held 22 seats, Labour 44, Liberals 3 and SNP 2.
15.  Between 1974 and 1979 there was an overall reduction in crime of 12½ per cent. See H. Ewing, HC Deb., vol. 982, col. 915 (15 April 1980).
16.  HC Deb., First Scottish Standing Committee – Criminal Justice (Scotland) Bill, 3rd sitting, col. 1180 (29 April 1980).
17.  HL Deb., vol. 404, col. 131 (29 Jan. 1980).
18.  Criminal Justice (Scotland) Bill 1979, cl. 4.
19.  Ibid.
20.  See HC Deb., First Scottish Standing Committee – Criminal Justice (Scotland) Bill, 12th sitting, col. 680 (3 June 1980).
21.  See *Scotsman,* 9 May 1980, and *Guardian,* 9 May 1980.
22.  See Campbell, 'Society under Surveillance', in P. Hain (ed.), *Policing the Police,* vol 2, John Calder, London, 1980 and Lord McCluskey at HL Deb., vol. 404, col. 745. (29 Jan. 1980).
23.  During the mid-seventies the Scottish Police Federation became increasingly involved in national (i.e. British) law and order politics, yet senior police officers still remained reticent, see P. Gordon, *Policing Scotland,* Scottish Council of Civil Liberties, 1980, ch. 8. For an analysis of the developing role of 'political policemen' in England, see Kettle, 'The Politics of Policing and

the Policing of Politics', in P. Hain (ed.), op. cit., 1980.

24. Cf. P. Gordon, op. cit., p. 91.
25. HL Deb., vol. 404, cols. 27–8 (29 Jan. 1980).
26. HC Deb., vol. 982, col. 812 (14 April 1980).
27. Nicholas Fairbairn, quoted in *Scotsman*, 21 April 1980.
28. See *Summary of Views of the Faculty of Advocates on the Criminal Justice (Scotland) Bill*, Edinburgh, April 1980.

## Chapter 7. The Poverty of the Royal Commission

1. See Martin Kettle, 'The Politics of Policing and the Policing of Politics' in P. Hain (ed.), *Policing the Police*, vol. 2, John Calder, London, 1980.
2. Cmnd. 4991, HMSO, 1972.
3. See Sir Brian MacKenna 'Criminal Law Revision Committee's Eleventh Report, Some Comments', *Criminal Law Review*, 605 (1972); articles in *Criminal Law Review* of June 1973; M. Manfred Simon's letter to *The Times* of 5 Oct. 1972; Lord Devlin 'Too High a Price for Conviction', *The Sunday Times*, 2 July 1972; and Lord Salmon's critical speech in the House of Lords (HL Deb., vol. 388, cols. 1603–10).
4. 'The Confait Case', Report by the Hon. Sir Henry Fisher (Dec. 1977), HC. (1977/8) 90, HMSO, 1977.
5. Ibid., paras. 2–17.
6. Ibid., para. 1.8.
7. Royal Commission on Criminal Procedure, Report, Cmnd. 8092, 1981, p. 2.
8. *State Research Bulletin*, vol. 2, no. 12 June/July 1979, p. 108.
9. E.g. Kettle, loc. cit., pp. 21–4.
10. Royal Commission on Criminal Procedure: Part 1 of the Written Evidence of the Commissioner of Police of the Metropolis (1978).
11. Brighton Conference, Sept. 1978.
12. Sir Cyril Phillips, 'The Work of the Commission and Policy Problems', at the Conference on the Report of the RCCP, University of Leicester, 11 July 1981 (Leicester Conference).
13. *Observer*, 11 Jan. 1981.
14. Royal Commission on Criminal Procedure, Report, pp. 10–12.
15. *Police*, 15 Oct. 1981, p. 2.
16. Royal Commission on Criminal Procedure, Report, para. 3.86.
17. D. J. McBarnet, *Criminal Law Review*, 1981, p. 448.
18. On the difficulties of securing redress for unlawful police action see Criminal Procedure in Scotland: Second Report, Cmnd. 6218, HMSO, 1975, para. 3.32 and Royal Commission on Criminal Procedure, para. 4.119–22.
19. Ibid., para. 4.75.
20. K. W. Lidstone, *Criminal Law Review*, July 1981, pp. 454–6.
21. See D. J. McBarnet, loc. cit.
22. See J. C. Alderson, 'The Scope of Police Powers', Leicester Conference, 1981.
23. Royal Commission on Criminal Procedure, Report, para. 4.125.

24. *Guardian*, 14 Jan. 1981.
25. *Rights*, vol. 5, no. 4, March 1981, p. 4.
26. McBarnet, loc. cit, p. 450.
27. *Rights*, loc. cit.
28. Royal Commission Research Study, no. 1, by Barrie Irving and Linden Hilgendorf, HMSO, London, 1980.
29. 'Studying the Exclusionary Rule in Search and Seizure', *University of Chicago Law Review*, vol. 37 (1970); see Marquita Inman, *Criminal Law Review*, July 1981, p. 475.
30. On the distinction between interviewing (to elicit information) and interrogating so as to obtain confessions or evidence, see R. J. Wicks, *Applied Psychology for Law Enforcement and Correction Officers*, McGraw-Hill, New York, 1974.
31. *The Times*, 9 Jan. 1981.
32. *Guardian*, Jan. 1981.
33. *New Statesman*, 2 Jan. 1981.
34. *Rights*, loc cit.
35. *Guardian*, 12 Jan. 1981.
36. Ibid., 14 Jan. 1981.
37. Ibid., 19 Jan. 1981.
38. *Police*, Feb. 1981, p. 15.
39. See *Criminal Law Review*, July 1981.
40. *Public Law*, Summer 1981.
41. See Royal Commission Research Study, no. 7, by David Steer, HMSO, London, 1980.
42. Criminal Procedure in Scotland: Second Report, Cmnd. 6218, HMSO, 1975.
43. *Rights*, loc cit.

## Chapter 8. *Community Policing and Scarman on the Riots*

1. Evelyn B. Schaffer, *Community Policing*, Croom Helm, London, 1980, ch. 5.
2. Tony Gibson, *People Power*, Penguin Books, Harmondsworth, 1979.
3. Ibid., p. 53; Schaffer, op cit., p. 70.
4. Schaffer, op. cit., p. 71.
5. Ibid., p. 72.
6. See 'Community Involvement', *Strathclyde Police Review*, 1970, p. 1.
7. N. J. Shanks, *Police Community Involvement in Scotland*, Scottish Office Central Research Unit, 1980, p. 4.
8. Lothian Borders Police: Review of Community Involvement, 1981.
9. Shanks, op. cit.
10. Lothian and Borders Police: Review of Community Involvement, 1981, p. 4.
11. Shanks, op. cit., p. 7.
12. *Financial Times*, 12 Sept. 1981.
13. J. C. Alderson, *Communal Policing*, Devon and Cornwall Constabulary, 1980, p. 7.

14. Ibid., p. 46.
15. J. C. Alderson, *Policing Freedom*, Macdonald and Evans, 1979, p. 46.
16. *New Society*, 29 Jan. 1981.
17. See C. Moore and J. Brown, *Community versus Crime*, NCVO, London, 1981, ch. 4.
18. Alderson, 1980, op cit., pp. 7 and 39.
19. Moore and Brown, op cit., p. 53.
20. Ibid., p. 61.
21. Ibid., p. 75.
22. E.g., ibid., p. 23.
23. *Sunday Telegraph*, 12 July 1981.
24. *Sunday Times*, 6 Sept. 1981.
25. Moore and Brown, op. cit., p. 66.
26. *Guardian*, 9 July 1981.
27. Ibid., 3 Sept. 1981.
28. Ibid.
29. Ibid., 5 Sept. 1981.
30. Lord Scarman, *The Brixton Disorders, 10–12 April 1981*, Cmnd. 8427, HMSO, 1981 (Scarman Report), para. 2.38.
31. Ibid., para. 3.25.
32. On the causation of the disturbances see John Lea and Jock Young, 'Urban Violence and Political Marginalization: the Riots in Britain; Summer 1981', in *Critical Social Policy* vol. I, no. 3, Spring 1982, pp. 59–69.
33. Scarman Report, para. 3.101.
34. *Observer*, 18 Oct. 1981.
35. J. C. Alderson, 'The Case for Community Policing', Submission to Scarman, 1981, p. viii.
36. Scarman Report, para. 5.16.
37. See Pauline Morris and Kevin Heal, *Crime Control and the Police*, Home Office Research Study, no. 67. HMSO, 1981.
38. See M. Banton, 'Crime Prevention in the Context of Criminal Policy', *Police Studies*, 1, pp. 3–9.
39. J. C. Alderson, *Policing Freedom*, Macdonald and Evans, Plymouth, 1979, p. 191.
40. Ibid., p. 195.
41. J. C. Alderson, Interview with Authors, 14 Aug. 1981.
42. R. F. Sparks, H. G. Genn and D. J. Dodd, *Surveying Victims*, Wiley, New York, 1977, p. 152.
43. See W. Bieck, *Response Time Analysis*, Kansas City Police Department, Kansas City, 1977.
44. See Royal Commission Research Study, no. 7, by David Steer, HMSO, London, 1980, and R. Mawby, *Policing the City*, Saxon House, Farnborough, 1979.
45. Morris and Heal, op. cit., pp. 44–5.
46. Shanks, op. cit., p. 24.
47. R. Reiner, *The Blue-Coated Worker*, CUP, Cambridge, 1978; Scarman

Report, para. 5.48.
48. Alderson, Interview with Authors, 14 Aug. 1981.
49. Ibid.
50. Scarman Report, paras. 5.34, 5.48.
51. Alderson, Interview, 14 Aug. 1981.
52. Ibid.
53. J. Croft, *Crime and the Community*, Home Office Research Study, no. 50, HMSO, London 1979.
54. Alderson, op. cit., 1980, p. 46.
55. Alderson, op. cit., 1980, p. 8.
56. Sir Robert Mark, *Policing a Perplexed Society*, Allen & Unwin, London, 1977, p. 12.
57. *Guardian*, 22 Sept. 1981.
58. A. Blaber, *The Exeter Community Policing Consultative Group*, NACRO, 1979.
59. Moore and Brown, op cit. p. 24.
60. Ibid., p. 23, emphasis added.
61. Ibid., p. 24.
62. Blaber, op cit., p. 48.
63. See Frank Kitson, *Low Intensity Operations*, Faber & Faber, London, 1971.

## Chapter 9. *Alternatives and Conclusions*

1. Royal Commission on Criminal Procedure, *The Investigation and Prosecution of Criminal Offences in England and Wales: The Law and Procedure*, Cmnd. 8092-1, HMSO, London, 1979, para. 3.20.
2. *Law and Procedure*, Appendix 2.
3. *Powers of Arrest and Search in Relation to Drug Offences*, HMSO, 1970, para. 113.
4. M. McConville and J. Baldwin, 'Recent Developments in English Criminal Justice and the Royal Commission on Criminal Procedure, *International Journal of the Sociology of Law*, Winter, 1982.
5. D. Powis, *The Signs of Crime*, McGraw-Hill, New York, 1977, p. 104; see also N. Blake, *The Police, the Law and the People*, Haldane Society, 1980.
6. Royal Commission on Criminal Procedure, para. 3.25.
7. See Chapter 4 and M. Chatterton 'Practical Coppers, Oarsmen and Administrators: Front-line Supervisory Styles in Police Organisations', ISA Conference, Oxford, 1981.
8. Lord Scarman, *The Brixton Disorders, 10–12 April 1981*, Cmnd. 8427, HMSO, 1981 (Scarman Report), para. 4.75 and 5.46.
9. J. C. Alderson, 'The Scope of Police Powers', Leicester Conference, 1981.
10. See Blake, op. cit., p. 24.
11. Royal Commission on Criminal Procedure, Report, para. 3.26.
12. Royal Commission Research Study, no. 1, by B. Irving and I. Hilgendorf, HMSO, London, 1980.
13. See D. J. McBarnet, *Conviction: Law, the State and the Construction of*

*Justice*, Macmillan, London, 1981, ch. 3.

14. See Lord Devlin, *The Judge*, OUP, Oxford, 1979, p. 74.
15. Royal Commission Research Study, no. 1, op. cit., p. 153; see Royal Commission on Criminal Procedure, Report, para. 4.43.
16. *New Statesman*, 2 Jan. 1981.
17. See quotations in M. McConville and J. Baldwin, *Courts, Prosecution and Conviction*, OUP, Oxford, 1981, p. 127.
18. Ibid., chs. 7 and 8.
19. Royal Commission Research Study no. 4, by Paul Softley *et al.*, HMSO, London, 1980.
20. Irving and Hilgendorf, op. cit.
21. McConville and Baldwin, op. cit., ch. 8; see also R. Mawby, *Policing the City*, Saxon House, 1979, pp. 109–32; P. Softley *et al.*, *Police Interrogation*, HORU Study no. 61, HMSO, 1980.
22. Monitoring the the Criminal Justice (Scotland) Act 1980 by the Scottish Home and Health Department in 1981 reveals that one in 250 of the population may expect to be detained on suspicion each year.
23. Madden admitted under interrogation to having stolen 'Dinky' toys but was in possession of a receipt for their purchase, see *Guardian*, 9 March 1981.
24. *Morris v. Beardmore*, [1980] WLR 283, p. 296; see K. W. Lidstone, *Criminal Law Review*, July 1981, p. 458.
25. *Law and Procedure*, Appendix 5.
26. See s. 26(2) Theft Act 1968; *Ghani v. Jones*, [1970] 1 QB; K. W. Lidstone, loc. cit., July 1981, p. 460.
27. Royal Commission on Criminal Procedure, Report, para. 3.33.
28. Lidstone, loc. cit., p. 460.
29. Royal Commission on Criminal Procedure, Report, para. 3.45.
30. See Chapter 3. In their study of Crown Court prosecutions McConville and Baldwin note that in 40 per cent of all cases prejudicial evidence came exclusively from the police and in nearly 25 per cent of other cases police witnesses formed a major part of the prosecution case, McConville and Baldwin, op. cit., ch. 6.
31. Ibid., pp. 124–5; see also Lord Devlin, op. cit., p. 74.
32. See Royal Commission Research Study, no. 4, op. cit. Table 2.2.
33. Royal Commission on Criminal Procedure, Report, paras. 4.117–135.
34. See P. Hewitt, *The Abuse of Power*, Martin Robertson, Oxford, 1982; G. H. Gordon, in P. R. Glazebrook (ed), *Reshaping the Criminal Law*, Stevens & Sons, London, 1978.
35. *R v. Inwood*, [1973] WLR 647.
36. In Scotland a system of recording both detention and voluntary help has been introduced administratively following the Criminal Justice (Scotland) Act. In telling suspects of their rights, the value of the detention forms is undermined by their dependence on signature not by the suspect but by the police officer.
37. Scarman Report, para. 7.9.
38. In the case of McFadden, Lord Jauncey ruled statements inadmissible on

hearing a tape-recording and deciding that questioning was so severe as to amount to cross-examination. (Perth High Court, 12 Aug. 1980, unreported).

39.   See McConville and Baldwin, loc. cit., 1982.
40.   Ibid.
41.   Royal Commission on Criminal Procedure, Report, para. 4.27.
42.   For political opposition to the presence of solicitors at interviews see evidence to the Royal Commission and McConville and Baldwin, op. cit., 1981, p. 175.
43.   Royal Commission on Criminal Procedure, Report. 4.92.
44.   [1977] Crim LR 725.
45.   See McConville and Baldwin, op. cit., 1981, p. 86.
46.   For details of force procedures see Royal Commission Research Study no. 11, by Mollie Weatheritt, HMSO, London 1980. *Law and Procedure*, ch. 5.
47.   S. McCabe and R. Purves, *The Jury at Work*, Oxford University Penal Research Unit, Blackwell, Oxford, 1972.
48.   McConville and Baldwin, op. cit., 1981, ch. 5.
49.   Ibid., ch. 4.
50.   See Royal Commission Research Studies, nos. 2 and 4, by B. Irving and P. Softley *et al.*, respectively, HMSO, London, 1980.
51.   Lord Devlin, 'The Practice of Judging', *The Listener*, vol. 101, 1979, pp. 441–2, quoted in McConville and Baldwin, op. cit., 1981, p. 97.
52.   McConville and Baldwin, op. cit., 1981, pp. 189–90.
53.   Royal Commission on Criminal Procedure, Report, para. 6.24.
54.   Ibid., paras. 6.36 and 6.37.
55.   S. Moodie and J. Tombs, 'The Scottish Prosecution System', Paper to Oxford Centre for Criminological Studies, 22 Oct. 1981.
56.   See McConville and Baldwin, op. cit., 1981, p. 31.
57.   *Guardian*, 15 March 1982.
58.   See Chapter 2, n. 14.

# Index